CHURCHILL

OTHER BOOKS BY JAMES C. HUMES

How to Get Invited to the White House
Speaker's Treasury of Anecdotes About the Famous
Roles Speakers Play
Podium Humor
Instant Eloquence

CHURCHILL

Speaker of the Century

James C. Humes

STEIN AND DAY/*Publishers*/New York

First published in 1980
Copyright © 1980 by James C. Humes
All rights reserved
Designed by Louis A. Ditizio
Printed in the United States of America
Stein and Day/*Publishers*/Scarborough House
Briarcliff Manor, N.Y. 10510

Library of Congress Cataloging in Publication Data

Humes, James C.
  Churchill: speaker of the century.

  Bibliography: p. 323
  Includes indexes.
  1. Churchill, Winston Leonard Spencer, Sir, 1874–1965.
2. Great Britain—Politics and government—20th century.
3. Churchill, Winston Leonard Spencer, Sir, 1874–1965—
Quotations. 4. Prime ministers—Great Britain—Biography.
5. Orators, English—Biography. DA566.9.C5H85 1980
941.082′092′4 [B]   79-3812 ISBN 0-8128-2710-4

To Ambassador John P. Humes,
whose hallmark of service as diplomat,
counselor, and friend is a sincerity
which bespeaks an eloquence all its own.

He mobilized the English language and sent it into battle.

—*John Kennedy*

Acknowledgments

"Study history, study history. In history lies all the secrets of statecraft." Winston Churchill delivered these passing words of advice when an eighteen-year-old American exchange student was introduced to him in 1953. From that fleeting encounter came the seed that would eventually grow into a book twenty-seven years later.

In the quarter of a century between my year at an English school and my beginning of this work, the youthful admiration of Churchill, the man, crystallized on Churchill, the master of words. The focusing was, no doubt, due to the recordings of his speeches, which the author played over and over again. But I was also influenced by members of Churchill's family and his friends who revealed to me the arresting fact that the man who was to become the "speaker of the century" only became so after years of practice and persevering to surmount various handicaps.

From Sir Shane Leslie, Churchill's cousin, I first heard in 1957 of the impact of Bourke Cockran in shaping the future Prime Minister's speaking style.

In 1963, Churchill's son Randolph told the author of his father's struggle to overcome his lisp and stutter, as well as his herculean attempt to give himself the equivalent of a university education.

When John Churchill, the artist and the Prime Minister's nephew, was a visitor to the author's house in Washington in 1969, he delivered a fascinating insight into his uncle's painting and its influence on his writing habits.

And it was Randolph Churchill's son Winston Churchill, II, who told this writer while a guest at his house in Chailey, Sussex, in 1970, that his grandfather was in his early years a poor extemporaneous speaker who froze up in the give and take of parliamentary exchange and repartee.

I am also indebted to the late Earl of Avon (Anthony Eden) who described to me in his Wiltshire home, Fyfield Manor, in 1971, his former leader's painstaking care in preparing his wartime addresses.

Another former Prime Minister, Alec Douglas-Home, now the Earl of Home, revealed some glimpses of Churchill in his second premiership when Home was Secretary of State for Scotland.

A conversation I had with Antony Montague-Browne, in 1966, was also of some assistance in furnishing impressions of Churchill's last years. Montague-Browne was Churchill's secretary and link to the public world in those final years of his life.

I am also very grateful to Dwight Eisenhower, our late President, for his comments to me in October 1962 at Gettysburg on how Churchill's talent for prophecies and judgments was inextricably linked to his habit of drafting, revising, and editing his own speeches.

On that same facet of his skill as well as other insights into his personality, I owe a special measure of gratitude to Kay Halle who for years has been a close friend of the Churchill family. Kay, who is known for her encouragement to young writers, was ever helpful to this author.

Kay's good friend and mine, the late George Thayer, who was a research assistant in the first two volumes of Churchill's official biography written by his son Randolph, led me first to the study of Sir Winston's formative years. It was George Thayer who first suggested that I attempt a short biography.

The decision to focus such a study on Churchill's growth and development as a speaker was, in no small way, a result of the encouragement from two Presidents, whom I had the honor of serving as a speechwriter: Richard Nixon and Gerald Ford.

Once I had begun the project I received constructive suggestions from many. On the other side of the Atlantic, David Lloyd-George, the Viscount Gwynedd, and also his father, Earl Lloyd-George, deserve thanks for their comments on the singular relationship between Churchill and their illustrious kin.

Most particularly do I want to thank my old friend, Lord Crathorne. No one was more helpful than Jamie Crathorne in steering me in the right direction. Some conversations I had with his father, the first Lord Crathorne, were also of assistance. Lord Crathorne had served as a member of the Churchill cabinet and as Chairman of the Conservative Party. His reminiscences when he was parliamentary secretary to Prime Minister Stanley Baldwin were especially interesting.

I am also appreciative of the talk I had with Grace Hamblin, a former secretary to the Prime Minister and now a part-time guide at Chartwell, which is near her home.

On this side of the ocean I owe thanks to so many that it is difficult in this space to include them all. I am grateful to Mrs. Karolyn Dickson, director of the Churchill Memorial at Westminster College in Fulton, Missouri. I was very honored to be the guest speaker at the Memorial on the 33rd anniversary of Churchill's "Iron Curtain" address.

I am grateful, too, for the suggestions given to me by Brigadier General John Eisenhower, a friend and fine military historian.

Close friends such as Donald Whitehead, John Le Boutillier, Richard McCormack, Victor Lang, Jay Headly, and Trevor Armbrister bore with me as I struggled to complete the manuscript. So did my old friend and law school classmate, J. D. Williams whose staff assisted in the typing.

Christine and Lauren Hallquist also offered their typing and research skills.

Congressman Joe McDade and his staff helped me in securing the Library of Congress in tracking down various Churchill quotations. Marcie Powers and Vickie Mattison were of similar assistance.

Others who offered a friendly ear include Judge William Vogel, Susy Brandt, Ruth Seltzer, Charles Manatt, Ken Talmage, Robin West, John Mongoven, Jean Lawhon, and Stephanie Laszlo.

Most of all, I am deeply indebted to Sol Stein and his wife Patricia Day, who was my editor. Without them, this book might never have appeared. Whatever finish the book may boast can be credited to their editorial suggestions and judgments. Their faith in the worth of the book, as well as that of my agent Theron Raines, will never be forgotten.

Finally, I want to thank Dianne.

James C. Humes
Philadelphia, January 1980

CONTENTS

PROLOGUE

The historian Arnold Toynbee once wrote that the words of Winston Churchill spelled the difference between defeat and survival, not only of Britain but the cause of democracy everywhere. The observation was not original with him. The legend of Churchill has loomed so toweringly since the time of his leadership that we do not find it too difficult to accept that the resolute words of Winston Churchill in those dark days of 1940 persuaded President Roosevelt to extend crucial economic aid and dissuaded Adolph Hitler from attempting a costly invasion.

We all have in our mind's eye that marvelous Karsh photograph that caught the defiant Prime Minister at that perilous hour. But the facade does not reveal the real Churchill behind the myth.

Churchill was hardly destined to be an orator. He had little of the God-given talents for forensic brilliance. He was born with a congenital lisp and stammer. His voice lacked the rich resonance of the platform speaker and his five-foot five hunched frame was hardly an imposing presence.

Yet early in his life he determined that command of the English language would be his staircase to power and greatness. He would wield that mastery to advance his career and preserve the West.

DESTINY

He was history's child.
—*Lyndon B. Johnson*

It was only by a coincidence of destiny that Winston Churchill was born in Blenheim Palace, the estate of the Duke of Marlborough. Lord Randolph and Lady Churchill had planned to have their first child born in London, where the best doctors were available. The townhouse they had chosen on 48 Charles Street would not be ready to move into until the second week of December. Randolph's responsibilities in the House of Commons, to which he had been recently elected, required a city base. Randolph had been elected on February 4 and married on April 15 in Paris at a simple ceremony at the British Embassy there. If the passions of these two headstrong lovers, the younger son of a British duke and Jennie Jerome, the daughter of an American adventurer, made the birth of their first son "premature," it was not expected to be *that* premature. In fact, it happened so suddenly that the mother didn't even have time to get to her bedroom. Winston's unexpected arrival in a coatroom of Blenheim Palace at one-thirty in the morning on November 30, 1874, was such a surprise that baby linen had to be borrowed from the wife of a nearby attorney. Perhaps the birth was induced by Lady Randolph's going out on a bumpy carriage ride and then dancing at the Palace's St. Andrew's Eve Ball in the hours before the sudden delivery. Whatever the cause of Winston's unexpected entrance into the world, the place of his birth in the home of one of England's greatest heroes, the first Duke of Marlborough, must have shaped and colored the young Churchill's mind.

But what if Churchill had also inherited Blenheim Palace, in which he was born? This almost happened. If it had, and Churchill had become the tenth Duke of Marlborough in 1934, he would have had to quit his career in the House of Commons and he would never have become prime minister six years later. When, in the fall of 1895, the eighteen-year-old Consuelo Vanderbilt arrived at Blenheim as the ninth Duchess of Marlborough, the old dowager duchess, her husband's and Winston's grandmother, fixed her cold eyes upon her and said, "Your first duty is to have a child, and it must be a son because it would be intolerable to have that little upstart Winston become duke." Fortunately for Winston's sake and for history's, she produced an heir. Thus Winston Churchill, in failing to receive the title and estate of the first Duke of Marlborough, could win the duke's fame and glory. What this heroic ancestor did as a general leading a coalition against Louis XIV the descendant could also do as prime minister against Hitler.

If it was destiny that kept Winston Churchill in the House of Commons, it is perhaps also an odd turn of fate that made him choose such a career in the first place. Without the brilliant yet controversial career of his short-lived father, Lord Randolph, it is doubtful whether his son would have made politics his forum. Yet but for a snub, his father might never have concentrated on a political career. He did so after social banishment by Edward, the Prince of Wales.

While Edward went on a state visit to India with the Earl of Aylesford, Randolph's older brother and the ducal heir, the Marquis of Blandford bedded and won the affections of the earl's wife, the Countess Aylesford, a lady who had been Edward's inamorata. An irate Edward persuaded her husband, the earl, to bring divorce proceedings, naming Blandford as correspondent. With indiscreet if impassioned loyalty, Randolph reacted by threatening to make public the love letters of Victoria's son to Lady Aylesford. Edward was infuriated. He let it be known he would not set foot in a house that would entertain Lord Randolph. In a London that took its cue from the sportive prince, Randolph and Jennie became pariahs.

The rebuff triggered the change of Randolph from a social dilettante to a maverick politician. Excluded from the great houses of England, he decided to win recognition in the House of Commons.

When Randolph's comet-like career was cut short by early death, caused by what we now know was syphilis, about the only way the young Churchill could learn more about his father was to read his speeches and public papers. When a father who is a public figure dies young, the tendency for the orphaned son is to idolize and emulate the father to a far greater extent then when a more natural course brings out the inherent masculine rivalries between the two generations.

It was the father's social exile that also made his son's first memories ones of royal pomp and ceremony in a regal palace. To move Lord Randolph from the cold social atmosphere of London, the Duke of Marlborough accepted the post of viceroy in Ireland, taking his son along as secretary. Churchill's first memory is that of his mother at a receiving line at the Dublin palace: "She stood on one side to the left of the entrance . . . a dark, lithe little figure standing somewhat apart, and appearing to be another texture to those around her, radiant, translucent, intense. A diamond star in her hair, her favorite ornament — its lustre dimmed by the flashing glory of her eyes."

Such early childhood visions nurtured dreams of glory. It is no wonder Churchill's favorite interest as a child was playing with his toy soldier collection; he could pretend that he was a king, or even better, the first Duke of Marlborough, the Captain-General John Churchill, who beat the French on the German battlefield of Blenheim.

His maneuverings of miniature soldiers far surpassed those of the usual childhood game. He organized wars. The metal battalions were pushed into action. Peas and pebbles caused great casualties, forts were stormed, cavalries charged, bridges were destroyed. Once, his cousin Clare Sheridan wrote, he built a small log fort with an actual ditch and drawbridge. But she was quickly evacuated when the rocks began to fly in an all-too-real storming of the castle.

Churchill's youthful fantasies of fame were almost his undoing. Visiting an aunt on a holiday from Harrow School, he played escaping from his younger brother. Jack, and a cousin who were chasing him suddenly closed in on him as he was crossing a bridge over a ravine. Determined to avoid capture, Winston jumped off the bridge, hoping to break his fall by latching on to a tree. The tree gave no hold and he fell 30 feet. Unconscious for three days, Churchill was lucky he escaped with a ruptured kidney instead of a broken neck.

It was only the first of the many close calls with death that reinforced Churchill's belief that he was destiny's child. The first time he reflected on his luck was in Cuba as a young military observer attached to the Spanish army in 1895. A barrage of rebel gunfire opened up on the cavalry contingent he was traveling with. A bullet that passed inches from his head cut down the horse immediately behind him. For the occasion of his twenty-first birthday, it was a signal entry into manhood.

Two years later in the high mountains of India, a band of Pathan tribesmen ambushed him and his regimental leader. The adjutant was slashed to death. Surrounded and alone, Winston held them off with pistol fire and escape to a hiding place, avoiding capture and certain death.

His next brush with death was in the Sudan, where he participated in probably the last cavalry charge known in military annals, in the battle of Omdurman. Into the masses of four-deep, sword-wielding Dervishes, his troop, the 21st Lancers, galloped. Several men to the left of Churchill were hacked to death. Churchill himself killed several Dervishes in hand-to-hand combat, preventing his own decapitation.

The best example of his phenomenal luck was in the Boer war. Churchill, as a captured war correspondent in 1889, escaped from a prison in Pretoria, South Africa. From his hideout in a lavatory he made his break and vaulted over the wall when the sentry turned his back. Landing in a garden, he knelt behind the shrubs, with Boers walking in close proximity. After an hour, past dusk, he hopped a railroad train and jumped off near dawn. Tired, hungry, and lost, he threw caution aside and knocked on a house door, saying he was a Dutch clergyman. At any other house his lisping English accent would have meant immediate recognition and capture, since there was a price on his head. Amazingly, the house he picked was the only habitation in 20 miles that belonged to an

English fellow countryman, who hid him in a mine until an escape route could be worked out.

Then, in World War I, after he had been dismissed as First Lord of the Admiralty for the Dardanelles disaster, he had himself assigned as a battalion major to the war in France. One day, while he was supervising trench defenses, a note was delivered to him by his commanding general. Only testily did Churchill agree to leave his post. Minutes after his departure a bomb obliterated the spot in the dugout on which he had been standing. Writing about the incident later, he observed ". . . a hand had been stretched out to move me in the nick of time from a fatal spot."

Later, when he was called back to the cabinet by Prime Minister David Lloyd George, he again eluded certain death. He had developed, in the latter days of the war, the habit of getting up early, completing his work at the War Ministry in the morning, and then flying over the Channel to France to have a firsthand look at the need for munitions and supplies. By early evening he would be back at his Whitehall desk. Even by today's standards, such a daily commuting practice would be astonishing; then, it was almost suicidal. Once his engine caught fire over the Channel. Another time his plane somersaulted while taking off. A little later, while at the controls, Churchill found his control stick jammed, and he crashed a hundred feet from the hangar. He stepped from the burning wreck. Despite his injuries, he was addressing the House of Commons two hours later.

Like a racing car driver, he couldn't resist flirting with danger. As he wrote his mother after his shootout in the mountain frontiers of India, "it may be foolish but I play for high stakes." In sport, he could fling himself with the recklessness of one sure of his luck. Even in middle age, he continued his daring as a horseman eager to jump any wall or as a polo player ready to play with one arm strapped. In war, he had felt no bullet or bomb had had his "number" on it.

A car in New York City almost had that number. While on a speaking tour in 1931, he was run down by a taxi and rushed to a hospital. Despite multiple injuries he was soon up continuing his speaking engagements. To Churchill, only his luck explained his survival. As he himself stated about the course of his life, "One can see how lucky I was. Over me beat invisible wings."

Even if there are those who would argue that such a line of fateful incidents is not all that uncommonly meaningful, it was significant to Churchill. He believed that by both birth and background he was to have his appointed role in history. His string of luck in escaping death only reinforced his faith that destiny was saving a place for him. As he said at 22, "I have faith in my star—that is, that I am intended to do something in the world."

But paradoxically, he also thought he was going to die young. The shadow of his father's early death at the age of 45 loomed black and heavy before him. On his birthday in 1899 he wrote, "I am 25 today—it is terrible to think how little time remains." His father had become Chancellor of the Exchequer and Leader of the House of Commons before he was 37; his son had scarcely more than a decade to reach similar heights. In his youth he often told friends, "We Churchills are a frail-stemmed lot." Only in his middle years, past the age of his father's death, did he begin to think perhaps he inherited the robust constitution of his mother's Jerome side. Then the feeling began to develop that his racehorse owner of a grandfather, Leonard Jerome, might have been right when he said, "The pace is the sire's, the stamina comes from the dam [mare]."

The two beliefs—early death and eventual destiny—instead of counteracting, fed each other. Confident of his luck, he took chances. He had to; his time was short. Whatever the occasion, he chose excitement over safety, challenge over security, and the unknown over certainty. In the classroom he would not hesitate to contradict or correct a master. On the athletic field he would choose the spotlight of swimming or fencing over the crowd of team activities like rugby or cricket. Of such group sports only polo, which commanded the dash and daring of a brave horseman, could offer much appeal. In the army he would volunteer for front-line action and afterward write critiques of the commanding general's strategy. Politics would be no different. As a freshman member of Parliament he would attack his own party's senior ministers even in their conduct of a war. He would change parties not once but twice. In fact, once he formed his own and ran as a party of one.

When he was a child, however, the adult generation of teachers and parents saw only recalcitrance in his rebellion. To them, it suggested more dunce than destiny.

As the son of Britain's youngest Chancellor of the Exchequer since Pitt and descendant of its greatest general, Churchill, however, knew fame had to be his lot.

Lady Violet Bonham-Carter, his old friend and daughter of Prime Minister Herbert Asquith, wrote:

> Again and again, watching his life and fortune, it has seemed to me Winston had a private wire with fate. His course often appeared to be shaped either by accident or by impulse. It was always unpredictable, sometimes inexplainable in terms of reason, yet following it, it is hard not to believe it was directed by that beam which some call destiny and others instinct, by a power which intervened between him and events, which not once but many times preserved his life to serve its purposes. What he called "intuition" was in fact obedience to the beam which shaped his course.

It was Lady Bonham-Carter, as Violet Asquith, to whom Churchill at a dinner party said, "Curse ruthless time! Curse our mortality! How cruelly short is the allotted span for all we must cram into it! We are all worms. But I do believe I am a glowworm."

2

YOUTH

Winston Churchill is a born actor.
—*Prime Minister David Lloyd George*

But for his firm belief in his own destiny, Churchill might never have emotionally survived the traumas of a childhood grim even by Victorian standards. Classroom days were a long travail rendered harsh by draconian schoolmasters and lonely by a neglectful mother and indifferent father. Winston, before he was eight, was sent away to school at St. George's in Ascot. Although it was not unusual for upper-class British parents to board their children away from home at such an early age, it is surprising that Lord and Lady Randolph knew so little about this dreadful school or its perverted headmaster. The Reverend H. W. Sneyd-Kynnersley, whose Dickensian name almost suggests the nature of the school, combined obsequiousness to his aristocratic clients with bestiality to their offspring. If a young boy received poor grades, he had the habit of taking him to his room, stripping him, and beating him until "the wretched boy's bottom was a mass of blood."

Sneyd-Kynnersley was a psychopath who merged a bent for sodomy with sadism. At one point he forced Churchill to run at full tilt for hours round and round in dizzying circles. A visitor, noticing the red-haired youth, said, "Who on earth is that?"

"Why, that's young Churchill," the headmaster replied. "It's the only way we can keep him quiet."

That sort of punishment, however, not to mention the continual floggings, did not subdue the Churchill spirit. In fact, Winston took revenge by finding the headmaster's prize straw hat and kicking it to pieces. Churchill's miserable career at St. George's was predicted by his first Latin lesson on opening day. Told to

13

memorize the declension of *mensa*, meaning "table," Winston was puzzled at the vocative case.

"It means," said the master, "O table! You would use it in addressing a table or in invoking a table."

"But I never do," replied the confused Winston.

"If you are impertinent, you will be punished, and punished, let me tell you, very severely," was the stern reprimand.

The school's effect on the child was not noticed by his parents. Lord Randolph, now England's most talked about and caricatured politician, and his wife were again caught up in the social swirl. The attitude of the Prince of Wales, as Disraeli had predicted it would, thawed, and Randolph's success brightened. Queen Victoria, Edward's mother, had signaled the change by inviting the Churchills to Windsor.

Winston's parents may not have been concerned about the child, but his beloved nanny, "Woom" (for woman), was. She, no doubt, saw the bruises from birching and recommended a change. So, after two years at Ascot, Winston was enrolled at Brighton, a school run by two genteel spinsters where, if the treatment was kind, the academic standard was equally soft. Even with a less rigorous regimen, young Winston almost died from a dose of double pneumonia, possibly a delayed reaction to his abusive ordeal at Ascot. His lungs soon regained their strength, yet his heart remained sick. Winston was a lonely boy who yearned for any parental display of interest. At age ten he began avidly to follow accounts in the newspaper of the father he didn't know.

School was a prison term until vacations. The only things that continually stirred his interest in the classroom were poetic readings or theatrical recitations. In his letters to his mother, Churchill reveals that he enjoyed learning a poem by Sir Walter Scott called "Edinburgh After Flodden" and later Milton's "Paradise Lost." Even more fun were the plays the school put on such as Gilbert and Sullivan's *Mikado,* which Winston beseeched his mother to attend and even to act in.

His favorite gift as a child, besides his burgeoning tin soldier collection, was a toy theater one of his two American aunts gave him, which, as he wrote to his mother, was a "source of unparalleled amusement." The happiest moments of his Brighton years were his acting leads. He played the title role in *Robin Hood* and later had principal roles in dramas by Aristophanes and Molière. Perhaps the highlight of his three years at Brighton was his appearance as Dick Dowlas in Colman's play *The Heir at Law*. As the school's best actor, he was given the leading role in this 1808 melodrama. He brought down the house with his continued misreading of the line "I will send my carriage." Instead of "carriage" he said "carrot," which, as it was the color of his flaming hair, triggered gales of laughter. He was not so successful in his planned production of *Aladdin,* which, despite S.O.S. messages to home for more props, proved too ambitious for the school's capability.

Theater became the outlet for his pent-up frustrations. It was an avenue for his imagination and an escape from his lonely exile. In the world of make-believe, he could be that important personage he evidently was not in the eyes of his parents. Winston did, however, gain esteem in his own eyes. In acting, a lack of inhibition was an asset, and when Winston joined that with his exceptional memory, he found a talent that far exceeded that of his classmates.

His memory was to give him his first academic success, and indeed his only one, at Harrow, the public school he entered in 1888. He had hardly been enrolled when he, though assigned to the form for the slowest learners, announced his bid for the school prize in recitation. He wrote his father, "I am learning 1000 lines of Macaulay." His dearest wish would have been for his father to come to hear him. In another letter he begged for his mother to come, but neither of his parents was in attendance on his day of triumph, when the top prize was carried off by a boy in a bottom form.

Winston almost didn't bring it off. The day before presentation he found out the required number of lines was actually twelve hundred. Using every spare minute, he mastered the additional quatrains in the *Lays of Ancient Rome* and won the coveted prize, to the surprise of the school. As the voice of Horatius, he spoke lines that would be etched in the heart and mind of Churchill, the future statesman.

> Then none was for a party
> Then all were for the state,

Then the great man helped the poor
And the poor man loved the great;
Then lands were fairly portioned
And the Huns were fairly sold;
The Britons were like brothers
In the brave days of old.

Fifty-five years later Churchill, as prime minister, would close a wartime address to a group of Dominion leaders with these verses of Macaulay.

Though Churchill's name in the Harrow rolls today carries the letter P, for prize, after it, this was his only scholastic accomplishment. Indeed, he would never have been accepted into the school but for his father's public eminence. To qualify he had been given a passage of Latin prose to translate. After two hours his only ink contributions to the blank page were his name and two smudges. The headmaster, the Reverend J. E. C. Welldon, not eager to lose Lord Randolph's son, overlooked the lack of answer in a decision that would one day render the name of Harrow glorious around the world.

The ginger-headed youngster must have made Dr. Welldon doubt his decision many times. Once, when Churchill was summoned to the headmaster's study, the boy was told, "Churchill, I have grave reason to be displeased with you." Churchill's insouciant reply was, "And sir, I have very grave reason to be displeased with you."

The school did not sense the talent in Churchill, but unwittingly honed it. Condemning him to repeat the lowest form for his inability in Latin, they forced him to take over and over again Mr. Somervell's English class. Mr. Somervell would diagram sentences with different colors used for the parts of speech—noun, verb, object, adjective, and different layers for the subordinate clauses—relative, conditional, conjunctive, and disjunctive. Even fifty years later Winston could see in his mind's eye the "black" subject, the "red" verb, or the "green" object. As he himself wrote, "Thus I got in my bones the essential structure of the ordinary British sentence which is a noble thing." He added, not totally in jest, "Naturally I am biased in favor of boys learning English. I would make them all learn English; and then I would let the clever ones learn Latin as an honor and Greek as a treat. But the only thing I would whip them for is not knowing English. I would whip them hard for that. . ."

As a Harrovian, the resourceful Winston found a way to make his proficiency in English compensate for his deficiency in Latin. He struck a deal with a young Latin whiz who couldn't put his mind to writing the assigned English compositions. In return for this linguist's translations, Winston ghosted his essays. One of these struck the fancy of the headmaster, who called the Latin scholar into his study to amplify upon his interesting conclusions. Afterward the shaken youth told Winston he'd like the conclusions a bit less dazzling. It was not to be the last time people found Churchill's brilliance unsettling.

Under the pseudonym Junius Junior, Winston wrote for the school paper, the *Harrovian.* Just as he later took ministers to task for their inadequacies in meeting various contingencies, he attacked the condition of the school pool, workshop, and gym. The headmaster, who suspected that the identity of the anonymous writer was none other than Lord Randolph's son, gave him an indirect warning:

My boy, I have observed certain articles which have recently appeared in the *Harrovian* of a character not calculated to increase the respect of the boys for the constituted authorities of the school. As the *Harrovian* is anonymous, I shall not dream of inquiring who wrote these articles, but if any more of the same sort appear, it might become my painful duty to swish you.

Unbowed, Winston persuaded his editor to print one more broadside letter:

All these things that I have enumerated serve to suggest that there is "something rotten in the State of Denmark." I have merely stated facts—it is not for me to offer explanation of them. To you, sirs, as directors of public opinion, it belongs to bare the weakness. Could I not propose that some of your unemployed correspondents might be set to work to unravel the mystery, and to collect material wherewith these questions may be answered?

The school itself has an ancient history; even the gymnasium dates back to a Tudor. In those days they were not want to Risk [this was a pun of Churchill's; Tudor Risk was the name of the first gymnasium superintendent] the success of the school Assault-at-Arms in the manner it was done on Saturday last. For three years the Assaults have been getting worse and worse. First, the Midgets, then the Board School, and finally the Aldershot Staff (not regular teams) have been called to supplement the scanty programme. It's time there should be a change and I rely on your influential columns to work that change.

The boy who really took the heat for printing these columns was not Winston but the *Harrovian* editor, Julian Amery. Once Churchill, citing "the inexcusable decay of the gymnasium," excoriated a writer who had risen to defend the state of the facilities. Churchill wrote: "I will not pause to criticize his style nor comment on his probable motives, though I am inclined to think that both are equally poor." Amery, in deleting some of his more scathing words, added this note: "(We have omitted a portion of our correspondent's letter, which seemed to us exceed the limits of fair criticism. —Eds. *Harrovian)*"

Amery had been introduced to the rambunctious Churchill in a startling way. One day he found himself pushed from behind into the pool. Amery, though small for his age, was an upper former and, in addition, one of the best athletes in the school. He was not thus inclined to accept with equanimity such an unceremonious dunking by this puggish upstart. As Amery took his revenge, Winston realized his mistake and said in defense, "My father is small too and he is a great man." Indeed, at that time Lord Randolph was Secretary of State for India, and, half a century later, Amery was to be given that post by the boy who dunked him. Amery, later recalling his days of editing Churchill, spoke of Churchill's early journalistic flair even though he admitted he had to blue-pencil out some of his writer's best jibes.

That Churchill soon displayed a knack for turning out columns is not surprising. For years he had been poring over the newspapers for comment about his politically prominent father. Blessed with his retentive memory and solid grounding in the English sentence, Churchill found writing the critical essay no difficult task. In his head echoed the phrases of impassioned parliamentary speeches and the journalists' wry comments on them the next day. In his days at Harrow, Churchill soaked up more in his own reading than he did in the classroom.

Prose was not the only literary outlet for Churchill at Harrow. He also penned at least one epic ballad of mock-heroic style, called "Ode to Influenza." The "bug," which had been plaguing the school, was treated as if it were the spread of the Huns or Vandals.

In the twelve-stanza poem, he manifested both the political acumen and the patriotism of a future war leader.

> Fair Alsace and forlorn Lorraine
> The cause of bitterness and pain
> In many a Gallic breast
> Receive the vile, insatiate scourge
> And from their towns with it emerge
> And never stay or rest.
>
> In Calais port the illness stays
> As did the French in former days
> To threaten Freedom's isle
> But now no Nelson could o'er throw
> The cruel, unconquerable foe
> Nor save us from its guile

And in the closing peroration we hear the voice of him who was to rally Britain to its finest hour:

> God shield our Empire from the might
> Of war of famine, plague or blight

> And all the power of Hell
> And keep it ever in the hands
> Of those who fought 'gainst other lands
> Who fought and conquered well.

Perhaps we also hear the echo of Milton or Shakespeare in *King John*. Stirring lines of martial beat and patriotic fervor early made an impression on Churchill that was never to be erased.

Anthems also made their mark on him, like the "Battle Hymn of the Republic," which he would order played at his funeral, and the Harrow School Song. Fifty years later he was chanting to his son these lines he loved:

> God give us bases to guard or beleaguer
> Games to play out whether earnest or fun
> Fights for the fearless and goals for the eager
> Twenty and thirty years on.

If Winston had not always an ear for the tune, he had for the rhymes and rhythm. He absorbed lines and phrases of poems and ballads as today's teenagers soak up rock and pop music lyrics. Words were his escape, and he would declaim without benefit of prompting or stage.

During World War II, when he was visiting Franklin Roosevelt, the presidential party made its way by car from Washington to Camp David (then Shangri-La). As they went through Frederick, Maryland, Harry Hopkins recited the opening verse of "Barbara Frietchie," the gray-haired lady who defied the Confederate troops:

> Up from the meadow green with corn
> Clear in the cool September morn . . .

Then Churchill, to the amazement of the Americans, proceeded to recite the rest of the thirty-stanza poem, urging them to chime in with the punch line:

Shoot if you must this old gray head
But spare your country's flag, she said.

Though most people think memory is a matter of gift, it can, like a muscle, be developed, as most actors will tell you. Churchill, by ever committing verses to heart, expanded his capacity for recall. The next term, after winning his prize for reciting Macaulay, Churchill tackled a more ambitious goal, the Shakespeare award, which that year meant the study of *The Merchant of Venice, Henry VIII,* and *A Midsummer Night's Dream.* Here memory was not the only factor. Notes had to be worked up on the plays' history, background, and literary symbolism and allusion. Clearly Winston, who really became a scholar only upon leaving school, was at a disadvantage. Nevertheless, he came in fourth, beating out boys who were older and in senior forms.

After that effort, Winston could quote whole Shakespearean scenes by heart. He would often rattle schoolmasters by interrupting and correcting them for misreadings. One can imagine the reaction of the pedagogue who declaims, "Is this a dagger which I see before me, the handle toward my head?" only to have this freckle-faced urchin pop up and say, "Actually, it's 'toward my hand'."

During World War II Sir Laurence Olivier and Vivien Leigh invited the prime minister to see their production of *Richard III.* He shook the cast as he had his Harrow masters by reciting all of the lines during the play. Later, at dinner, the Oliviers discovered he knew the whole of *Henry IV, Henry V,* and *Henry VIII* by heart. Indeed, by reciting various passages aloud, Churchill made Olivier, by his own admission, recast at least one of his renditions in accordance with the Churchill version.

Years later, Richard Burton told Jack Paar of Churchill's phenomenal knowledge of Shakespeare. During the 1950s, when Burton was playing *Hamlet,* he had an encounter with Churchill. From the first row he could hear a dull rumble, which was the prime minister reciting the play's lines. Burton tried speeding up and then slowing down, but he couldn't shake Churchill off. When he tried to cut, an explosive expostulation would erupt. During the intermission Burton exuded relief when he saw

Churchill's seat empty and assumed its occupant had left the theater. Only minutes later, there was a knock on his dressing-room door, and a well-known voice asked: "My Lord Hamlet, may I use your lavatory?" And the speaker did.

Even though Churchill was then eighty, glimpses could be seen of the little boy who early saw in poetry and drama the opportunity of taking center stage. It was his love of declamation that gave Churchill a head start in mastering the fundamentals of English expression. The actor in the boy would shape the orator in the man.

3

SOLDIER

The first virtue of a soldier
is the discipline of endurance.
                    —*Napoleon*

The decision that Churchill enter Harrow instead of Eton had been made for reasons of health. Harrow, whose nickname is "the hill" for its command of a knoll, was considered a wiser choice for a frail-lunged boy than the boggy Eton which Lord Randolph had attended. That Winston went to Sandhurst, the British West Point, however, was more luck than logic. In those years of becoming a soldier, Winston Churchill was to become a man.

One day while Winston was home on vacation, his father made one of his rare visits to the nursery playroom. There Winston, with his array of miniature might, a collection of 1,500 toy soldiers, was conducting maneuvers. Lord Randolph stood solemnly inspecting the terrain. Finally, he asked Winston, "Would you like to go in the army?" "Of course," Winston answered. What else would you expect a young descendant of Marlborough to say when he was in the midst of his own military operations?

The father's reasoning, if just as impulsive, was no less obvious. As the grandson of a duke, the boy could not go into trade, as business was then called by those of the upper class. An aristocrat in Victorian days had only three suitable careers: the church, the law, or the military. In Randolph's eyes, the unpromising child seemed too obstreperous for a spiritual vocation and too obtuse for a legal one.

But choosing a military career and qualifying for it are two different things. First, the boy had to be accepted into the Army Class at Harrow, which prepped for the Royal Military Academy at Sandhurst. Many boys with much higher scholastic ratings than Winston failed the rigid preliminary examination, in which one of

25

the tests was to draw a map of some country. The night before the exam Winston put all the maps of his atlas into a hat and then pulled one out; it proved to be New Zealand, and he set out to memorize it. Amazingly, the first question asked him the next day was to draw a map of New Zealand.

Years later, Mr. Moriarity, the teacher, confessed that he had never seen such an intricately detailed map drawn freehand in all his life. Winston, who had concentrated his memory on the one country, had filled in streams, narrow-gauge railroads, and bridges. Later a frequent habitué of the French casinos in the Riviera, Churchill himself once said of his long-shot success: "It was like hitting the jackpot at Monte Carlo." But for that lucky strike, which pulled up his total average in the other tests, Winston would have been eliminated from the Army Class and would never have made it to Sandhurst.

Sandhurst saw the first stirrings of manhood in Churchill. A sober sense of purpose was beginning to replace the attitude of capricious dissent. Perhaps the influence of the stern and spartan Academy had its effect. But of greater impact was the realization by Winston that failure at Sandhurst spelled the end to any dreams of destiny. His father, who had cut short his brilliant political career by an impulsive and headstrong resignation on principle, was already a shadowy figure declining under the ravages of his debilitating disease. Winston sensed he would soon have to make it on his own. He was eighteen and becoming a man.

In Victorian England, young men started to earn their living in their teens. Even today in Britain, where a college education, even for the upper classes, is the exception, not the rule, 18 is the age at which most men begin their life as adults. Winston was still at school but there was now a maturity in the way he applied himself to the courses at hand. Courses like Tactics, Fortification, Topography, and Military Law commanded his full attention. He learned how to blow up bridges, construct breastworks, and make contoured maps. He studied major battles of great wars, and the one he found most fascinating was the conflict at Gettysburg in the American Civil War.

His newly found seriousness of purpose had its results. Winston finished twentieth in a class of 130. If this wasn't the brilliance of a Douglas MacArthur or Robert E. Lee, who at West Point finished first and second respectively, it was better than Omar Bradley and Dwight Eisenhower, who in a class of 160 were forty-fourth and sixty-first. Such comparative rankings may be meaningless, but the contrast to Churchill's record at Harrow is significant. He had moved from the bottom ranks there into the upper at Sandhurst. An often delinquent schoolboy had become a diligent cadet. What he had learned was the secret of Napoleon, whose maxim he later would often quote: *"L'art est de fixer les objets longtemps sans être fatigué."* It was thus he acquired the ability to throw himself into an unfamiliar field or subject and master its essentials. If out of his experience at Sandhurst he never became a general, it made him a generalist, the sine qua non of any great leader.

Winston's son Randolph, describing his Sandhurst years, says, "He had to fight every inch of his road through life; nothing came easily to him, not even oratory and writing, in which he was later to excel. To achieve success, he had to develop that intense power of concentration which, as it grew, was to serve him and his fellow countrymen so well."

Perhaps, as he later would imply, Churchill's sudden maturing was aided by his father's early decline and death. A couple of years after Lord Randolph died Winston wrote, "Solitary trees, if they grow at all, grow strong; and a boy deprived of a father's care often develops, if he escapes the peril of youth, an independence and vigor of thought which may restore in afterlife the heavy loss of early days." The year 1895 made Winston feel very solitary indeed. On January 24 his father, who for months had been a pitiful spectacle, finally passed away. The tragedy of Lord Randolph's death, as former Prime Minister Lord Rosebery wrote, was that "he died publicly inch by inch." His conduct on the floor of the House of Commons was strange, with outbursts followed by flashes of inexplicable silence. His friends had to suffer through these aberrations while his foes ridiculed him. The mental effects of a disease only dimly suspected by those outside the family invited more scorn than sympathy.

Upon Randolph's death Winston became the man of the house, with a mother to console and a younger brother to supervise. There were other deaths that year that removed from his life old familiar sources of strength and stability. His grandmother Jerome, of whom Winston was a special favorite, died in April. Most important was the death in July of Mrs. Everest, his old nanny, who was more than his surrogate mother. She was, excepting only his wife, the one in his life who gave him the most unconditional love. At Harrow, to the surprise and sneering gibes of his classmates, he had invited his old nanny down and walked hand in hand with her across the campus, showing her the sights. A classmate wrote years later that it was one of the greatest acts of courage and compassion he had ever seen. For years before her death his nanny had been in retirement, her days brightened by letters from her beloved Winston. He was the only Churchill to attend her funeral. Even though he had only an officer's pay, a meager £120 a year, upon leaving Sandhurst he made an arrangement with a florist for the constant upkeep of her grave. To the end of his life Winston kept her picture on his desk at Chartwell.

From his father's death in January to his being shot at in Cuba on his twenty-first birthday, 1895 was the year of Churchill's coming of age. He left Sandhurst and discovered what he should do with his life; it was not soldiering. In August, a speech by his cousin, the Duke of Marlborough, eulogizing Lord Randolph prompted this passage in a letter from Winston to his mother:

It is a fine game to play—the game of politics—and it's well worth waiting for a good hand before really plunging.

At any rate, four years of healthy and pleasant existence, combined with both responsibility and discipline can do no harm to me, but rather good. The more I see of soldiering the more I like it, but the more I feel convinced that it is not my metier.

But at the same time Winston realized that the narrowness of his Sandhurst education had not prepared him for political life. His had been the specialized training of a military officer. There were gigantic gaps in his knowledge, wide spaces of ignorance that had to be filled fast. When he was stationed at his first post with the Queen's Own Hussars at Aldershot in Hampshire, his mother had suggested he make himself an expert on "the supply of horses." Churchill demurred, writing his mother:

No—my dearest Mamma—I think something more literary and less material would be the sort of mental medicine I need. . . . You see—all my life—I have had a purely technical education . . . as a result my mind has never received that polish which for instance Oxford or Cambridge gives. At these places one studies questions and sciences with a rather higher object than mere practical utility. One receives in fact a liberal education. . . . I have now got a capital book—causing much thought—and of great interest. It is a work on political economy by [Henry] Fawcett. When I have read it, and it is very long, I shall perhaps feel inclined to go still farther afield in an absorbing subject. But this is a book essentially devoted to "first principles" and one which would leave at least a clear knowledge of the framework of the subject behind—and would be of use even if the subject were not persevered in.

Then I am going to read Gibbon's *Decline and Fall of the Roman Empire* and Lecky's *[History of] European Morals.* These will be tasks more agreeable than the mere piling up of statistics. . . .

It is clear that his mother was no longer the remote figure of his boyhood in which "She shone for me like the Evening Star. I loved her dearly—but at a distance." The young widowed Lady Randolph still dazzled, but she now employed her radiance to help guide her son just as she had his father. In a man's world her son now succeeded his father as a focus for her own ambitious dreams. She was, after all, not only an American in the midst of the British aristocracy, but also a widow without the base of her husband's position or the security of a large inheritance. Her only asset was her unfading beauty and her will to use it. Though vain and self-centered, Jennie had a shrewdness that belied a seemingly brittle shallowness.

The new object for her maneuverings was not an unstriking figure. This youngest lieutenant in the service of Victoria was, if not tall, yet lithe and supple. His head, if too large for his body, fit Plutarch's conception of the look of leadership. The head was set off by a pug nose, large blue eyes, and a pink and white skin that would make any girl envious. A shock of reddish gold hair just about matched the braid on his Hussar uniform.

But in 1895, this newly turned-out Hussar cavalryman found himself all dressed up with no place to go. There was no field on which to make a name. Hardly a cloud jotted the horizons of the Empire. The last war Britain had fought was in the Crimean Peninsula in 1854. The only place any fighting was now going on was in Cuba, and one could scarcely call a minor rebellion a war. But it promised more excitement than the round of parties young officers filled their two-month vacations with, and so Winston went, but only after his mother obligingly scraped up some extra funds out of her limited income to pay for his passage.

Though his stint as a military observer with the Spanish army gave him his first taste of gunfire, perhaps his more significant initiation was his first venture as a journalist. Winston engaged the editor of *The Daily Graphic,* for whom his father had once written a few articles, to pay him for a series of dispatches at £5 a piece.

For an untrained eye, young Churchill was prescient. He sensed the paradox that would describe almost every revolution in the following century. As he put it: "I liked the rebellion, but not the rebels." In other words, though he thought the cause was just and would soon prevail, he had little faith in the movement's leadership, which he thought might manipulate the people to its own ends. "Though the Spanish administration is bad," he wrote, "a Cuban government would be worse, equally corrupt, more capricious and far less stable. Under such a government revolutions would be periodic, property insecure, equity unknown."

Winston might have observed only three days of the Cuban conflict, but he picked up some habits that would last a lifetime. The first was his taste for Havana cigars, and the second his discovery that the Spanish siesta, taken at midday with clothes removed, could add at least three or more productive hours to the day in the nighttime. Without the ever-present cigar, the Churchillian image of imperturbability in the face of crisis might not have been so completely effected, and without the midday nap, his Herculean round-the-clock World War II efforts could never have been accomplished.

When Churchill returned, he soon learned that the unit of the Fourth Hussars had been called to India. Most of his fellow officers welcomed the assignment to this Kiplingian subcontinent where life spelled one continuous round of polo and parties. But to Churchill, it was almost an exile from the real scene of the action—London and the House of Commons. On his way from Southampton to Bombay he revealed to a shipmate his feelings of frustration in cricket terms: "We Churchills peg out early, we must get our innings in fast."

But at Bangalore, situated more than 3,000 feet above sea level, it was not innings, but chukkers of polo. Garrison life centered around the equestrian sport, which called for the brave and daring horsemanship that produced a superb cavalryman. Drills and reviews were just routines that marked the hours before the daily five o'clock match. Evening mess at eight-thirty and the hours that followed in the cool night were opportunities for officers to rehash the day's game.

Though Churchill, because of a dislocated shoulder he had injured while reaching for the iron ring on his disembarkment at the quay in Bombay, had to play polo with his arm strapped, he was an excellent player. He would be playing until age 52, when he participated in a match in Malta. In fact, one account of his superlative equestrian skills comes from no less an authority than the young Aga Khan, who in his training as a British officer had occasion in India to observe Lieutenant Churchill. Churchill loved playing polo, but he was soon bored talking about it. His mind was elsewhere, reaching out for the mental stimulation that was absent in the banalities of bungalow chatter dwelling only on the flesh, be it equine or feminine.

The idea of thirteen or fourteen more years of this Indian tour of army duty was unbearable. It would be a virtual prison sentence for almost the remaining years of what he felt sure was his allotted life span. How would he ever be able to pick up his father's fallen political banners? When he read that an ex-officer had stood successfully as a Conservative in West Bradford, a constituency where Lord Randolph's views were popular, he was bitter with the belief that it should have been he. Still other thoughts that he was unworthy of his father's mantle plagued him. He had not been an Oxford scholar and, with his inadequacies in Greek and Latin, never could be.

The only answer was for Churchill to educate himself. He would set up what F. Scott Fitzgerald would later call "a university of one." He would use the three or four hours in the torrid midday, when his fellow officers played cards, to read what he would have studied at Oxford or Cambridge. To his mother he sent urgent letters asking for books. The first to arrive was Edward Gibbon's *Decline and Fall of the Roman Empire,* which his mother said had been his father's favorite, and which he had already begun reading at Aldershot. Then came Macaulay's various histories, which he had heard were almost easy reading and afforded an accessible overview of British institutional and political history; he would follow up those with philosophers both ancient and modern, Plato and Aristotle, together with Darwin and Lecky.

Of all the efforts in Churchill's life, this achievement of self-education was the most formidable. He had no teacher, no guide, no intellectual soulmate to bounce ideas off of or share thoughts. He would teach, discipline, and grade himself.

As if he were at a university, he gave himself assignments such as reading twenty pages of Gibbon along with fifty of Macaulay a day. The reason for this was more than just to simulate an academic atmosphere. He found he could absorb more if he interspersed his readings among several authors. At the same time he asked his mother to send him copies, beginning with his birthdate of 1874, of the *Annual Register* (the parliamentary equivalent of the *Congressional Record*). As an intellectual exercise, he would not read the debates until he had first read the bill in question and mastered its implications. Thus he would record his own views on bills such as slum clearance, the purchase of Suez Canal shares, and compulsory vaccination before reading the debates pro and con. In this way he graded the logic of his own views. He became his own university.

Churchill's regimen of studies comprised more than history and politics. For biology he read Darwin. In the realm of philosophy, he added the German Schopenhauer to the Greeks Plato and Aristotle. In economics he added Malthus and Adam Smith to his study of Fawcett. In religion he pondered over Winwood Reade's *The Martyrdom of Man*. All in all, his studies covered hundreds of books.

Soon he came to look forward more to his midday lessons than his late afternoon polo. What had started as a discipline became a diversion. As soon as he arrived back in his bungalow he would get out his books, pour out some brandy and soda, light up a cigar, and read away. "He read," as his friend Lady Violet Bonham-Carter noted of this period, "as the hungry eat, neither from habit nor from duty, but from need; these books entered his system and became part of him."

In his novel *Savrola,* written a few years later, Churchill describes the library of the hero with a glance at his own bookshelves in Bangalore:

The room was lit by electric light in portable shaded lamps. The walls were covered with shelves, filled with well-used volumes. To that Pantheon of Literature none were admitted until they had been read and valued. It was a various library, the philosophy of Schopenhauer divided Kant from Hegel, who jostled the *Memoirs of St. Simon* and the latest French novel; Rosselos and La Curie lay side by side; eight substantial volumes of Gibbon's famous *History* were not perhaps inappropriately prolonged by a fine edition of the *Decameron,* the *Origin of Species* rested by the side of a block-letter Bible; *The Republic* maintained an equilibrium with *Vanity Fair* and the *History of European Morals*. A volume of Macaulay's *Essays* lay on the writing table itself; it was open and that sublime passage on Gibbon whereby the genius of one man has immortalized the genius of another was marked in pencil. "And History, while for the warning of vehement, high and daring natures, she notes his many errors, will yet deliberately pronounce that among the eminent men whose bones lie near his, scarcely one has left a more stainless and none a more splendid name."

It is no whim that makes the historians Macaulay and Gibbon co-stars of the bookcase, with the latter given top billing. In a comment in 1947 on one of his first books, *The River War,* Churchill wrote, "I affected a combination of the style of Macaulay and Gibbon, the staccato antitheses of the former and the rolling sentence and genitival endings of the latter, and I stuck in a bit of my own from time to time."

To see what Churchill meant by the two styles, compare these social commentaries by the two historians. Macaulay says: "The Puritan hated bear-baiting, not because it gave pain to the bear but because it gave pleasure to the spectators." Gibbon, in more stately prose: "Whenever the offense inspires less horror than the punishment, the rigour of the penal law is obliged to give way to the common feelings of mankind."

The influence of Gibbon would finally edge out that of Macaulay in the sentences of Churchill, who became fond of prepositional endings. Such genitival conclusions have an air of finality to them. ("The laws of a nation form the most instructive portion of the history. The winds and waves are always on the side of the alert navigator." Decent easy men who supinely enjoyed the gifts of the founder.") Churchill also observed the Ciceronian tricolon of the Gibbon sentence. ("In every deed of mischief he had a heart to resolve, a head to contrive, and a hand to execute.") What Churchill particularly admired was the balance of the Gibbonian sentence, that suggested an aura of detached impartiality. Gibbon would concede the virtues of an emperor with the "although" or "while" subordinate clause, and then excoriate him in the main part of the sentence. ("While Theodoric indulged the Goths in the enjoyment of rude liberty, he servilely copied the institutions and even the abuses of the political system which had been framed by Constantine and his successors.")

Churchill was impressed by Gibbon, but he was more amused by Macaulay. The more quotable Macaulay lent himself more to conversation and speech. ("People who take no pride in the achievements of remote ancestors will never achieve anything worthy to be remembered with pride by remote descendants." "From the very beginning England was a democratic aristocracy and aristocratic democracy." "Timid and interested politicians think more about the security of their seats than the security of the nations.") But even in his bungalow at Bangalore Churchill began to sense what he later voiced, that "Macaulay was the prince of literary rogues," who could on occasion sacrifice substance to style. Macaulay himself hinted this in his phrase, "I shall cheerfully descend below the dignity of history."

Macaulay's writings, though, made up in acid what they lacked in authority. And this wit, joined with the wisdom of Gibbon, became the staple of Churchill's conversation and even his letters. His brothers complained of his affected style. Churchill himself recognized it.

At one point he started to write to his mother, "The voyage may be made by literature both profitable and agreeable," but upon thinking better he crossed it out, commenting, "what a beastly sentence," and adding, "I suppress with difficulty an impulse to become sententious. Gibbon and Macaulay, however much they improve one's composition of essays or reports, do not lend themselves to letter writing."

Neither did such august style lend itself to after-dinner conversation in the nightly conviviality with other officers. When Churchill offered a pontifical discourse once too often, his mates did literally suppress him. A Churchill monologue for close to an hour so vexed his fellow officers that they grabbed him, pinned him to the floor, and then shoved him under a couch, where they imprisoned him to let their whist playing continue undisturbed.

But Churchill remained undaunted in his course. If he was considered a bit odd, he had always accepted eccentricity as the badge of his individuality. At Harrow his impertinence had made him an outsider; now his intellectualism did. The difference was that in India, Churchill commanded some grudging respect. There, he obviously was not the typical officer in the queen's service. He enjoyed the wine and fellowship of the mess and the team comradery in match and field, but he had little interest in gossip or girls. He had more important conquests to make. What he wanted was the world, or at least to make his mark on the world. To do that he had to understand the world, the forces that shaped it and moved it. If he was going to have his place in the world, he had first to learn where he stood in the scheme of things. With this growing realization, Churchill grew mentally as well as physically into manhood.

4

APPRENTICE SPEAKER

Mend your speech a little,
Lest it may mar your fortunes.
—*Shakespeare*
(King Lear)

For a young man who wanted to climb the peaks of the world, Churchill was burning with frustration. As a soldier, he had never been in a war except for his brief observer role in Cuba. And as a would-be politician, he had never been called on to deliver a speech except for one escapade while he was still at Sandhurst. .

The cadets at Sandhurst were antagonized by the crusading zeal of one Mrs. Ormiston Chant, who wanted to bring reform to the London music halls. Mrs. Chant took offense at the raucous behavior at the theater bars, where young blades in search of a night on the town could mingle with the dancers and chorus girls. Such bars, particularly the one at the Empire theater in Leicester Square, were naturally a magnet for soldiers on leave as well as for many "ladies of the evening."

Mrs. Chant, who saw it as her God-appointed duty to close these dens of iniquity, mobilized church and temperance groups in a drive to shut down the theater bars by taking away their license to serve liquor. Soldiers were not the only ones to see this puritanical, or better yet Victorian, prudery as an infringement of civil liberties. In some segments of the press and public it was viewed as a constitutional issue which was, not unlike that of Prohibition, the attempt by sanction of government to regulate personal behavior.

Churchill, who even in youth had held the Temperance League in minimal esteem, followed the dispute closely in the newspapers. One day he spied a letter written by a man who was forming "The Entertainments Protection League." A meeting of the Executive Committee was announced for six o'clock on the following Wednesday at the London Hotel. Sensing an opportunity

39

that could catapult him into the public spotlight, Churchill wangled a two-day leave and boarded a train for London. The day before the meeting was spent composing a reasoned argument against such misguided moralism. But when he arrived at the hotel armed with his notes he found no meeting—only one rather forlorn figure in the lobby of the seedy hotel. The gentleman embarrassedly confessed he was "The Entertainments Protection League." The setting was not the splendid forum Churchill had anticipated. Not that evening was he to have an oratorical triumph before an enraptured audience. Since he was not to perform, he hocked his watch, bought a good dinner, and went to one of the celebrated music halls to watch others perform. He returned to Sandhurst on the slow night train to be greeted by his fellow cadets anxious to hear the blow-by-blow account of his forensic victory. With shrugs, smiles, and knowing winks he managed, without actually lying, to convey a tour de force in the fight for constitutional liberty.

The real facts of the situation revealed themselves during the next few days. The momentum for any campaign was all on the other side. The London County Council, responding to the pressure of Mrs. Chant's attacks, had forced the management of the Empire Theater to erect barricades between its bar and the adjoining promenade, where good-natured and free-spirited women were wont to parade themselves.

After some prompting by Churchill, it was decided that a delegation from Sandhurst should go down and demonstrate against the hanging of the canvas partitions, which would block feminine passersby from the attention of the young men drinking at the bar. By chance, a great many young bloods of London had the same idea—to be on hand when Mrs. Chant and her legion of do-gooders were to proclaim a new era of moral enlightenment for the old Empire Theater. What resulted was the inevitable collision between self-annointed saints and would-be sinners. The regular variety show on the Empire stage was not the star attraction that evening. The exciting performance was in the aisles, where young men jostled with matronly ladies trading taunts and epithets. At one point Churchill, in evening dress, shouted, "Follow me and charge the barricades." A merry scrambling for the rear ensued, and the hated canvas screen was ripped down.

Now Churchill saw the chance to give that speech he had prepared for the Entertainments Protection League audience which had never materialized. Mounting the stage, he asked the dancers to step aside and yelled for the audience's attention. Although the hubbub temporarily abated, the crowd was not in the mood to absorb lengthy constitutional arguments. So he shifted to an ad hominem attack against "the prowling prudes," a phrase he had lifted from a *Telegraph* editorial. Then he closed with this rousing peroration:

> Where does the Englishman in London always find a welcome? Where does he first go, when, battle-scarred and travel-worn, he reaches home? Who is always there to greet him with a smile and join him with a drink? Who is ever faithful, ever true? The ladies of the Empire promenade! Gentlemen—you have seen us tear down these barricades tonight; see that you pull down those who are responsible for them at the coming municipal election.

Churchill, however, could not list this forensic frolic as a credit for a serious political career. In fact, when a few editorials against "young hooliganism" appeared, he lay low, managing to keep his identity as the chief instigator away from the press. What Churchill yearned for was a proper speech in the right forum where he could at last be taken seriously.

Four years later when he returned from India to England for his first home leave, he was almost bursting with the set of beliefs he had fashioned from his crash course on history and politics, but what group wanted to hear the views of a twenty-two-year-old?

One day, soon after his arrival home, he dropped in at the Conservative party's main headquarters and introduced himself. To the head of the office he allowed that he was thinking of a political career. To his amazement, he was asked if he would be willing to make a speech at a local Tory function. In *My Early Life,* Churchill writes of his elation: "It appeared there were hundreds of indoor meetings and outdoor fetes, of bazaars and rallies—

rallies—all of which were claimant for speakers. I surveyed this prospect with the eye of an urchin looking through a pastry cook's window. Finally, we selected Bath as the scene of my official maiden effort."

The occasion was a meeting of the Primrose League in Bath. The League, organized by Randolph Churchill in memory of Benjamin Disraeli, promoted allegiance to the Crown, the Empire, and the British Constitution. It drew its membership from Tory loyalists. Bath, which took its name from the spring that had been enjoyed in Roman times, was a fashionable place to retire. Thus many in the audience would have had personal acquaintance with Lord Randolph Churchill, who had been dead for only two and a half years. Indeed, the attendance would be swelled by the local announcement in the press that Randolph's son would be the featured speaker.

The thought filled Winston with anxiety as well as pride. The inevitable comparison worried him. He was no university graduate with a grounding in the classics or experience in the Oxford Debating Union. Not only did he lack the polish of a finished speaker, he had the handicap of a funny lisp and an awkward stammer.

Before he had left for India he had been so concerned about the effect of such an impediment that he had made an appointment with Britain's leading voice specialist, Sir Felix Semon. "How can I ever be a minister," cried young Winston, "when I cannot say any words that end with s?" Sir Felix, who had often been retained by Queen Victoria and other members of the royal family, had been helpful in solving the voice problems of actors and opera stars. But to Winston, he could offer only the mixed report that there was no organic defect. That meant that his impediment could not be corrected by an operation, but only modified by "constant practice and perseverance."

One of Winston's first female friends, a Miss Muriel Wilson, whom he intermittently saw on his leaves home from India, wrote later how determined he was to cure himself of his lisp. Just as Demosthenes would walk on the beach trying to speak with a mouthful of pebbles, Winston would walk up and down the long drive of her house, rehearsing phrases in the manner of an Eliza

Doolittle such as, "The Spanish ships I cannot see for they are not in sight." The daily practice did more for rhetoric than romance, for this beautiful heiress shifted her interests elsewhere and found another mate for marriage.

Princess Bibesco, who knew Winston as a young man, described his odd combination of lisp and stammer this way: "His delivery was defective and, strange to say, he stuttered in a manner peculiar to himself. His speech was not indistinct—there was no trace of harelip in the firmly drawn mouth—but something seemed to make him chew and turn over every word several times before allowing it to escape from his lips. It was as if he wanted to suck all the juice out of it and savor its taste to the fullest; a kind of satisfied grunt accompanied this operation." Winston, in trying to overcome his defect, was overcompensating. The halting rhythm of his delivery helped mask the stutter. In constantly pausing he slowed his delivery and managed to make it one of continual stammer. So by this practice of deliberately hesitating throughout a speech, he turned his stutter into a matter of style. The advantage of this style was the lessening of any anxiety over an occasional stammer, since it was expected. The stutter was now his oral signature.

The lisp, however, posed greater problems. To emphasize it would have courted ridicule. Since he could not overcome it, he tried to slide around it. In words beginning with *s,* he developed a compromise sound that was neither *th* nor *s.* By keeping the tongue from the teeth, which turned "say" into "thay," he managed to simulate a weak *s* that lacked sibilance.

All of these efforts had been well under way by the time of the Bath speech. In fact, he had posted a letter to his mother when he arrived in India that told about his participation in a mock court trial on shipboard, in which he played defense counsel in a breach-of-promise suit. "My impediment did not seem to interfere with my articulation at all and of all who spoke, I was the best heard."

Winston's concern as the date for his Primrose League appearance neared was more about the substance than the style. The real question was what should he talk about? At twenty-two years of age, he had neither the fame of exploit nor the authority of expertise. What could he say on colonial life in India that Rudyard

Kipling had not said better? Anyway, at a meeting of Conservative party followers, he could hardly attack the present government. Yet a speech of praise offered little hope of being memorable.

These were his thoughts as he mulled over the speech in his mother's London townhouse at Cumberland Place. In the end he decided to surmount the problem by meeting it head-on. He would start by alluding both to his inexperience as a speaker and to the difficulty of finding anything to talk about in good times.

". . . if it were pardonable in any speaker to begin with the well-worn and time-honored apology 'unaccustomed as I am to public speaking,' it would be pardonable in my case, for the honor of addressing an audience of my fellow countrymen and women is the first honor of the kind I have ever received. . . . But every pleasure has its corresponding drawback, just as every rose its thorn, and the corresponding drawback in my case is that it is exceedingly difficult to find anything to talk about. . . ." Churchill would go on to sketch the beauty of tranquil times, following up by quoting the words of a popular song of the day:

> Every eyelid closes
> All the world reposes
> Lazily, lazily, drowsily, drowsily
> In the noonday sun.

"But sleepy, comfortable peace," he would remind them, "involved comfortable progress and led eventually to comfortable prosperity and that . . . although bad for the speaker . . . was good for the people."

"Parliament," he would say, "is dull but by no means idle." With this transition, he could give his attention to the highlights of the ruling Conservative party's legislative program. For contrast, he compared what the Liberals and Radicals would do if they were in power. Here was the chance for some choice sallies:

"Radicals who were never satisfied, and Liberals, always liberal with other people's money."

"The Radicals," he would say, reminded him "of the man who, on being told ventilation was a good thing, smashed every window in his house and died of rheumatic fever."

"Conservative policy was a look-before-you-leap policy." He would declaim that the British workingman had more to hope "from the rising tide of Tory Democracy than the dried-up drainpipe of radicalism." "Tory Democracy" was a theme dear to Winston's father, and he would couple it with the catchy phrase "dried-up drainpipe" of radicalism.

Then how to end the speech? In his novel, *Savrola,* the title character acted the part for him:

What was there to say? Successive cigarettes had been consumed. Amid the smoke he saw a peroration which would cut deep into the hearts of the crowd; a high thought, a fine simile, expressed in that correct diction which is comprehensible even to the most illiterate and appeals to the most simple; something to lift their minds from the material cares of life and to awaken sentiment. His ideas began to take the form of words, to group themselves into sentences; he murmured to himself; the rhythm of his own language swayed him; instinctively he alliterated.

Puffing Havanas instead of cigarettes, Churchill wrote out an appeal that would stir patriotic hearts in that Jubilee year of 1897 (Victoria's sixtieth year on the throne).

They were not wanting, those who said that in this Jubilee year our Empire has reached the height of its glory and power and that now we should begin to decline, as Babylon, Carthage and Rome had declined. Do not believe these croakers but give the lie to their dismal croaking by showing that the vigor and vitality of our race is unimpaired and that our determination is to uphold the Empire that we have inherited from our fathers as Englishmen, that our flag shall fly high on the sea, our voice be heard in the councils of Europe, our sovereign be supported by the love of her subjects. Then shall we continue to pursue that course marked out for us by an all-wise hand and carry out our mission of bringing peace, civilization, and good government to the uttermost ends of the earth.

Churchill knew he had a speech that would please the audience even if it ran ten minutes more than the fifteen allotted to him. He needed the extra time to reveal his familiarity with current national issues. But what good would his efforts be if London and the British political world were not also made aware of his potential? To that end, the twenty-two-year-old Winston took a step rare in that pre-media age; he sent copies of his speech beforehand to the London press. *The Morning Post,* amused by such young bravado, sent a reporter to Bath to cover this son of the late Lord Randolph. As fate would have it, young Churchill met up with the reporter on the train going down to Bath from London. In the two-and-a-half-hour train ride Churchill overwhelmed his compartment mate with a dress rehearsal of his speech. Over and over he repeated the phrase and theme he wanted the journalist to highlight: "England would gain far more from the rising tide of Tory Democracy than the dried-up drainpipe of Radicalism." The newsman, swept up by Churchill's expansive enthusiasm, filed a long account of the Bath speech for his London paper. He found that the Bath audience who heard Churchill on the picnic grounds outside that Georgian manor house (now the American Museum in Britain) were enthralled. They were impressed by the message but even more by the man, or more accurately the boy, who bore it. After all, the "progressive Toryism" of Lord Randolph was not strange to them. What was intriguing was this combination of innocent earnestness and sardonic worldliness in his son.

The speech stirred talk among political observers. Shortly afterward G. W. Steevens, a columnist for *The Daily Mail,* interviewed Churchill for a series he was doing on future leaders of the twentieth century. His prophetic words describe Churchill at that time:

> In years he is a boy; in temperament he is also a boy, but in intention, in deliberate plan, adaptation of means to ends, he is already a man. . . . But Mr. Churchill is a man with ambitions fixed, with the steps toward their attainment clearly defined with a precocious, almost uncanny judgment as to the efficiency of the means to an end. . . . From his mother he derives his American strain; he adds to this a keenness, a shrewdness, a

half-cynical, personal ambition, a natural aptitude for advertisement and happily a sense of humor.

He may or may not possess the qualities which make a great general, but the question is of no importance. In any case they will never be developed for if they exist, they are overshadowed by qualities which might make him, almost at will, a great popular leader, a great journalist, or the founder of a great advertising business.

In those three careers, there is one common quality without which success is impossible. That is the ability for the imaginative putting together of words in a form that persuades and excites. It should be no surprise that Steevens perceived that talent in the young man he interviewed. All his life, whether declaiming in schoolboy recitals, writing in the *Harrovian,* or reading the histories of Gibbon and Macaulay in his Bangalore bungalow, he was fascinated with the impact of words and determined to wield them with mastery. But as much as he enjoyed the actor, valued the journalist, and venerated the great historian, it was the orator who commanded his deepest interest.

To answer Plutarch's riddle, he would rather be the hero who does the deed than the herald who describes it. To have the fame of a statesman, he needed the skills of an orator. He wrote in 1897, "Of all the talents bestowed upon men, none is so precious as the gift of oratory. He who enjoys it wields a power more durable than that of a great king. He is an independent force in the world. Abandoned by his party, betrayed by his friends, stripped of his offices, whoever can command this power is still formidable." These were the opening words of an article never published, entitled "The Scaffolding of Rhetoric."

For months, Winston had been studying the great orators in British history: the muscular, soldierlike prose of Oliver Cromwell, the lofty wisdom of Edmund Burke, the conversational simplicity of John Bright. He would read aloud the Earl of Chatham's plea for conciliation with America and of his son, the younger Pitt, the refusal to negotiate with Napoleon. He would contrast the witty elegance of Disraeli with the majestic thunder of his foe Gladstone.

His studies led him to these conclusions about the art of oratory: first, that it is an art, an acquired art. Although one may be born with the temperament and talents of an orator, he must practice and develop those talents.

In the building of an oration, or "the scaffolding of rhetoric," Churchill saw four factors: the right words, a certain rhythm, the mounting of an argument, and the use of analogy. The first he labeled "diction." "It is the best possible word to fit the meaning." As an example, he cited the uncommon word "dour" to describe the Scotch. We may also think of his characterization of the growing American involvement in the war in 1941 as "benignant."

Secondly, he cautioned against the employment of long words for rhetorical effect. "The shorter words of a language are usually more ancient. Their meaning is more ingrained in the national character, and they appeal with greater force to simple understandings than words recently introduced from the Latin and Greek. All the speeches of great English rhetoricians—except when addressing highly cultured audiences—display a uniform preference for short, homely words of common usage. So as long as the words can fully express their thoughts and feelings, it suffices to mention as a famous example the name of John Bright."

We might expect the man who wrote "We shall fight on the beaches. . ." or "Give us the tools and we will finish the job" to value the virtues of simplicity. But to a twenty-two-year-old, who was almost a half-century away from delivering such lines, such an insight could come only from close studies of the great orations.

Another feature he sensed from reading aloud the famous speakers of the past was the peculiar rhythm of a good rhetoric. It is not quite prose and it approaches poetry. "The sentences of the orator when he appeals to his art become long, rolling, and sonorous. The peculiar balance of the phrases produces a cadence which resembles blank verse rather than prose."

Then, under the title "Accumulation of Argument," Churchill described the assembling of "a series of facts . . . brought forward all pointing in a common direction. The end appears in view before it is reached. The word anticipates the conclusion and the last words fall amid a thunder of assent.''

Fourth, he cited the impact of the analogy. We have already witnessed young Churchill's example of the lover of fresh air who broke all his windows and then died of overexposure. Churchill also cites the Bishop of Derry's remark, ''A strong nation may be no more confiding of its liberties than a pure woman of her honor.''

But to Churchill, the style of the orator is not nearly as important as his sincerity. ''Before he can inspire them with any emotion he must be swayed by it himself. When he would rouse their indignation, his heart is filled with anger. Before he can move their tears, his own must flow. To convince them he must himself believe. His opinions may change as their impressions fade, but every orator means what he says at the moment he says it. He may be often inconsistent. He is never consciously insincere.''

Of all the talents and skills of oratory, sincerity is the one Churchill did not have to learn or cultivate. He had to work on his delivery and build up his vocabulary. To develop his style, he emulated the balance of Macaulay, the rolling sentence of Gibbon, and the perorations of Pitt and Gladstone. But he never had to learn to speak from his heart, and he never feared to say what he believed.

5

WRITER

Writing is said to be the
best and most excellent modeler
and teacher of oratory.

—*Cicero*

All the study of oratory and development of his speaking talents would be of no avail to Winston if he were never elected to Parliament. Such a career was not a practical prospect for the young Hussar lieutenant, who in all likelihood could be assigned for the next twelve or so years to a garrison in India. Even if the Conservative party central office might now regard the son of Lord Randolph as an attractive political hopeful, particularly after his Bath speech, he could hardly resign his commission on the strength of such a tenuous possibility. The infelicitous fact was that, by education and training, Winston was fitted only to be a soldier. What was to be his livelihood if he left the army? Indeed, even if he gained a seat in the House of Commons after one or two tries, he would still require some means of support. In those days ordinary members of the House of Commons received no salaries. Even the compensation of ministers was hardly more than minimal. In an era that still regarded politics as ideally a gentlemanly pursuit that was less a vocation than an avocation, the present-day professional politician had not yet emerged.

Business was hardly a field in which Winston manifested inclination or acumen. In trying to maintain the polo ponies, a requisite expense in an Army officer's life, he had shown no abundance of fiscal judgment in taking on usurious debts to Indian moneylenders. With only a modest inheritance, he would have to find some way of making money or else find himself condemned to the purgatory of some remote military station.

In his inventory of talents, only one had commercial potential—his ability with words. If he could not keep books, he could write them. The balance of a sentence came more easily to Winston than the balance of a checkbook. From his extensive readings he had a solid conception of how to write. All he needed was something to write about.

One day, on home leave while at a racecourse and about three pounds ahead in his afternoon's wagers, he found something to really bet his life on. A newspaper headline caught his eye: a story that proclaimed that fighting had broken out on the northwestern frontier of India. The Pathans, a mountain tribe, were raiding the village settlements and storming the outlying military posts. Sir Bindon Blood was called on to put down the uprising. Winston saw his chance for glory in joining the expedition. He had met Sir Bindon at a dinner party at Deepdene, the home of Lord Beresford. Lord Beresford's wife, the fabulous Lily, who still insouciantly styled herself Duchess of Marlborough, was in the second of her three marriages. (The real Duchess of Marlborough at the time was another American, the former Consuelo Vanderbilt, who had been enjoined to produce an heir so that the "upstart" Winston would never become Duke.) The American Lily,* who had taken a great interest in Winston, somewhat to the consternation of Lady Randolph, had introduced him to General Blood. Winston was intrigued by the dashing and much-decorated officer and not the least by his famous name. Sir Bindon was descended from the notorious Thomas Blood, who had tried to steal the crown jewels from the Tower of London in the reign of Charles II, which was in the lifetime of the first Sir Winston Churchill, a cavalier courtier of that "Merry Monarch." Winston had extracted a promise from General Blood that if he ever commanded another expeditionary force on the Indian frontier, he would let Winston join him.

So Churchill, remembering the pledge, rushed from the race track to a telegraph office and wired Blood, reminding him of his promise. And then, before he could receive a "no," he boarded

---

*The American Lily is not to be confused with the Jersey Lillie, the beautiful Mrs. Langtry, who was the favorite of the Prince of Wales. This Lily was plain but rich. Her real name was Lillian, but she disliked its rhyme with *million,* which suggested the assets of the former Mrs. Lillian Hammersley of New York.

the first ship for Bombay. There he found an equivocal answer from Blood, reading "Very difficult; no vacancies; come up as a correspondent; will try to fit you in. B.B."

Winston had already signed up as a correspondent for *The Daily Telegraph* for a meager fee of five pounds per column. To this he added an Indian newspaper, the Allahabad *Pioneer,* for another couple of pounds. With those credentials he took the five-day, 2800-mile train ride to the northwest frontier, after persuading his reluctant commanding officer at Bangalore to agree to an extension of his home leave.

On arriving at his destination, he found himself part of the Malakan Field Force, who would search out the Pathan villages, burn them, and return to base, not without harassment from the guerrilla tribes. His dispatches, entitled anonymously "From a Young Officer," attracted public attention for their vivid descriptions of battle scenes.

The fighting was over in a few weeks, but not before Winston had valiantly acquitted himself in holding off and escaping from a band of Pathan pursuers. Back at the dreary garrison routine at Bangalore, Winston, in a move unheard of in the journalism of that era, decided to turn his series of news dispatches into a book. The result was the bestselling *Malakand Field Force.* Among the fascinated readers in England was the Prince of Wales. Edward wrote:

My dear Winston, I cannot resist writing a few lines to congratulate you on the success of your book! . . . Everybody is reading it, and I only hear it spoken of with praise.

The first lines of the book bear reading:

The historian of great events is always oppressed by the difficulty of tracing the silent, subtle influences, which in all communities precede and prepare the way for violent outbursts and writings. He may discover many causes and record them duly, but he will always be sensible that others have escaped him. The changing tides of public opinion, the undercurrents of interest, partisanship, and caprice, the whirlpools of illogical sentiment or ignorant prejudice exert forces so complex and numerous that to observe and appreciate them all, and to estimate the effect of each in raising the storm, is a task beyond the intellect and industry of man.

The sentences could have opened almost any of his many books. Although the young student of Gibbon is heard, it is all Winston Churchill. If the voice is that of an historian, it is also that of the man of action. Winston, who knew he was very lucky to have survived the bloody frontier skirmishes, pondered the soldier's answer to duty and pursuit of glory:

To some the game of the war brings prizes, honour, advancement, or experience; to some the consciousness of duty well discharged; and to others—spectators perhaps—the pleasure of the play and the knowledge of men and things. But here were those who had drawn the evil numbers—who had lost their all, to gain only a soldier's grave. Looking at those shapeless forms, coffined in a regulation blanket, the pride of a race, the pomp of empire, the glory of war appeared but the faint and unsubstantial fabric of a dream; and I could not help realizing with Burke: "What shadows we are and what shadows we pursue."

Winston, however, to the dismay of would-be detractors, did not include himself in his field accounts. Although General Blood would cite his bravery under fire, he kept his observations to the doings of the main army. It was an objective and largely unpolitical appraisal of the terrain, the parties involved, and their aims and tactics.

In the *New Yorker,* Robert Lewis Taylor wrote that Churchill's battle descriptions compared with the best of Stendhal's, Stephen Crane's, or even Tolstoy's in *War and Peace.*

The bullets passed in the air with a curious sucking noise like that produced by drawing the air between the lips. . . . The company whose operation I watched—Lieutenant Lockhart's— killed one of these [tribesmen] with a volley and we found him sitting by a little pool, propped against a stone. He had been an ugly man originally, but now that the bones of his jaw and face were broken in pieces he was hideous to look upon. His only garment was a ragged blue linen cloak fastened at the waist. There he sat, a typical tribesman, ignorant, degraded and squalid, yet brave and warlike, his only property his weapon, and that his countrymen had carried off.

The adjectives of the early journalist were to be heard in the later statesman. "Squalid" is one of them. Others that would recur in his writings and speeches are "somber," "resolute," "austere," and "unflinching." Such a series of adjectives coupled in a description is more the fashion of the writer than of the public speaker.

For example, listen to Churchill's closing words in denouncing the Munich settlement, when he scores Conservative party members for blindly supporting the Chamberlain government:

What is the use of sending members to the House of Commons who say just the popular things of the moment and merely endeavor to give satisfaction to the government whips by cheering loudly every ministerial platitude, and by walking through the lobbies oblivious of the intrusions they hear? People talk about our parliamentary institutions and parliamentary democracy; but if these are to survive, it will not be because the Constituents return *tame, docile, subservient* members and try to stamp out every form of independent judgment [author's italics].

Or mark Churchill's words in a speech during the Battle of Britain:

These *cruel, wanton, indiscriminate* bombings of London are, of course, a part of Hitler's invasion plans.

If his early writings suggest the later prose of the warrior-statesman, they also reveal his beliefs. In one beautifully illuminating passage, the young Churchill searches out the roots of valor:

The courage of the soldier is not really contempt for physical evils and indifference to danger. It is a more or less successful attempt to simulate these habits of mind. Most men aspire to be good actors in the play. There are a few who are so perfect that they do not seem to be actors at all. This is the ideal after which the rest are striving. It is one very rarely attained.

Three principal influences combine to assist men in their attempt: Preparation, vanity, and sentiment. the first includes all the force of discipline and training. . . .

Then vanity, the vice which promotes so many virtues, asserts itself. He looks at his comrades and they at him. So far he has shown no weakness. He thinks, they are thinking him brave. The dearly-longed-for reputation glitters before his eyes. He executes the orders he receives.

But something else is needed to make a hero. . . . It is sentiment which makes the difference in the end. Those who doubt should stroll to the camp fire one night to listen to the soldier's songs. Everyone clings to something that he thinks is high and noble; or raises him above the rest of the world in the hour of need.

Romantic idealism, lust for fame and glory, readiness for sacrifice and self discipline—what else explains Churchill's volunteering for service on the dangerous Indian frontier? And what else could explain the efforts of his firsthand battle reports, carefully and painstakingly written down in the evening hours when the troops had returned to their outpost base exhausted from their daylight search-and-destroy missions?

When the fighting ceased, near what is now the Afghanistan border, Churchill did not welcome his return to the peaceful Bangalore routine. After rewriting his Malakand dispatches into a book, he turned his energies to fiction. With his *Malakand Field Force,* he had proven to himself and the world that he could not only make a living as a journalist, but perhaps even prosper. Fiction was an entirely different medium to master. For some time he had been enthralled by Anthony Hope's bestselling swashbuckler, *The Prisoner of Zenda,* published in 1894. He was not unaware that Benjamin Disraeli had used the novel to climb into politics. Disraeli's *Coningsby* was regarded a classic, and *Sybil,* in a sense, was almost a manifesto of "Tory Democracy."

In a scant two months, Churchill wrote a seventy-thousand-word tale of political intrigue; a swiftness that more experienced novelists might have envied. Anthony Hope had located his story in mythical Ruritania, so Churchill made the equally mythical Laurania the setting for *Savrola.* The title is the name of the young political leader who heads the opposition to the military dictator Molara in a Balkan-type or "banana" republic.

The literary reactions to the young soldier's first effort in fiction were mixed. The *Times* said it lacked the lightness of Anthony Hope's style and could not hope to compare with Robert Louis Stevenson. The *Saturday Review* said, "His events are real, his people abstractions." Even Churchill, in later years, asked his friends not to read it.

But the book should be read not as successful fiction, but as a revealing insight into Churchill himself. Psychologically it is almost autobiography, and in a political sense it is prophecy. In Molara, the insensitive autocrat who could not communicate with his people, there is Winston's father as he seemed to his son. The description of Molara through his wife's eyes give a lifelike portrait of Lord Randolph just before his fall from power:

> Of late things had been less bright. The agitation of the country, the rising forces of Democracy, added to the already heavy business of the Republic, had taxed the president's energies to the full. Hard lines had come into his face, lines of work and anxiety, and sometimes she caught a look of awful weariness, as of one who toils and yet foresees his labor will be in vain.

Savrola's attitude toward Molara is ambivalent. He abhors the tyrant, yet retains a certain admiration for him. He wants to remove him from office but will not have him murdered. For Savrola, Molara is a father figure.

Molara's wife, Lucille, is clearly modeled after Lady Randolph. Churchill himself suggests this when he reveals that her French nickname is "Jeannette," which is what Jennie Jerome was often called by her circle of friends in Paris.

As she stood there in the clear light of the autumn evening, she looked divinely beautiful. She had arrived at that stage of life when to the attractions of a maiden's beauty are added those of a woman's wit. Her perfect features were the mirror of her mind. . . .

Her salon was crowded with the most famous men from every country. Statesmen, soldiers, poets, and men of science had worshipped at her shrine. She had mixed in matters of State. Everyone talked to her of public business. . . .

Here we are no longer in Laurania, but London; and Lucille Molara is playing the great role which, in the eyes of her son, should have been that of Jennie Jerome, if his father's career had not been cut short.

Savrola, the title character, is everything in a hero Winston wanted to be—brave, intelligent, well-read, and eloquent, who combines all the rational outlook of a philosopher with that of the "human man who appreciates all earthly pleasures."

Savrola rose. "Come in," he said, "I do not allow such considerations to affect my judgement. The lives of men are at stake; the time is short. . ."

He hoped for immortality but he contemplated annihilation with composure. Meanwhile, the business of living was an interesting problem.

Molara, the dictator, asks his wife, Lucille, to gain the confidence of Savrola, the young leader of the opposition, in order to thwart any plans of an overthrow. Molara later catches the two in an embrace. A fight ensues, but Savrola, in Hamlet-like hesitation, cannot bring himself to kill the assailant-dictator.

The president's death does come at the hands of Socialist revolutionaries. Their leader, Kreutze, a rabid German, has an almost prophetic resemblance to another Teuton Churchill would combat as prime minister.

It is the descriptions of and insights into the political world that make Churchill's attempt at fiction well worth reading.

Savrola, referring to British gunboat diplomacy: "It is a Conservative Ministry; they must keep things going abroad to divert the public mind from advanced legislation."

Or this comment on the political fickleness of the business community: "The idea of bombardment was repugnant to the fat burgesses who had joined the party of revolt as soon as it had become obvious that it was the winning side."

And this description of the mindless professional soldier: "General Sorrento was one of those soldiers, not an uncommon type, who fear little but independent responsibility."

What astonishes is the prescience of the young Churchill. In the sedate era of Victorian calm—twenty years before the Russian revolution—he prophetically paints the sad but familiar pattern of twentieth-century political strife: the military rightist government is destroyed and then replaced, not by democratic institutions, but by a dictatorship of the left. To friends at the time, Churchill described his book this way: "I chose as a theme a revolt in some imaginary Balkan or South American republic and traced the fortunes of a liberal leader who overthrew an arbitrary government only to be swallowed up by a socialist revolution." Of course, it could be said that Churchill was foreshadowing the defeat that would happen to him after his victory over fascism in 1945.

A critic for the *Spectator* who did like *Savrola* noted that Churchill "displayed a genuine rhetorical gift of expression."

Savrola exhorts: "We have exalted liberty; it remains to preserve her."

In Savrola's speech to City Hall, one detects a hint of Churchill's Fulton, Missouri, speech a half-century later, when he introduced his famous Iron Curtain passage with this line: "A shadow has fallen upon the scenes so lately lighted by the Allied victory."

> When I look at this beautiful country that is ours and was our father's before us, at its blue seas and snowcapped mountains, at its comfortable hamlets and wealthy cities, at its silver streams and golden cornfields, I marvel at the irony of fate which has struck across so fair a prospect the dark shadow of a military despotism.

Though we may expect oratory in a political novel, we are unaccustomed to the flavor of rhetoric in military chronicles or history. But Churchill began to write with a touch of the orator before he ever became politician. Lady Violet Asquith Bonham-Carter suggests that this was because Winston, as a journalist, historian, or even novelist, had the dual vision of both the actor and the observer. His was a heroic, dramatic, and personal view of history. As the historian Alan Bullock put it, "It is exactly what you would expect of the great man of action." It was "almost another form of action."

If not that, it was at least a substitute for action. And when Churchill received his £3,500 for the delivery of the manuscript, he found himself again suffocated by the torpor of Indian life. He tried, without success, to get himself transferred to the Sudan, where Lord Kitchener was in the midst of stamping out a rebellion by the Mahdi and his "Dervish" followers. Then, while on home leave in England in the summer of 1898, Churchill found help from an unsuspected quarter.

Lord Salisbury, who as prime minister had maneuvered the downfall of his Chancellor of the Exchequer, Lord Randolph, had picked up in his London Club Winston's account of the Malakand Field Force. Salisbury, Wellington's godson, was entranced by the book and wrote the author asking him to drop by 10 Downing Street for a visit the next time he was in London. Winston, expecting the usual perfunctory ten-minute chat, was kept for an hour by the busy premier. At the end, Salisbury, who obviously found the son of his old rival and colleague engaging, asked him if there was anything he could do for him. "Yes," replied Churchill, "send me to Sudan."

Lord Kitchener was not overjoyed with the addition to his staff of young Churchill, who had been forced upon him by an insistent War Office and prime minister. The general had enough problems without having in his entourage a lieutenant who had developed the unmilitary practice of offering advice to his superiors and then putting it into print. Churchill was immediately assigned to a detail handling a decrepit mule and two donkeys.

Winston, however, soon manipulated his way to the front. The man who as wartime leader would share atomic secrets was to participate in the last cavalry charge known in military annals. The Battle of Omdurman took place as Lord Kitchener and his armies made their desert trek to Khartoum, the Sudanese capital, on the Nile, where the martyred hero General Gordon had been slain only two dozen years before. Attached to the 21st Lancers, Churchill, on a dawn patrol, was the first to sight the assembling Mohammedan mass of about 40,000 riflemen, swordsmen, and spear carriers, whose suicidal religious fanaticism gave rise to the phrase "whirling Dervishes." He rushed a warning back to Kitchener. In the confrontation that followed, the battle was won by the historic charge made by Winston and others, who pierced and broke the four-deep lines of the Mahdi followers.

Churchill then penned an account of Kitchener's Nile campaign and entitled it *The River War.* The reviews of the 950-page book were generally favorable. The *Outlook* went so far as to say that the author "came very near doing for the Sudan what Kinglake did for the Crimea."

The structure of the book is worth studying. The first third is a careful background exposition, with scarcely one expendable sentence. The rising British colonial presence is sketched, along with the region's tribal and religious history. Churchill, in *My Early Life,* compared writing a book to building a house. "The technique is different, the materials are different, but the principle is the same. The foundations have to be laid, the data assembled, and the premises must bear the weight of the conclusions." The same background buildup of facts so apparent in his *World Crisis*

(World War I) and *The Second World War* became a feature of his speech organization. The perorations of his 1940 speeches still reverberate in the ear, but they are only the roof of a sound structure. Churchill began his speeches and books with a logical formation of facts. He would persuade the head before pulling the heartstrings.

But if the journalist's workmanlike penchant for background and facts would shape his future speeches, the would-be orator infused his writing with the ring of rhetoric. Churchill's attack on Kitchener's desecration of the Mahdi crypt is perhaps his first use of irony as political invective:

> By Sir H. Kitchener's orders, the Tomb has been profaned and razed to the ground. The corpse of the Mahdi was dug up. The head was separated from the body and to quote the official explanation, "preserved for future disposal," a phrase which must in this case be understood to mean that it was passed from hand to hand until it reached Cairo. Here it remained, an interesting trophy, until the affair came to the ears of Lord Cramer, who ordered it to be immediately re-interred at Wadi Haffa. The limb and trunk were flung into the Nile. Such was the chivalry of conquerors! No man who holds the splendid tradition of the old Liberal Party, no man who is in sympathy with the aspirations of Progressive Toryism, can consistently consent to such behavior.

Although such frank criticism of Britain's foremost general would hardly be beneficial to a young lieutenant's military career, it did strengthen his credentials as journalist and writer. *The River War,* while not a popular bestseller like *The Malakand Field Force,* was a more solid work of history. The soldier was no longer an amateur writer but a professional journalist. With such a livelihood he was ready to launch a political career. Moreover, Churchill's early repertorial experience would shape the rhetoric of that career. His speeches would reveal the journalist's knack of giving the audience all the facts without boring them in the process. Churchill would also write out the whole speech for an occasion rather than speak from a few notes. His words, premeditated rather than extemporaneous, would be more stately than conversational, more the language of history than the street harangue.

6

CANDIDATE

I am a child of the House of Commons.
— *Winston Churchill*

When Churchill returned from the Nile War in 1899, he decided the time had come to say farewell to arms. He would live by his pen and seek the first opportunity to stand for Parliament. With the £10,000 he had banked from his recent book sales, he could now resign his commission and devote his life to politics. Compared to war, politics was, he wrote, "almost as exciting and quite as dangerous. . . . In wars you can only be killed once but in politics many times."

The chance for action soon came in a by-election at Oldham, a marginal constituency for Conservatives, located in the heart of industrial Lancashire. By-elections are notoriously hazardous to the candidate belonging to the party in power. In these special elections, he has the thankless duty of defending an administration that often is becoming progressively unpopular. As Churchill himself noted, "All the woes of the world, all the shortcomings of human society, . . . are laid upon him and he is vociferously urged to say what he is going to do about them."

Nevertheless, Churchill jumped at the chance to stand at this northern England factory district when asked by the Conservative party central office. The peculiarities of the Oldham election had a certain romantic appeal for him. First, because it was a by-election, he would have the attention of the whole nation. Second, he was to run in tandem with a trade union organizer as his fellow Conservative against two Liberals. The Labour party had not yet emerged, and although most politically minded unionists made identification with the Liberal party—inviting the nickname Lib-Labs—a few, like Jim Mawdsley, a spinner by trade, chose the Conservative party

69

banner much the same way as some blacks in America might run today as Republicans. Churchill, a "Tory Democrat" like his father, welcomed the chance to stand side by side with Mawdsley, and so prove that old class conventions could be broken and that the Conservative party could represent the workingman.

It was an early version of the odd couple, this young grandson of a duke dressed in a swallowtail coat and sporting a gold-topped cane and the cloth-capped sturdy-threaded middle-aged laborer. The press dubbed them "the Scion and the Socialist." This strange coalition of candidates, in the minds of Conservative party strategists, was a clever formula for victory in this industrial area over two strong Liberal candidates.

Conservatives in the House of Commons were particularly optimistic about Churchill's prospects. As a son of Lord Randolph and descendant of the Duke of Marlborough, he bore a familiar name, and to it, as a soldier who had acquitted himself well in action and written some books in the process, he had added some fame. If he could channel all his abundant energies into the campaign, he could win and might even bring that "Socialist" along with him.

Fresh from his heroics at the great cavalry charge in the Sudan, Winston brought to his campaign in Oldham all the cocky enthusiasm of youth. When his Liberal opponent, Walter Runciman, accused him of being "a swashbuckler around the world," Churchill retaliated in his next speech by impugning his opponent's patriotic loyalty to the local regiment. He asked whether "this is the sort of welcome you will give the Lancashire Fusiliers when they come home from Omdurman. Mr. Runciman has not the experience of the Lancashire Fusiliers; his contests have been more pacific. The difference between Mr. Runciman and the Lancashire Fusiliers is that, while they are fighting at Omdurman for their country, he was fighting at Gravesend for himself. And another difference between them is that while the Fusiliers were gaining a victory, Mr. Runciman at Gravesend was being defeated."

For the most part, Churchill chose as his theme the continuing glory of the British Empire and ignored the concerns of the

Lancashire textile workers. "I have no fear for the future," Churchill proclaimed in one speech:

> I see the British nation marching steadily forward on the path of progress, combining the glamour and glitter of an ancient theme, the dignity and splendor of a royal court with the might of a free and contented people and the justice of equal laws. A strong yet merciful nation, armed with imperial power, comforted with the spoils of commerce and enriched with the rewards of industry, beating all rivals, beating down all enemies in war—thus we shall march onward in triumph to glory.

In the four-man race, Winston was the center of attraction. His was the brightest personality and his were the best-delivered speeches. He even had the last-minute help of the celebrated Lady Randolph, who made the election-day rounds in a two-horse open carriage. For the occasion she had shed her widow's black for a brilliant blue frock with matching parasol.

True, it was a tough constituency. The two Liberal candidates were rich and well-financed. In addition, the Conservative government's support of a tithe to subsidize the Anglican clergy did not set well in northern England, reared on John Wesley and no-nonsense Low Church doctrines.

Churchill, at the last minute recognizing the unpopularity of his party's position, declared that if he were elected he would vote against the tax. This repudiation of his party's policy did not help, and it may have hurt. Arthur James Balfour, the Conservative Leader of the House of Commons, made this acid remark: "I thought he was a young man of promise, but it appears he is a young man of promises."

Churchill's expediency on the church matter, however, was only symptomatic of a larger problem. He was not really sure of his own political views and was more or less casting around for the line that would go over best with the Lancashire voters. That is not to say that he was insincere, only immature. He had not yet developed a message or program that was peculiarly his. Although he proved to be an energetic and forceful speaker, he lacked something to "say." He had the technique but not the theme.

Actually, most politicians remain political adolescents, searching for roles like actors, but never finding out who they are or what their mission should be. Winston Churchill, at age twenty-five, entered as a Conservative at Oldham more out of consanguinity than choice. His father had been a Conservative leader of the House of Commons, but Lord Randolph had also positioned himself as a Tory Democrat, one who would entertain and support progressive legislation while at the same time championing the causes of the monarchy, the constitution, and the empire. Winston knew what his father had stood for ten or fifteen years ago, but he had not yet translated that into a meaningful philosophy for himself.

If sheer energy should be rewarded by victory, Churchill should have won easily. Day and night he campaigned before gatherings extolling "the virtues of the government, the existing system of society, the Established Church, and the unity of the Empire," sometimes culminating with the claim "Never before were there so many people in England, and never before had they so much to eat."

In the harsh soot-stained life of industrial Lancashire, the words struck the wrong chord. But Oldham warmed to the young man, if not to his language. Only narrowly defeated, he ran ahead of the spinner, Jimmy Mawdsley. Yet, in the end, they both lost.

A month after Churchill's defeat, war broke out in the Transvaal, where Boer president Paul Kruger had challenged British interests. Immediately *The Daily Mail* bid for Churchill's services as a war correspondent. In October 1899, he sailed for Africa. On arriving at Capetown he caught the boat train, which would enable him to make a shortcut to the battlefront; but the armored train he was traveling on was ambushed by Boers, resulting in derailment. Churchill volunteered to organize the moving of one of the destroyed cars off the track while British soldiers kept the attacking Boers at bay. Just as he freed the engine, allowing it to take those wounded in the fray to receive needed medical attention, he was surrounded by Boer horsemen. Their leader, later identified as General Botha, first premier of the Union of South Africa, made

Churchill surrender his revolver. He was taken to the prison in Pretoria, whence he made the dramatic escape, previously recounted. When a tired and weary Churchill luckily asked for refuge in the only habitation for miles around that contained friendly English faces, John Howard, manager of the mine where Churchill was hidden, introduced the fugitive to Dewshap, his foreman, who hailed from Oldham in Lancashire. "Don't worry," Dewshap told Churchill, crushing his hand in a miner's hearty clasp, "they'll vote for you next time."

And Churchill did return to Oldham, but not before he had helped his cousin, the Duke of Marlborough, lead forces into Pretoria, where Churchill personally tore down the Boer flag that flew over the prison where he once had been captive.

A little later Churchill got word from Conservatives that they wanted him to stand again in the "Khaki election," so called because of Conservative hopes to turn wartime jingoism into immediate votes. This time Churchill would be more than just a star attraction; he was becoming a national hero after his escape from the Boer prison. London music halls were singing this ditty:

> You've heard of Winston Churchill
> This is all I need to say
> He's the latest and the greatest
> Correspondent of the day.

We think of the term "war correspondent," remembering the Ernie Pyle and Quentin Reynolds bylines of World War II stories, but the first to make the role a glamorous and exciting profession were Richard Harding Davis and Winston Churchill. Davis, whose handsome profile inspired the old Arrow shirt image, had heard Churchill expound at a London military dinner when he was still at Sandhurst. Davis, who was intrigued by the conversation of the younger man, thought Churchill had the makings of a bright career. Davis became famous in the American war with Spain in 1898, and Churchill won attention with his exploits in the Sudan and worldwide recognition with his South African adventure. In fact, it might be argued that Churchill was the first media sensation to exploit his fame for his political career.

Churchill had taken from Africa his dispatches as a war correspondent and compiled them into a book entitled *London to Ladysmith*. While not as popular as *Malakand Field Force* or as respected as *The River War,* it did contain some prophetic predictions suggesting apartheid.

Churchill writes that the British government is associated in the Boer farmer's mind with violent social revolution. "The servant is to be raised against the master; the [black] Kaffir is to be declared the brother of the European, to be constituted his legal equal and to be armed with political rights."

He goes on to quote a Boer's conversation with him while he was in jail: "Educate a Kaffir; ah, that's you English all over. No, no old chappie. We educate them with a stick."

Churchill adds that there was "no more agreement but argument growing keener and keener; a gulf widening every moment." The final result, Churchill noted, was but "a matter of time and money—expressed in blood and tears." The phrase, which suggests 1940, was actually written in the final weeks of the last century.

As the nineteenth century closed, Churchill's vision of imperialism was not so simplistic. Nevertheless, he still thought empire would be his winning issue at his reelection try at Oldham.

All the way home on the voyage from Capetown to Southampton in July 1900, Churchill spent his time drafting his remarks for the coming campaign in Oldham. In the words of a fellow passenger, Winston would, with no apparent inhibitions or embarrassment, stand at the prow of the ship and, in the style of Demosthenes, rehearse his speeches "by haranguing the waves and winds."

When he arrived in England, he had hardly had time to attend his mother's wedding to George Cornwallis-West, a handsome military officer of Winston's own age, before he was off to Lancashire to campaign in Oldham. He was greeted with a spectacular welcome. Crowds lined up and the band struck up the melody to "See the Conquering Hero Comes" as he came in by open carriage to the town hall. When the door of the carriage was opened to help him down, he vaulted over the other side to the street. In the assembly hall, he told for the first time of his escape. When he mentioned the name of Mr. Dewshap, the Oldham man who had helped him hide in the coal mine, there were shouts from the audience, "His wife is here." Applause and yells filled the hall. A young girl in the front row expressed the sentiments of Churchill's supporters. She wore a sash with the words emblazoned "God bless Churchill, England's noblest Hero."

The ensuing campaign of the next two months was not to prove easy. After the glitter of the initial homecoming faded, nasty rumors began to be circulated by Churchill's Liberal opposition that he was a coward who in escaping, had somehow deserted his English officers at the Pretoria prison. A captain who was with Churchill at Pretoria was asked to write a letter refuting the canard. In addition, Joseph Chamberlain, the monocled Colonial Secretary, was imported to campaign on behalf of young Winston, the son of his old friend, Randolph. Chamberlain, who was known as the British Empire's "architect," declared, "Lord Randolph's son has inherited some of the great qualities of his father—his originality and his courage."

His opponents in this campaign were the same Runciman and Emmot who had bested him and Mawdsley a year earlier. Since then Mawdsley had died, and Crisp, a stockbroker, would be Churchill's Conservative running mate. At first Churchill must have pondered how to join the issue of empire to his campaign. After all Runciman and, to a lesser extent, Emmot were Liberal "imperialists" or hawks who supported the Conservative ministry's conduct of the war. Yet it was on these credentials of his Boer War experience that Churchill had to wage his fight if he was going to win in this pro-Liberal industrial constituency.

Churchill shaped the issue of the campaign this way. "The Liberals," he argued, "have no policy of their own and they do not object to our policy except that they would like to carry it out themselves." The fight, he said, was merely between "the genuine turtlesoup of Tory Imperialism and the mockturtle soup of Liberal Imperialism."

The Oldham voters apparently preferred the genuine article, for enough of them split their votes to give Churchill a second-place victory behind the Liberal Emmot. But it was his fame more than his Tory philosophy that carried the day in working-class districts. For Conservatives over the country, Churchill was the hero of the hour. Prime Minister Salisbury sent his congratulations. Balfour asked him to speak for him at his campaign in Manchester. For the next three weeks, as the various contests of the Khaki election were held, Churchill was the featured guest of honor.

From the banquet circuit in Britain, he went to one arranged in America by a Major Pond. By cashing in on his current celebrity status, he hoped to establish himself in the international lecture field. Throughout his tour across the United States and Canada, he was publicized by impresario Pond as "the hero of five wars, the author of six books, and the future prime minister." Although at least two wars and three books were added for good measure, the last turned out not to be hyperbole.

The future prime minister was feted in New York by Mark Twain, who introduced Churchill as an Englishman by his father and an American by his mother—"no doubt a blend that makes the perfect man." Then Twain signed signed his books for Churchill with the advice, "To be good is noble; to teach others how to be good is nobler and no trouble." The date of that inscription, January 22, 1901, was the day Queen Victoria died.

On February 2, the day the old queen was being buried, Churchill sailed from Boston. An era had passed. At the accession of the new king, Parliament would reconvene. On the same day that Edward VII opened Parliament, February 14, 1901, Winston Churchill took his seat for the first time in the House of Commons.

There was almost as much curiosity over the conduct of the new member from Oldham as there was over the demeanor of the new king. Winston, dressed in a somewhat extravagant style of wing collar and bow tie, was clearly borrowing from the wardrobe of his father. He had the same large eyes and square forehead, with the same habit of throwing up his head and laughing loudly at anything that amused him. His father's contemporaries also saw a bit of Randolph in the way he would walk through the lobby at great speed, with his hat swinging in his hand like a cane.

It was not expected that Winston would deliver his maiden speech for some time. After all, his father, Lord Randolph, had waited for about two months after he entered the House of Commons. Yet almost from the first day Winston could be seen making notes at his desk and then stuffing the pieces of paper in the hat beside him. Always in a race with time and destiny, Churchill was not about to sit back and wait for a month or even a week before rising to be heard. Yet Churchill viewed a maiden speech with more than a little apprehension. He was used to speaking from a prepared text at a podium or lectern when he faced his audience.

In the House of Commons, tradition frowned on the reading of a prepared manuscript. Although in a speech of great technical complexity, such as a budget speech, the House would make concessions, usually the most that was allowed was a sheaf of notes because to read from a manuscript would destroy the appearance of "formal conversation." Parliamentary debate is supposed to be just that, a debate; an exchange of views, not a series of monologues.

Churchill knew this, and tried to prepare his address accordingly. His opportunity would present itself during the debate on the conduct of the Boer War. So, in his London flat, he carefully wrote out, memorized, and practiced his speech, reflecting upon his South African experiences.

The House of Commons chamber in which he would speak was unchanged since the days of his father, who was regarded as one of the four or five greatest parliamentarians of the previous century. He had never actually heard him speak in the House of Commons, but he had read all of his speeches. For a new member he was well versed in the traditional parliamentary vocabulary: to refer a bill "upstairs" meant to a committee; "another place" was the phrase for the House of Lords; speeches made outside Westminster were said to be delivered "out of doors"; "the right honourable friends" referred to leaders of his own party, "the right honourable gentlemen" to leaders of the other party; "the honourable and gallant member" was used for those who had served in the military, "the honourable and learned member" for those who were members of the bar. He knew that speeches should be addressed exclusively to the Speaker, and that the mace on the table was the symbol of the king in Parliament; but that when money matters were discussed, the mace was put under the table, the Speaker left, and the House went into committee under a chairman so as to assert the Commons's power over the purse.

So on the third day after his seating, Churchill rose to be recognized, but at the same time another member was also demanding the floor. The Speaker recognized not Churchill but a Liberal member, David Lloyd George. Churchill knew from the newspapers that Lloyd George, increasingly a thorn in the Conservative government's side, had prepared a moderately phrased amendment to the government policy that King Edward had read in his opening address on February 14. In fact, the amendment was announced in the "order paper" of the day's proceedings. Yet Lloyd George crossed everybody up by saying right away in his speech that he did not propose to move the amendment. Instead, he launched into a bitter attack on the methods of warfare used by the British command in the war in South Africa.

Churchill was almost thrown into despair. In no way could he think of how to adapt his memorized remarks to follow those of Lloyd George. Yet he had to speak—the Speaker would look to him next. His moment would soon be at hand; he had told his whole family to expect his maiden speech this day. His mother and four paternal aunts, Lady Wimborne, Lady Tweedmouth, Lady Howe, and Lady de Ramsey, were in the galley. He sat, trying furiously to weave possible transitions from the remarks of Lloyd George to his own. Finally a Conservative colleague, Thomas Gibson Bowles, came to his rescue and whispered, "Churchill, you might say of Lloyd George that 'instead of making his violent speech without moving his moderate amendment, he would have better moved his moderate amendment without making his violent speech.'" As Churchill later wrote, "Manna from heaven could not have been more welcome in the wilderness."

As Lloyd George sat down, the Speaker recognized the gentleman from Oldham.

I understand that the honourable member to whose speech the House has just listened had intended to move an amendment to the Address. The text of the Amendment which had appeared in the papers was singularly mild and moderate in tone; but mild and moderate as it was, neither the honourable member nor his political friends had cared to expose it to criticism or to challenge a division upon it, and indeed when we compare the moderation of the Amendment with the very bitter speech which the honourable member has just delivered, it is difficult to avoid the conclusion that the moderation of the Amendment was the moderation of the honourable member's political friends and leaders, and that the bitterness of his speech was all his own.

Then Churchill, with a nod to his benefactor, said:

It has been suggested to me that it might perhaps have been better, upon the whole, if the honourable member, instead of making his speech without moving his Amendment, had moved his Amendment without making his speech.

When the expected applause and laughter followed, Churchill paused and, with both a graceful and gallant allusion to the Boers, managed to put down Lloyd George and the Liberal critics while at the same time disassociating himself from the hard-line pro-government position:

Moreover, I do not believe that the Boers would attach particular importance to the utterances of the honourable member. No people in the world received so much verbal sympathy and so little practical support as the Boers. If I were a Boer fighting in the field—and if I were a Boer I hope I should be fighting in the field [here Joseph Chamberlain on the government bench said, "That's the way to throw away seats"]—I would not allow myself to be taken on by any message of sympathy, not even if it were signed by a hundred honourable members.

Churchill continued by making some observations on the future of South Africa. He appealed for clemency in dealing with the rebels, advocating magnanimous terms for them that would secure for them their ethnic identity and their Calvinist religion.

Of course we can only promise, and it rests with the Boers whether they will accept our conditions. They may refuse the generous terms offered them, and stand or fall by their old way—"death or independence."

Here the members from Ireland cheered, but Churchill anticipated them with this turn of argument:

I do not see anything to rejoice at in that prospect. . . . If the Boers remain deaf to the voice of reason and blind to the hand of friendship, if they refuse all overtures and disdain all terms . . . we can only hope that our own race . . . will show determination as strong and endurance as lasting. . . . It is wonderful that the honourable members who form the Irish party should find it in their hearts to speak and act as they do in regard to a war in which so much has been accomplished by the courage, the sacrifices, and above all, by the military capacity of Irishmen.

Then he sounded his peroration:

Whatever we have lost in doubtful friends in Cape Colony, we have gained ten times or perhaps twenty times over in Canada and Australia, where the people—down to the humblest farmer in the most distant province—have, by their effective participation in the conflict, been able to realize, as they never could realize before, that they belong to the Empire and that the Empire belongs to them.

One last word remained:

I cannot sit down without saying how very grateful I am for the kindness and patience with which the House has heard me, and which has been extended to me, I well know, not on my own account but because of a certain splendid memory which many honourable members still preserve.

Despite Joseph Chamberlain's grumbling, the general verdict, as Churchill wrote later, was "not unfavorable." There was applause from all sides of the House, and Churchill was congratulated not only by Chamberlain on the Conservative side but also by Asquith on the Liberal, both of whom assured him they saw some of Lord Randolph's great qualities in his son.

The Tory *Daily Express* called Churchill's maiden address "spellbinding." In a more objective tone, the Liberal *Daily Chronicle* wrote, "Mr. Churchill is a medium-sized, undistinguished young man with an unfortunate lisp in his voice . . . and he lacks face . . . but he has some inherited qualities, candour and independence."

The lion in Churchill had not surfaced. There was no voice of the reformer, no prophet of the future. No tribune of the people yet stirred inside him. He had not yet shown himself worried by any particular injustices that cried out for solutions. He still reflected the aristocrat's naive belief that, on the whole, everything was right with the world.

But in two months, Churchill went from the defense to the attack. The more he studied the government's military policy, the more he sensed inconsistencies which his own military experience had revealed to him. The Secretary of State for War, Mr. William Broderick, in reaction to criticism of the British army, had proposed a full-scale army reform which would make Britain, like the Kaiser's Germany, in essence a military nation. Churchill, with a clairvoyance far beyond his twenty-seven years, saw that Broderick's proposal would end Britain's reliance on the navy and thus alter the whole course of her future foreign policy.

For the next six weeks Churchill would throw himself into organizing his attack against Broderick's policy. Then, when the army budget was introduced, he would be ready with his speech. For the first time he would not just be saying the right words; he was going to say what he thought was right. It was a speech he had to deliver to be true to his own heart and convictions.

On May 12, 1901, Churchill rose to deliver his attack on government policy. He began by alluding to his own father's dismissal after fighting in vain for military economy:

I am very glad the house has allowed me, after an interval of fifteen years, to lift again the tattered flag I found lying on a
stricken field.

He then made his case that having three army corps could lead
to world war:

One is quite enough to fight savages, and three are not enough
to begin to fight Europeans. . . . In former days, it was possible
to limit the liabilities of the combatants. But now, when mighty
populations are compelled against each other, each individual
severally embittered and inflamed—when the resources of
science and civilization sweep away everything that might mitigate their fury, a European way can only end in the ruin of the
vanquished and the scarcely less fatal commercial dislocation
and exhaustion of the conquerors.

Churchill then argued for the maintenance of Britain as a naval
power:

The superiority of the navy is vital to our national
existence. . . . Yet this tremendous army expenditure challenges
the principle. . . . For the main reason that enables us to maintain the finest navy in the world is that whereas every European
power has to support a vast army first of all, we in this for-
tunate, happy island . . . may turn our individual effort and
attention to the Fleet. Why should we sacrifice a game in which
we are sure to win to play a game in which we are bound to lose?

Closing his hour-long address with this peroration, Churchill
warned his audience of the moral considerations in tripling the size
of the army:

There is a higher reason still. . . . We shall make a fatal bargain
if we allow the moral force which this country has so long executed to become diminished or perhaps destroyed for the sake of
the costly trumpery, the dangerous military playthings on which
the Secretary of State has set his heart.

In this speech the young Churchill displayed all the courage, ardor of conviction, and prophetic insight that would distinguish his greatest oratory. The child of the House of Commons had become a man.

7

CONSERVATIVE BACK-BENCHER

It is not flesh and blood but the heart
which makes us father and sons.

—Schiller

Never was Winston Churchill more the son of Lord Randolph than when he rose to attack his own government's plan to expand the army. It was not just the way he looked, with his polka dot tie, frock coat, and watch-chained waistcoat, or the way he would thumb his lapels when speaking. Even the ring he sometimes fingered was the same signet Randolph would rub in the midst of an address. More than the mannerisms, by attacking his own party leadership, Winston was following the maverick route of his father.

The example of Randolph was not the only paternal influence upon Churchill. As he moved closer to the anti-imperialist sentiments of the free-trading Liberals, he was guided by the urgings of an American politician named Bourke Cockran.

Cockran, an Irish-American politician out of Tammany Hall, seems an unlikely father substitute for the grandson of a British duke. But with Bourke Cockran, Winston had the fatherly fellowship he had never found in his own family. Cockran, of leonine appearance and robust charm, was considered one of the great conversationalists of his day. Lord Ripon, whose dining companionship had included such stars as Thomas Carlyle and William Gladstone, found Cockran more scintillating than they. In Churchill's life Cockran was one of the very few he did not lecture, but instead listened to.

Churchill wrote in 1932, "In pith, rotundity, in antithesis and in comprehension, Bourke's conversation exceeded anything I have ever heard."

Cockran, a tall, commanding figure with large deep-set eyes that flashed imperiously, had captivated Winston's mother Jennie at a

Paris soirée shortly after his father's death. While their affair in the spring of 1895 was in progress, Winston, just graduating from Sandhurst, wrote his mother of his plans to visit Cuba as a military observer. Jennie naturally asked her current lover to look after Winston when he stopped over in New York City on his way to Cuba.

Cockran, a widower at the time, was forty-one years old and a Democratic member of Congress. Cockran met Winston's boat and whisked him off to a dinner party he staged in honor of his English guest at which leading members of the New York bar were present. The next day, Cockran took Churchill to watch a celebrated murder trial then in progress. Cockran, a famous trial lawyer himself, gave this advice on forensic technique: "To present a case you have to pick the strongest argument on your side and concentrate on that—build and mount that to an indisputable conclusion."

That Churchill owed more to Cockran for his oratorical style than to any other man seems clear. The stately elegance of a Cockran speech is what we now call Churchillian. In 1957 Adlai Stevenson, who had never heard of Cockran, was astonished when Winston told him of his debt to Cockran. The same year Winston's cousin, Sir Shane Leslie, told the author in Washington that Cockran's advice inspired much of Churchill's early ideas on oratory as expressed in the unpublished "Scaffolding of Rhetoric."

In that pamphlet, Churchill wrote of the necessity of laying the factual foundation of an argument before culminating with the high climactic peroration. He echoed Cockran's advice to find the strongest reason for a point of view and then amass all the facts behind that one reason. One strong reason wins the mind more than two or three. When the mind is persuaded, the orator should then go to the heart of the final summary.

Bourke Cockran was not just a good orator. He was one of the greatest in an age when rhetoric was a polished art and resounding oratory a popular entertainment. Born in Ireland and educated in France, Cockran was a student of the classics and history, with a particular love for Edmund Burke, to whom his family had claimed some ties. Cockran had emigrated to America and, quickly winning success as a lawyer, was adopted as a candidate by the Tammany Democratic Party organization.

But Cockran was no ward-heeling politician. He was an erudite scholar whose gifts of imposing looks, wide range of voice, and prodigious memory were focused on oratory. Archie Butts, military aide to President Taft, described the impact of Cockran in his diary:

> One is fascinated by his power of oratory. He looks like a lion ready to spring when he is speaking. His voice is like a low rumble of thunder, then has the sweetness of the lute in it. . . .

> As we left the banquet hall and were going home in the motor, the President said, "Archie, you now see the difference between declamation and oratory. I believe Cockran is the greatest orator using the English language today."

Taft was not the only leader to voice that sentiment. Senator Chauncey Depew, long considered America's greatest after-dinner speaker, deemed Cockran the finest orator he knew of. Across the ocean, a distinguished member of the British parliament, the journalist and author T. P. O'Connor, who was himself regarded as one of the most brilliant speakers in the House of Commons, wrote: "I have long held that Bourke Cockran was the most eloquent orator of his time among the English-speaking peoples, if not of all nations—more eloquent than Gladstone or Bright, more eloquent than Gambetta."

No wonder, then, that the young Churchill found himself under Cockran's spell, for he had the gift Churchill yearned for. Moreover, Cockran was the first older man who took a profound interest in Churchill's career, and it was done not out of a friendship with his late father, but out of a feeling of real spiritual kinship with the young man himself. His own mother adored Cockran; Churchill would worship him.

Churchill was also Cockran's guest when he returned from his Cuban tour as a military observer in 1895. From India Churchill corresponded with him, and in South Africa he asked Cockran to intercede, with his American influence, to secure his release from prison. When Churchill went on an American speaking tour in in December 1900 after his sensational prison escape and triumphant return to England, it was Cockran who met him in New York and lined up dinner parties and receptions for the young hero.

Some of their time together was spent in heated political discussion. The American-Irish Cockran thought the British policy on the Boers and their war to sustain it was morally wrong. Under the barrage of Cockran's arguments Churchill's own position began to shift. He began to reassess his Conservative government's policy on South Africa. As a result Winston began to show, in his speeches, a lot of sympathy for the Boers as a people. Some old-line Tories resented his kind words for a nation that was killing British soldiers.

Yet the issue that would pull Churchill away from the party of his father was economic, not colonial, imperialism. Here again, the free-tariff convictions of Bourke Cockran had their impact.

In July 1903, Bourke Cockran was invited to speak at the National Liberal Club in London on tariff reform. The Liberals wanted an internationally known speaker to counter the arguments of Joseph Chamberlain, the monocled Conservative leader, who was calling for a return to a stronger protective tariff system. Cockran was considered an ideal choice. Members of the club had heard Cockran was an even greater speaker than William Jennings Bryan, who, in any case, was too much of a populist for the British establishment. Cockran's speech opposing former President Cleveland at the 1892 Democratic national convention was said to be a finer address than Bryan's famous "Cross of Gold" speech at the 1896 convention. Cockran did not disappoint his National Liberal Club audience. His resplendent speech mesmerized his audience, which included young Churchill.

Your Free Trade system makes the whole industrial life of the world one vast scheme of cooperation for your benefit. At this moment, in every quarter of the globe, forces are at work to supply your necessities and improve your condition. As I speak men are tending flocks on Australian fields and shearing wool which will clothe you during the coming winter. On Western fields men are reaping grain to supply your daily bread. In mines deep underground, men are swinging pickaxes and shovels to wrest from the bosom of the earth the ores essential to the efficiency of your industry. Under tropical skies dusky hands are gathering from bending boughs luscious fruit, which, in a few days, will be offered for your consumption in the streets of London. Over shining rails locomotives are drawing trains; on heaving surges sailors are piloting barks; through the arid desert Arabs are guiding caravans, all charged with the fruit of industry to be placed here freely at your feet. You alone, among all the inhabitants of the earth, encourage this gracious tribute and enjoy its full benefit, for here alone it is received freely, without imposition, restriction, or tax, while everywhere else barriers are raised against it by stupidity and folly.

However impressive Cockran's reasoning for free trade, it was the lavish richness of his style that dazzled Churchill. Soon after, Churchill and a few like-minded young Conservative back-benchers began to speak out against Chamberlain, a stalwart of the Balfour government. These dissidents included Ian Malcolm, Lord Hugh Cecil, and Ivan Guest (Churchill's cousin, who later became Lord Wimborne). The press's nickname for the heretical four was either the "Malcontents" or "Hughligans," even though Churchill, and not Malcolm or Cecil, was the ringleader.

It was Churchill who coined the most stinging epigram against the Chamberlain policy. Standing in the back benches, he glared at the venerable Chamberlain and said, "Mr. Chamberlain loves the workingman; he loves to see him work."

In the fall of 1903, Churchill took his best friend at the time, Lord Hugh Cecil, for a barnstorming tour to follow in the wake of Chamberlain, who was speaking from town to town in favor of "Free Trade Within the Empire." In Birmingham, Chamberlain's home, Churchill was warned that hostile mobs awaited him if he dared to show his face. The scare only quickened the Churchill sense of adventure. Coolly, Churchill had his carriage driven into the midst of the people. Then, in plain sight of all, he imperturbably lit a cigar and casually made a path to the speaker's platform. At first stunned, the crowd relaxed and cheered him for his poise.

Not all his Conservative audiences acted so magnanimously. In one town Lord Hugh and Winston found themselves locked out of the Conservative club. From the front windows a number of indignant older faces stared down, brandishing their fists at the young duo. Churchill just shrugged it off and led his friend to a local pub.

At his own constituency of Oldham, the Conservative Association passed a revolution saying that he had "forfeited its confidence." In March 1904, Churchill rose in the House of Commons to speak against the Chamberlain policy. The reaction of the Conservative party was one unparalleled before or since in parliamentary history. Prime Minister Balfour and the rest of the Conservative members walked out in protest, with each one except the dignified Balfour pausing at the exit door to jeer at the young Churchill.

In the days to follow, Winston was the subject of many taunts from his fellow Conservatives. One M. P. named Claude Lowther asked him if he had contracted beri-beri during his time in South Africa. He documented his diagnosis by saying, "I made the remark because I have heard that the most characteristic symptom of the disease is a terrific swelling of the head." If Churchill failed to find an appropriate response to that barb, he did retaliate when another member, a Colonel Kenyon-Slaney, had the audacity to call him a traitor.

I have noticed that when political controversy becomes excited, persons of choleric dispositions and limited intelligence are apt to become rude. If I was a traitor, at any rate I was fighting the Boers in South Africa when Colonel Kenyon-Slaney was slandering them at home. I had the honor of serving in the field for our country while this gallant, fire-eating colonel was content to kill Kruger (the leader of the Boers) with his mouth in the comfortable security of England.

In becoming the *enfant terrible* of the Conservative party, Winston was treading the same route his father had close to three decades earlier. Indeed, his first break with the party leadership, his speech on military economy in May 1901, was on the same issue that triggered Lord Randolph's final rupture with the Conservative ministry in 1886.

The issue was the defense budget. The enlarged military programs of Lord Salisbury's Conservative government, such as tax reform and reorganization of the local poor councils, endangered Randolph's provisions for Tory Democracy. The Admiralty adjusted to Randolph's demands for cuts, but the War Office refused. On December 13, 1886, Lord Randolph had written to Salisbury: "You will shortly have to decide whose services you want to retain—those of your War Minister or those of your Chancellor of the Exchequer." In five days the flippant jest had hardened into a threat. On the fifth day, December 20, Randolph had been having an audience with Queen Victoria at Windsor Castle. Following an informative conversation with Her Majesty on state business in which he breathed no hint of a possible rupture, Randolph had retired to a guest bedroom where, on royal notepaper, he requested "to be allowed to give up my office and retire from the government." The letter broke not only the rules of royal etiquette, but also those of common sense. The ultimatum was delivered without Randolph's consulting any potential political allies. He did not even tell his wife. Without any spadework or concerted political action, he was unconsciously courting the rejection Salisbury wrote in reply. Randolph then went from his club to the editorial office of the *Times*, where he insisted his letter of resignation be made public.

His wife, as well as the queen, learned of the sensational news in the morning paper. For different reasons, both were upset. Victoria was angry at being used, his wife at being neglected. In one capricious throw of the dice Randolph had staked his political life, and with the fatalistic shrug of a gambler he accepted his loss and fall from power.

In these early years of his parliamentary career, the ghost of the father stalked the son. If Winston lacked the mustache and bulging eyes of his father, he made up for it by aping Randolph's curious stoop and shuffling walk. Indeed, long after the shadow of the father had vanished, Winston was still wearing the same polka-dot bow tie and lurching forward with the same stooping gait.

He had moved out of his mother's house at Cumberland Place to his own dwelling in Mayfair, which he shared with his brother Jack. Everything he collected and assembled represented his father's world. The entrance hall was covered with cartoons of his father from *Vanity Fair* and *Punch*. The carved oak chair at his desk was the one his father had been presented with by the city of Manchester. Even the brass inkstand on the writing surface was a legacy from Lord Randolph. There was not only a print of Lord Randolph, taken in the lobby of the House of Commons, but near it a portrait of Randolph's horse which had won the coveted Oaks Cup. Opposite the desk were shelves of books, mostly taken from Lord Randolph's library. Most of Winston's waking hours in the small house were spent at the desk poring over his father's speeches and letters during the writing of Lord Randolph's biography.*

If Winston was inspired by Randolph's rapid rise to early success, he was haunted by his father's tragic demise. The sad eyes that stared from Randolph's picture were a spur to the son to fight his father's battles and vindicate his memory. Thus it was not surprising that Churchill, in these years, embarked, as a young alienated Conservative, on a biography of his father that would defend Randolph's brand of "Tory Democracy" and justify his reasons for breaking with the leadership. In a sense, he was unconsciously reinforcing his own rationale for leaving the party that had rejected his father.

The word "meteoric" had been applied so many times to Randolph's life as to become trite. But how else can one describe in one word his rapid rise and sudden fall? For a short period from 1884 to 1886, the British parliament saw Lord Randolph's drama played out—ascent, apogee, and then fall. In quick succession he went from aristocratic playboy to a gifted parliamentarian to burnt-out wreck. The venereal disease he contracted in a casual encounter in Paris does not fully explain his demise. It was symptomatic of his self-destructiveness.

---

*The agent who negotiated the contract for Winston was his father's friend, Frank Harris. Somewhat of a literary rogue, Harris wrote about his dealings with the great in a salacious autobiography that was a big seller in the 1960s.

Many of the older Conservatives who remembered Lord Randolph now saw in his son, as he led the younger rebels in an attack against the leadership, the same mold of outspoken dissidence and brilliant instability. His older critics, however, failed to perceive a difference in their characters.

If both Churchills thought their time on stage was brief, Randolph was almost indifferent, while Winston was frenetic. The fitful and erratic father lacked the unflagging zeal of his son. The quicker mind of Randolph would yield to Winston's greater capacity for energy and persistence; the steel of the son's character would in the end outshine the brilliance of the father's.

But as Winston tried to establish himself as a rising politician with a future to be reckoned with, he could only see his own liabilities. While Winston read over Lord Randolph's papers and speeches in writing the biography, he could only envy his father's gift for facile expression. Since his days at the Oxford Debating Union, Randolph had been a talented extemporaneous speaker, but while he could just dash off his addresses, Winston would painstakingly have to grind out his drafts sentence by sentence. The reason Lord Randolph wrote his speeches out at all, his son stated in the book, was not for the sake of crafting the polished oration, but rather for recordkeeping. Lord Randolph wrote his first and final copy with hardly a line or word crossed out. Winston, who had to write many drafts, writes admiringly in his biography of Lord Randolph:

He seems to have written with scarcely a correction and without hesitation of any kind, as fast as he would set pen to paper. Indeed, I fancy that he wrote his speeches chiefly as an exercise of memory and to fix them clearly in his mind and did not by any means make them up with pen in hand. Once written, they could be repeated almost without notes and quite without alteration.

Imagine his sense of inadequacy mingled with envy as Winston wrote these words. For him, the preparation of every sentence was an effort and the delivery of every phrase a strain. How could one who had neither the mental gifts nor the intellectual training of his father ever become the parliamentarian his father was? How could he, now approaching his thirties, ever become a Chancellor of the Exchequer by the time he was thirty-six?

In April 1904, while he was still, every day, writing by pen the biography of his father, Winston suffered a disaster in an evening session of the House that almost convinced him that he had little potential as an orator or as a leader of the Commons.

As the front benches of the Conservative party were still smarting from his attacks during the past winter on Chamberlain's protective tariff policies, Winston would commit a ranker heresy by supporting the developing labor union movement. Here even his friend Lord Hugh Cecil and the other "Hughligans" thought he was moving too far to the left.

The speech that signaled his break with the Conservative party was to be the most painful experience in his parliamentary career. The address concerned the Trade Disputes Act. Churchill's call for the safeguarding of union organization rights was decidedly a left-wing speech. But it was not Conservative criticism, such as that of *The Daily Mail* which called it "radicalism of the reddest type," that embarrassed Churchill. Churchill was humiliated because, at the end of the hour-long speech he had committed to memory, he faltered.

"It lies with the government," he said, "to satisfy the working classes that there is no justification. . . ." Then he forgot his closing paragraph.

Having lost the thread of his argument, he looked around, confused, while struggling to find in his pocket a slip of paper that contained a relevant note. Finally, with a strange chopping gesture of his hand, he sank into his seat whispering, "I thank the honourable members for listening to me." Then, in chagrin, he covered his face with his hands. Members were struck by the comparison to Lord Randolph's halting delivery in those last years following his resignation from power. Such talk only deepened his son's agony. Winston knew that his father in his prime was in such command of rhetoric that even if he forgot, which he never did, he could "wing it" extemporaneously with even more telling effect.

Actually, Winston's collapse was due to an experiment. Stung a few months earlier by Conservative Prime Minister Arthur Balfour's jibe that his carefully prepared speeches were a "powerful but not very mobile artillery," Winston had tried to rely just on notes or paragraph headings. The result was this fiasco. From that day, April 22, 1904, Churchill would always carry with him ample notes, if not the full text, in case he forgot the address he had worked out beforehand. (In later years someone who noticed that Churchill rarely consulted his notes asked why he bothered to carry them. Churchill replied, "I carry fire insurance but I don't expect my house to burn down.")

If the arguments of Bourke Cockran moved Winston closer to the free trade position of the Liberals, it was the influence of Lord Randolph that made him more readily adopt some of the "Radicals'" ideas on the workingman and his growing problems in coping with the Industrial Age.

The "Tory Democracy" of Lord Randolph in the 1880s was a call to the newly franchised working classes in the cities to join the party of the patricians and squires of the countryside. In the biography, Winston tells how Lord Randolph had staked his hopes on the workingman's impatience with the fashionable liberalism of aristocrats who fulminated against slavery abroad and the treatment of peasants in Ireland, Boers in Africa, and Greeks under Turkish rule, but were indifferent to the industrial serfdom at home. Winston, with a rapidly developing social conscience of his own, described the mood of the biography this way:

The long dominion of the middle classes which had begun in 1832 had come to its close and with it the almost equal reign of liberalism. All sorts of lumbering tyrannies had been toppled over. Authority was everywhere broken. Slaves were free. But hunger and squalor was also free; and the people demanded something more than liberty.

Lord Randolph's interest in working and housing conditions made him, with the man on the street, the most popular figure in a Conservative party long dominated by reactionary landowners. To that extent, he was the successor to Benjamin Disraeli, who "dished" Whigs, as the Liberals were then called, by advocating wider extensions of suffrage. Disraeli was the founder of the modern Conservative party. To build his political following, Disraeli had combined a mild progressivism with a fervent patriotism. There was no more staunch defender of the monarch, the Empire, or even the established church than this Anglican Jew. Disraeli was an imperialist who gained the Suez Canal for the Empire and made Victoria, who was charmed by his courtly flattery, Empress of India. Disraeli's imperialism shrewdly tapped the romanticism of an emerging lower middle class, whose patriotism outstripped that of the more educated classes.

Though Lord Randolph's appeal to nationalist feelings mostly consisted of his opposition in the 1880s to Liberal Prime Minister Gladstone's support of home rule for Ireland ("Ulster will fight and Ulster will be right"), he was the acknowledged heir to the Earl of Beaconsfield, as Disraeli was known when he retired from the House of Commons to the House of Lords. Like Disraeli, Lord Randolph was a romantic figure who pleased the crowd more than the caucus. Randolph's oratorical gifts were assets, however, that the Conservative party leadership could ill afford to exploit. In addition, Randolph created his own political base by forming the Primrose League. The clubs were approximate British equivalents of the American Legion, the Elks, and the D.A.R. (Of course, the Primrose League would have been offended at being compared to a society with "Revolution" in its name.) But if the D.A.R. conjures up an image of ample-bosomed women with ribboned medallions bedecking their fronts, the comparison is not inapt. Randolph sensed the hunger in the industrial middle class. Enshrouded by drab routine, it hungered for elaborate titles and symbolic paraphernalia. With the enthusiastic support of Lady Randolph, he developed a following well beyond the limits of his own constituency.

In the days when the penny daily newspaper was just coming into its own as grist for the masses, the dashing Lord Randolph and his stunning American wife made splendid copy. And on the campaign platform, the resplendently tailored Randolph was as elegant as he was eloquent. As his son wrote:

He had the showman's knack of drawing public attention to everything he said or did. Before the end of 1882 a speech from Lord Randolph had become an event to the newspaper reader. . . . Wit, abuse, epigrams, imagery, argument—all were "Randolphisms." No one could guess beforehand what he was going to say or how he would say it. No one else said the same kind of things in the same way.

If the young people and the newly franchised urban workers of the great towns and cities relished the Randolphian jibes at the expense of the stately Gladstone, the educated classes, as they read the *Morning Post* or *Times,* would often harrumph at the lack of parliamentary decorum and dignity.

Even the leaders of his own party feared Lord Randolph, but they also needed him. His rapier attacks were the Conservative's most cutting weapon against pious liberalism. His most celebrated assault was his "chips" speech that mocked Gladstone's favorite recreation of chopping down trees. The "chips" were the souvenirs the Liberal leader would hand out to admirers who journeyed to visit the "Grand Old Man" at his country estate.

. . . For the purposes of recreation he has selected the felling of trees; and we usefully remark that his amusements, like his politics, are essentially destructive. Every afternoon the whole world is invited to assist at the crashing fall of some beech or elm or oak. The forest laments, in order that Mr. Gladstone may perspire. . . .

It has always appeared to me somewhat incongruous and inappropriate that the great chief of the Radical party should reside in a castle. But to proceed, one would have thought that the deputation would have been received in the house, in the study, in the drawing-room, or even in the dining-room. . . . The working men were guided through the ornamental grounds, into the wide-spreading park, strewn with the wreckage and the ruins of the Prime Minister's sport. All around them, we may suppose, lay the rotting trunks of once umbrageous trees: all around them, tossed by the winds, were boughs and bark and withered shoots. They came suddenly on the Prime Minister, in scanty attire and profuse perspiration, engaged in the destruction of a gigantic oak, just giving its last dying groan. They are permitted to gaze and to worship and adore and, having conducted themselves with exemplary propriety, are each of them presented with a few chips as a memorial of that memorable scene.

Is not this, I thought to myself as I read the narrative, a perfect type and emblem of Mr. Gladstone's government of the Empire? The working classes of this country in 1880 sought Mr. Gladstone. He told them that he would give them and all other subjects of the Queen much legislation, great prosperity, and universal peace; and he has given them nothing but chips. Chips to the faithful allies in Afghanistan, chips to the trusting native races of South Africa, chips to the Egyptian fellah, chips to the British farmer, chips to the manufacturer and artisan, chips to the agricultural labourer, chips to the House of Commons itself. To all who leaned upon Mr. Gladstone, who trusted in him, and who hoped for something from him—chips, nothing but chips— hard, dry, unnourishing, indigestible chips. . . .

With each derisive voicing of "chips," Randolph's audience could almost sense another ax blow against the towering oak of the British political forest, William Gladstone. No wonder the rank and file of the Conservative party were captivated by Lord Randolph. He was an electric personality, a sight never to be forgotten on the parliamentary bench or campaign rostrum, with his pop-eyed, walrus-mustached face dominating his slender, aristocratic frame.

Winston knew the words of the "chips" speech by heart. Although he rarely conversed with his father, much less witnessed his performance on the stump, he could still hear in his mind's ear all the intonations of the Randolphian invective. For the rest of his life the catchy epithet or smart epigram that was the staple of his father's speech repertoire would crop up in Winston's speeches.

The comment about Attlee that "he was a modest man with much to be modest about" was a gibe his father would have made.

So was his catch phrase in the 1950 general election: "Abadan, Sudan, and Bevan — they are a trio of misfortune." Though he had not Randolph's knowledge of the classics, Winston inherited his father's love for playing with words. In the midst of World War II, he wrote to F.D.R.: "From Malta to Yalta, we will not falter."

Winston, who in his early political career found interruptions and heckling disconcerting, knew all his father's parliamentary exchanges by heart. He particularly enjoyed reading aloud his father's flights into invective and abuse. His studies reaped a rich harvest in his World War II denunciations of Hitler and Mussolini. ("This whipped jackal, Mussolini, who to save his own skin has made all Italy a vassal state of Hitler's Empire, comes frisking up to the side of the German tiger with yelpings not only of appetite — that could be understood — but even of triumph.") Against lesser villains such as members of the opposition, the Randolphian penchant for invective sometimes backfired. Labourites never forgave Churchill when, just after World War II, he likened a bureacracy under British Socialists to "the Gestapo apparatus." Perhaps the cruelest example of his Randolphian wit is the description of Labourite Prime Minister Ramsey MacDonald in 1931.

> I remember, when I was a child, being taken to the celebrated Barnum's circus, which contained an exhibition of freaks and monstrosities, but the exhibit on the program which I most desired to see was the one described as the "Boneless Wonder." My parents judged that the spectacle would be too revolting and demoralizing for my youthful eyes, and I have waited fifty years to see the boneless wonder sitting on the Treasury Bench.

If some critics felt that such invective offended parliamentary niceties, his father would have applauded. Lord Randolph, in the polite Victorian Age, had been the most notorious breaker of the gentleman's code in his use of the savage personal attack.

As the Conservative back-bencher wrote his father's biography in the first years of the new century, he became more and more convinced that it was Lord Randolph's witty gibes, such as the "chips" speech, that forced Lord Salisbury to advance "young

Randy" in the party hierarchy. Randolph Churchill entertained the popular press and captured the enthusiasm of those workers who now had a vote.

With such popular backing, Lord Salisbury, amid disgruntled mutterings from ranking members, had been compelled to give due recognition to Lord Randolph. In 1885 he became the Secretary of State for India in the short-lived Conservative government. A year later, when the Gladstone rule toppled over the Irish question, Prime Minister Salisbury offered his junior colleague the number two position in the Conservative government—Chancellor of the Exchequer and Leader of the House of Commons. Yet when Randolph was finally handed a starring role in what could have been a long-running show, he had not the constancy nor the stability to sustain the challenge. He had no staying power. Randolph himself was aware of that. A Liberal friend asked him, "How long will your leadership last?" "Six months," Randolph replied. "And after that?" "Westminster Abbey." It lasted less than six months, and there was no Westminster Abbey. He impulsively resigned his chancellorship and so forfeited that lasting niche that could have been his in British history.

Eighteen years later, the son of Lord Randolph would make his final break with the Conservative party. The leader of that party would be Arthur Balfour, whose uncle, Lord Salisbury, Lord Randolph had challenged. Less than a month after he forgot his memorized speech, an event which *The Daily Mail* had headlined "MR. CHURCHILL BREAKS DOWN," Winston took the ultimate step and crossed over to the opposition. Undaunted by that forensic failure, Churchill had been making arrangements with another constituency to run as a Liberal while still sitting on the Conservative side. On May 31, 1904, Winston entered the chamber of the House of Commons, strode swiftly up the aisle, bowed to the Speaker, and turned sharply right to the Liberal benches. He sat down with the Liberals next to David Lloyd George in a seat that his father used to occupy when the Conservatives were in opposition.

Now a Liberal, Churchill lost no time in ripping Prime Minister Balfour for not setting a date for general elections which, according to all signs, would turn out the floundering Conservatives and end their decade of dominance in Parliament.

To continue in office for a few more weeks and months there is no principle which the government is not prepared to betray, and no quantity of dust and filth they are not prepared to eat.

When the general election was finally held in 1905, the Liberals won by a landslide. The Liberal leader rewarded young Churchill with the position of Undersecretary of State for the Colonies. At the age of thirty-one he had now left the party of his father and had charted another route for political power. As he was finishing *Lord Randolph Churchill* to send to the printer, Winston was completing his filial quest of the man with whom he had had hardly more than a handful of real conversations all his life. He had brought a legend to life and, in doing so, freed himself from the thralldom of emulation. The phantom of his youth was now reduced to a historical fact. He had exorcised the ghost of his father.

When Winston left the Conservatives to join the Liberals in 1904, he switched from the party of his father to a party whose views were closer to the other paternal influence in his life. Bourke Cockran was an anti-imperialist who opposed the American war with Spain in 1898 and the tariff protection policy of big business. Though an American politician, he held views that were much the same as those of traditional British liberalism.

Yet Cockran influenced his protégé even more in oratory than in political theory. Churchill would change political labels in his long career, but did not alter his unique brand of rhetoric.

The rich imagery and regal sweep of the Cockran speech became the style of Churchill. The eloquence of Cockran permeated Churchill as no other man's ever would. As Sir Shane Leslie* told the author, "Cockran was not just an idol for Winston, but a father." Cockran was the first figure in his life to treat Winston as an adult, to take his budding political opinions seriously, and to discuss the power of words. If Churchill had any teacher of oratory it was Bourke Cockran. In one of his last trips to America, Churchill said:

*Sir Shane Leslie was the son of John Leslie and Leonie Jerome, the sister of Winston's mother, Jennie.

When I first came over here in 1895 I was a guest of your great lawyer and orator Mr. Bourke Cockran. I was only a young Cavalry subaltern but he poured out his wealth of mind and eloquence to me. Some of his sentences are deeply rooted in my mind. "The earth," he said, "is a generous mother. She will produce in plentiful abundance food for all her children if they will but cultivate her soil in justice and in peace."

It was a phrase he would repeat countless times in his life, including his "Iron Curtain" address in Fulton, Missouri. But more than just the greatness of words, Cockran gave Churchill the wisdom of greatness. "Only a speaker who is sincere," Cockran would often say, "can be eloquent, because sincerity is the name of eloquence."

It was advice his real father would never have given. Lord Randolph, whose most quoted maxim was, "It is the duty of the Opposition to oppose," was a better parliamentarian than philosopher, with speeches that had more edge than depth. Yet the two men, Lord Randolph, who died in 1895, and Bourke Cockran, who would die in 1923 at the age of sixty-nine, played major roles in shaping what is memorable in Churchill's words and writings. From one he learned the art of invective and epigram, and from the other the art of the elegant sentence and majestic diction. In a sense, the aphoristic Lord Randolph and the stately Cockran were to his speaking what Macaulay and Gibbon were to his writing.

These two politicians, the one a searing memory and the other a continuing mentor, shaped not only Winston's oratory but his opinions. Though of different backgrounds and temperaments, Lord Randolph and Bourke Cockran were not unalike politically. Each defied his party, Randolph resigning in 1886 and Cockran by campaigning for McKinley against William Jennings Bryan in 1896 and then for Theodore Roosevelt in 1912. Each saw himself pitted against the forces of reaction. Randolph, the Tory Democrat, by advocating better employment and welfare conditions, was fighting for the poor; Cockran, the Jeffersonian Democrat, by championing antitrust and lower tariffs, was combating the rich. Without their example of political independence and social conscience, Winston Churchill might never have left the

Conservative party. The Winston Churchill who now was to become a leader in the Liberal government and its program of progressive legislation was the spiritual heir of both Randolph Churchill and Bourke Cockran.

8

LIBERAL REFORMER

Lloyd George and Churchill are the
men of tomorrow.

—*Eli Halevy*

Churchill became a Liberal just as the Conservatives' long-held domination of Britain was about to end. The opportune timing did not mitigate Conservative bitterness at his defection. In the Liberal sweep of 1908, Churchill was a junior minister. Such an appointment under the British constitution required that the newly designated minister immediately stand for election. Thus, even though the General Election had just been completed, a vacancy in a special election had to be found in order that Churchill could now stand as a subcabinet officer. Churchill went first to contest a Conservative-held seat in Manchester, where he immediately caught the imagination of the electorate. For one thing, he had donned a new specially tailored felt hat, which some of his supporters wore in emulation. Then he had festooned the halls and meeting places with mammoth posters proclaiming "Winston Churchill" in letters five feet high. With him he carried copies of his new biography of Lord Randolph, which was just hitting the bookstores at the first of the year. The flamboyance of the young parliamentarian did not sit well with his Conservative opposition, who regarded him as an apostate. Churchill entered the arena punching hard:

I am glad that the [Conservative] Parliament elected in 1900 is about to be dissolved. Few Parliaments in our modern experience have been less worthy of respect. A majority elected under the spell of patriotic emotion, upon a rational issue, in the stress of an anxious war, has been perverted to crude and paltry issues of party. . . . Seven more years of tinker, tax, and trifle. Seven years of shuffle, shout, and sham. Do not be taken in again.

The staccato style of his campaign attacks held echoes of Randolph:

We know perfectly what to expect—a party of great vested interests, bound together in a formidable confederation; corruption at home, aggression to cover it up abroad, the trickery of tariff juggles, the tyranny of a party machine, sentiment by the bucketful, patriotism by the imperial pint, the open door at the public house, dear food for the millions, cheap labour for the millionaire.

Supporters of the Conservative candidate, Joynson-Hicks, a loyal solicitor, started circulating a document stating Churchill's previous positions as a Tory. Churchill secured one of the pamphlets and was ready when some of the hecklers, waving the circulars like flags, yelled: "Answer it! What about it?"

Churchill, waiting patiently at the platform for the furor to build, replied, "It's true, it's all true. I said all those things because I belonged to a stupid party which I have left because I did not want to go on saying stupid things." Then, amid cheers, he tore the pamphlet into shreds with an expression of contempt for the cause he had once advocated.

In a constituency that had been considered a Conservative citadel for twenty years, Churchill could win only narrowly. He had help, though, from Manchester's sizable Jewish community. Churchill won their minds with his forthright embrace of a Zionist homeland, and he won their hearts by his style of campaigning. When his opponent, of Calvinist persuasion, piously pledged never "to electioneer on the Lord's Day," Churchill brazenly did, and he won the election by 5,639 to 4,398.

Churchill, now Under Colonial Secretary in the new government, would have to defend Empire policy in the House of Commons since the senior minister, Lord Elgin, served in the House of Lords. His method of preparing and memorizing speeches for days ahead of time would now be put to the test. Carefully wrought orations were not easily inserted into the informal nature of Commons debate. Jibes disguised as queries could derail the prepared address. Such taunting questions had long been considered part of the parliamentary tradition. The "heckling" Churchill himself gave, however, came not in the give and take of questions, but in his speeches. Older members of the Commons found the practice rather unsportsmanlike. A clever or snide question deserved an answer in kind, of course. But to spend hours at home dreaming up cute epithets was almost cheating.

The Conservative leader, Balfour, himself a frequent target of Churchill's barbs, expressed the resentment:

> It is not, on the whole, desirable to come down to this House with invective which is both prepared and violent. The House will tolerate almost anything within the role of order which evidently springs from genuine indignation aroused by the collision of debate . . . But to come down with these prepared phrases is not usually successful. . . . If there is preparation, there should be more finish, and if there is so much violence, there should be more veracity of feelings.

As a minister, Churchill would now be in a vulnerable role. He would have to field uncomfortable questions and defend sticky or unpopular policies. The renegade Churchill would be watched for any mistakes. Realizing this, Churchill turned down the more prestigious post Prime Minister Campbell-Bannerman had offered him as Financial Secretary to the Treasury. Churchill felt toward the decimals of statistics the way his father had ("Those damned dots.") He chose the less weighty Under Secretaryship for the Colonies, where the major issue before the Commons was a new constitution for South Africa. Though African matters, because of his Boer War involvement, were an area he had fairly well mastered, nevertheless his first speech as a minister was a disaster.

A back-bencher had unexpectedly made a motion that Lord Milner, the former High Commissioner in South Africa, be censured for his flogging of Chinese coolie laborers. Churchill, who did not want to exacerbate the volatile feelings then raging in South Africa, tried to slide around the issue by urging the Commons to condemn the practice but not the man following it. The junior minister's defense of Milner was half-hearted. He seemed to be seeking popularity for himself at the expense of the older man. The Conservatives ripped his defense, not only for his inconsistency in argument, but for his inconsistency in loyalty. Conservatives such as his old Harrovian friend Julian Amery felt that the speech might finish his career.

Such predictions were premature. Churchill worked hard as a minister even though he was paired in uneasy harness with Lord Elgin, a crotchety former India proconsul twenty-five years his senior. A self-government charter for the Transvaal government was hammered out. Churchill's speeches on behalf of the African settlement were those of a statesman:

> There is a higher authority which we should earnestly desire to obtain. I make no appeal, but I address myself particularly to the right honourable gentlemen who sit opposite, who are long versed in public affairs and who will not be able all their lives to escape from a heavy South African responsibility. . . . I will ask them, further, whether they cannot join with us to invest the grant of a free Constitution to the Transvaals with something of a national sanction. With all our majority we only make it the gift of a Party; they can make it the gift of England.

Even though the Conservatives did not join in supporting the bill, Churchill, though still resented by the Conservatives, was no longer considered a gadfly. When he was appointed a privy councillor to the king at the uncommon age of thirty-three, it was a recognition by the Liberal party leadership of his emerging statesmanship.

Already Churchill was making his voice heard in the councils in what has been considered the most eminent assemblage of talent in a government administration. Besides Prime Minister Campbell-Bannerman, there were Asquith at the Exchequer, Sir Edward Grey at the Foreign Office, Lloyd George at the Board of Trade, and many other distinguished names, including such eminent intellectuals as Viscount Morley and Lord Bryce.

The Liberal government, in addition to having allies in the Irish Nationalists and fledgling Labourite party, was, in itself, two parties. On the one hand, there were the aristocratic old-line Liberals who wanted to keep the state out of the people's lives, and, on the other, the newer social Liberals or Radicals, who felt the state should play a larger social role. It was not unlike the North-South mixture of Rooseveltian and Jeffersonian Democrats in America.

It is a paradox that the upper-class Churchill soon became the most articulate spokesman of the middle-class Radicals. Churchill had left the Conservatives over the issue of free trade, a tenet of nineteenth-century liberalism, but he would become the twentieth-century Liberals' most effective champion of welfare state reforms.

The catalyst in this conversion was David Lloyd George. From Lloyd George, Churchill was to learn the language of radicalism. It was Lloyd George's native tongue. Born and brought up in a small Welsh hamlet by his uncle, the village shoemaker, the orphaned Lloyd George had early tasted poverty. Deprivation was, for him, not an abstraction, but a fact of life that colored his hostility toward the rich. Country squires, estate owners, and even the Anglican vicars were his sworn enemies.

The first time Churchill ever saw the face of poverty was at the time of election at Manchester. Strolling out from his hotel headquarters one evening with his administrative secretary, Edward Marsh, he wandered into slum sections replete with grimy tenements. "Fancy," Churchill said, "living in one of those streets— never seeing anything beautiful—never eating anything savoury— never saying anything clever." An entirely new world, known before to Churchill only from reports and statistics, opened before him.

Churchill had grown up in another world, of stately country homes and fashionable townhouses where the art of conversation and the ways of society were exquisitely practiced by gracious families unburdened by the drudgery and chores of household care; these were people who had the time to read, talk, and discuss the current affairs and fashions. It was, as Churchill once said, "the world of the few, and there were very few."

It was these few that Lloyd George attacked with the vehemence of an Old Testament prophet. When Lord Rothschild attacked Lloyd George's budget, this was the black-haired Welshman's impassioned answer:

We are having too much of Lord Rothschild. We are not to have temperance reform in this country. Why? Because Lord Rothschild has sent a circular to the Peers to say so. We must have more dreadnoughts [battleships]. Why? Because Lord Rothschild has told us so at a meeting in the City. We must not pay for them when we have got them. Why? Because Lord Rothschild says so. You must not have an estate duty and a super-tax. Why? Because Lord Rothschild has sent a protest on behalf of the bankers to say he won't stand for it. You must not have a tax on reversions. Why? Because Lord Rothschild, as chairman of an insurance company, said he wouldn't stand for it. You must not have a tax on undeveloped land. Why? Because Lord Rothschild is a chairman of an industrial housing company. You must not have Old Age Pensions. Why? Because Lord Rothschild was a member of a committee that said it couldn't be done. Are we really to have all the ways of reform, financial and social, blocked by a notice board: No thoroughfare: By order of Nathaniel Rothschild?

Churchill was fascinated by the Radical politician eleven years his senior. The volcanic Celt had great fire as a speaker. To the note of political passion, Lloyd George could add the fervor of a prophet. The man from Wales was a latter-day Amos, decrying the evils that had beset his pastoral people. The Welsh had been torn out of their idyllic past by the English Industrial Revolution. Into their world came the pits, railways, and steelworks, thrusting the shepherds, farmers, and their children into mines, factories, and slums, condemned to a life that would be joyless, brutish, and short.

To Churchill, David Lloyd George was a messenger of history, with a tablet of plans to sweep injustice from the land. In the crusade that Lloyd George captained, Churchill was enlisted as lieutenant. Both his former secretary, Robert Boothby, and Violet Bonham-Carter say that Lloyd George was the only contemporary politician ever to dominate Churchill. As Lady Violet said, "His was the only personal leadership I ever knew Winston to accept unquestioningly in his whole political career. He was fascinated by a mind more swift and agile than his own, by its fertility and resource, by its uncanny intuition and gymnastic nimbleness, and by a political sophistication which he lacked."

The author was told by retired Prime Minister Harold Macmillan in 1966 of the advice Lloyd George once gave Churchill, as well as himself, as a young member of the House of Commons. It included his shrewd technique for gathering an audience in a half-filled House when he was still a young junior minister with an undeveloped reputation:

Don't deliver an essay with so many points. No one can absorb it. Just say one thing. Maybe as a minister you can offer two points—as a prime minister perhaps three. Remember only few will actually listen to you. What you want is someone to go to the Smoking Room and say, "Macmillan made a very good speech." "Oh, what did he say?" will be the reply. Then he has to be able to say one thing—one point. Of course you say the point in many different ways over and over again with different illustrations.

And you must constantly vary your pitch—anger, sorrow, humor, sarcasm. Remember to say to yourself as you rise to speak, "Vary the pose and vary the pitch." Finally, don't forget the pause.

Don't lead off with all your best stuff. Wait till you build up an audience. You know how in a play the first minutes are taken up with talk by the butler or the maid. There is no murder in the opening moments because some of the audience is still being seated.

You can pull the same trick in the House of Commons. Before you start with your message ask one of the speakers who just finished. Say, "I have listened with great interest to your address, but there was just one point I didn't understand. Why did you say there is no difference from A or B?" He rises to explain. When he sits down, thank him if the House has filled up. If it hasn't, say, "I now understand but I still don't see the difference between C and D." He rises and a little angrily explains. The charade is repeated. Then with your audience full and ready, you can begin your own speech.

When it came to the art of political manipulation, Lloyd George was a virtuoso. He could not only move a crowd, but sway a caucus. As Lord James Bryce, a Liberal colleague of Lloyd George and Churchill, wrote in his *American Commonwealth,* only a rare leader can do both; but Lloyd George had the oratorical gift of a Daniel Webster on the stump along with the Lyndon Johnson talent of massive persuasion in private. About Lloyd George Churchill coined a phrase that would later become trite: "He could charm the birds out of the trees."

To critics who complained about Lloyd George's bent for cheap opportunism and demagoguery, Churchill was philosophical. He said to Violet Asquith, "He gets things done, doesn't he, and you have to admit he's a genius, a political genius." For one with so much character, Churchill was strangely tolerant of its lack in others if they had compensating strengths. At any rate, with his father now consigned to the bookshelf, it was the personality of Lloyd George that now filled his life.

William Gladstone once described the art of oratory as "perceiving a vapour arising from the people, condensing it, and passing it back in a flood." By such a definition, Lloyd George was a genius and Churchill a failure. Lord Morley wrote, "Whereas Winston knows his own mind, Lloyd George is always more concerned to know the minds of others." Lord Keynes wrote after the First World War, "Lloyd George is rooted in nothing; he is a void and without content; he lives and feeds on his immediate surroundings; . . . he is a prism . . . which collects light and distorts it and the most brilliant of the light comes from many quarters at once; a vampire and a medium in one."

But if Lloyd George was a reflector, albeit one of magnifying splendor, Churchill was a generator. What he lacked in Lloyd George's instinct, he more than made up in intellect. In Churchill's mind, the Lloyd George pension and tax proposals filtered, their pieces reassembling into a mental framework, a perfectly organized structure. While absorbing the ideas of others, he could put them into a rhetorical context of his own. In appropriating Lloyd George's plans, he transformed them into a philosophy that was totally his.

In Glasgow, on October 11, 1906, Churchill gave form to the idea of a middle way between socialism on the left and laissez-faire capitalism on the right:

> It is not possible to draw a hard-and-fast line between individualism and collectivism. You cannot draw it either in theory or in practice. That is where the Socialist makes a mistake. Let us not imitate that mistake. No man can be a collectivist alone or an individualist alone. He must be both an individualist and a collectivist. . . . Collectively we light our streets and supply ourselves with water. But we do not make love collectively and the ladies do not marry us collectively.

Churchill continued to delineate the role of the state that would be a model for Western democracies for the rest of the century.

> I should like to see the State embark on various novel and adventurous experiments. I am of the opinion that the State should increasingly assume the position of the reserve employer . . . the State must increasingly concern itself with the care of the sick, and the aged, and above all of the children. . . . I look forward to the universal establishment of minimum standards of life and labour; . . . but I do not want to see impaired the vigour of competition. . . . We want to draw a line below which we will not allow persons to live and labor, yet above which they may compete with all the strength of their manhood. We want to have free competition upwards; we decline to allow free competition upwards; we decline to allow free competition downwards. We do

not want to pull down the structures of science and civilization, but to spread a net over the abyss.

It must be remembered this was voiced over seventy years ago. Neither Prime Minister Campbell-Bannerman nor his successor Asquith was then contemplating such an ambitious program. The patrician Churchill had outlined an even greater agenda than the plebian Lloyd George would propose or later enact.

Even though a privy councillor of the realm had made a profoundly radical address, it did not disturb the older-generation Liberals of the party as did the strident class warfare of Lloyd George. When Campbell-Bannerman suddenly died and Asquith took his place as prime minister, Churchill moved up into the presidency of the Board of Trade, the chair Lloyd George vacated for Asquith's old post as Chancellor of the Exchequer. The promotion meant that Churchill had to stand again for election in the insecure seat of Manchester.

This time Churchill lost, perhaps, as he himself suggested, on account of the sudden entry of the suffragettes, led by Mrs. Pankhurst. Even though he gave them his personal assurances of his support, the feminists demanded a public confirmation of support by the prime minister, Asquith. Not gaining that objective, they staged their defiance until they were violently and often bloodily ejected from the hall. As Churchill himself wrote:

This was the beginning of a systematic interruption of public speeches and the breaking up and throwing into confusion of all Liberal meetings. Indeed, it was most provoking to anyone who cared about the style and form of his speech to be assailed by the continued, calculated, shrill interruptions. Just as you were reaching the most moving part of your peroration or the most intricate point in your argument, when things were going well and the audience was gripped, a high-pitched voice would ring out, "What about the women?" "When are you going to give the women the vote?" and so on. No sooner was one interrupter removed than another in a different part of the hall took up the task. It became extremely difficult to pursue connected arguments.

Yet within minutes of hearing the final returns of his defeat, Churchill was handed a telegram inviting him to contest the Scottish seat in Dundee, one of the great Liberal strongholds. At the Kinnaird Hall in Dundee, Churchill delivered a speech which would later be one of the most successful campaign speeches of his career. For weeks he chiseled, shaped, and polished the lines that would win highest praise from Lloyd George and Asquith. It refined and distilled even further the philosophy of the Glasgow speech. The passage contrasting liberalism and socialism was widely quoted:

> Liberalism has its own history and its own tradition. Socialism has its own formulas and aims. Socialism seeks to pull down wealth; Liberalism seeks to raise up poverty. Socialism would destroy private interest; Liberalism would preserve private interests in the only way they can be safely and justly preserved, namely by reconciling them with public right. Socialism would kill enterprise; Liberalism would rescue enterprise from the trammels of privilege and preference. Socialism assails the pre-eminence of the individual; Liberalism seeks, and shall seek more in the future, to build a minimum standard for the mass. Socialism exalts the rule; Liberalism exalts the man. Socialism attacks capital; Liberalism attacks monopoly. These are the great distinctions.

Amid favorable editorial reception to his address, Churchill won against his Conservative opponent. This time the suffragettes were less effective in the no-nonsense Scottish district. But if feminism was not a factor in Churchill's campaign, there was a new feminine interest in his life. One who was impressed by the Churchill address in Kinnaird Hall was Clementine Hozier. Clementine, who had met Churchill at a dinner party at Dundee, came from a political family strongly Liberal in their convictions. Eleven years younger than the thirty-three-year-old Churchill, Clementine was a granddaughter of the Earl of Airlie.

The tall and regal Clementine had a striking elegance, with classical features that could flash into animation. Everyone said she looked like a queen, and a queen she should have been, for her superbly sculptured face would have shone splendidly on a coin.

Her appearance was what first attracted Winston. She was in the statuesque mold of such beauties as Pamela Plowden, Murial Wilson, and the actress Ethel Barrymore, who sporadically diverted Churchill's thoughts from politics. (Before her death, Miss Barrymore told Churchill's son that she, though attracted to Winston, had turned down his proposal because she felt she could not adjust her career to his.) Clementine had a keen brain to match her beauty, and a political brain at that. A Radical with a sympathy for the suffragettes, Clementine was a friend with whom Churchill could sound out his ideas and practice his speeches. He would dedicate to her the printed collection of his speeches on Liberal philosophy, including the speeches at Glasgow and Dundee that were printed the next year. The collection came out just after they were married in a fashionable wedding at St. Margaret's at Westminster, which all the leading politicians attended.

For such a lusty and adventurous man, Churchill had been a circumspect bachelor. Perhaps the venereal disease of his father made him unusually wary of any physical liaison. Another reason is that Churchill had absolutely no capacity for small talk. Social occasions that gave no opportunity for stimulating conversation bored him. Churchill was describing himself when he wrote in *Savrola*: "Savrola did not dance; there were some amusements which his philosophy taught him to despise."

Yet this ballroom wallflower emerged as the most scintillating conversationalist of this century or, to be more precise, the world's most entertaining monologuist. Churchill was not particularly adept at reading and manipulating people, but as a one-man show, Churchill was incomparable. His audience, within the space of moments, could be dazzled by wit and stunned by prophecy. In words that glistened with alliteration and phrases studded with epigrams, Churchill would thunder warnings, whisper jests, and invoke the apt verse, all without inhibition or self-consciousness; but he needed an audience, the right kind of audience, for there was only one subject in his repertoire—politics or, in its antique form, history.

Young ladies were usually not likely to be charmed by such monologues. Violet Asquith was. She said that after listening to him she "knew what it meant to be seeing stars." Clementine was equally entranced. Years later, she was asked if she found Churchill handsome when she first met him. "No," she replied, "I found him interesting." Clementine Hozier, whose social conscience had been pricked by the squalor of the industrial slums, was fascinated by this prophet of the Liberal state. In turn, Churchill, a romantic idealist about love, had found the woman to share his life. So when a summer squall forced the young people to seek shelter in a gazebo on the Blenheim Palace grounds, he proposed. London did not consider it an advantageous marriage. Though, through her mother, she was a daughter of the Scottish aristocracy, Clementine herself was in straitened circumstances and had to support herself by being a governess. Yet if Churchill did not make a money match in the time-honored tradition of British politicians, he made a decision, which, as he would later say, was the wisest he ever made. Clementine was his haven and shelter throughout a tumultuous and stormy life. For all his egocentricity and idiosyncracies, Winston inspired in Clementine an all-consuming and steadfast devotion. In the lasting love of his marriage, he relived the happy fate of his ancestor the Duke of Marlborough, for whom Sarah, his duchess, was the romance of his life. When Sarah, in her widowhood, once received a proposal of marriage, she gave her husband this magnificent tribute: "If I were young and beautiful, instead of old and faded, and you could lay an empire at my feet, you would never shade the heart and hand that once belonged to John, Duke of Marlborough."

With those who loved and served him or came into his orbit, Churchill's conversation was a magnetic, spellbinding force. His parliamentary secretary, Robert Boothby, wrote, "It can be said of Churchill as it was of [Robert] Burns that his conversation is better than anything he has ever written; and those who have not had the opportunity of listening to it can hardly appreciate the full quality of the man." It is a strange paradox that one who was in private such a voluble and articulate talker was, in public, almost wholly dependent upon careful preparation and rehearsal.

During the campaign of 1908, Churchill was mostly setting Lloyd George's ideas to rhetoric, but with his ascendancy to the presidency of the Board of Trade, he could begin putting some of his ideas into action. When he first assumed the cabinet post, he complained, "Lloyd George has taken all the plums out of the pie." He set out looking for his own plums, even if they happened to be in other people's pies. To the disgruntlement of the Home Office, he championed the abolition of the sweatshop and instituted under his Ministry the setting of minimum wages and maximum hours for selected industries. Another reform was the establishment of labor exchanges to deal with unemployment. Still, most political attention was focused on Lloyd George, who as Chancellor of the Exchequer had called for a "people's budget," and whose tax proposals alarmed the landed interests. Lloyd George and Churchill, the renegade aristocrat who championed Lloyd George's budget, attracted an upper-class hatred unequaled until the time of Franklin Roosevelt. Just as Franklin Roosevelt and the Democratic Congress found New Deal legislation blocked by a Supreme Court appointed in a conservative past, so the Liberals, with their huge majority in the House of Commons, saw their proposals stymied by the House of Lords. Dukes, marquises, earls, viscounts, and barons, who owed their seats to the favor of a bygone monarch, were hardly likely to be sympathetic to radical legislation. In this hereditary Senate, the Tories held a comfortable majority and took their signals from the Conservative leader of the opposition, Arthur Balfour. In the ensuing confrontation between the irresistible force of progressive legislation and the immovable object of feudal tradition, a constitutional crisis flared. When Balfour argued that the House of Lords was "the watchdog of the Constitution," Lloyd George replied that it was only "Balfour's poodle."

The virtual veto of Lloyd George's budget by the House of Lords turned what had been the battleground into the issue itself. Taking to the hustings, Lloyd George called for the Lords' power to be shorn. "It was now," said Lloyd George, "the King and the People vs. the King and the Peers."

As an old Tory Democrat, Churchill was agonized by this frontal attack on the Lords. His democratic Radical side was appalled by the Lords' veto, yet the evisceration of an august institution disturbed his sense of tradition. Nevertheless, Churchill swallowed his misgivings and mounted the most telling attack yet on the Lords.

The House of Lords is an institution absolutely foreign to the spirit of the age and to the whole movement of society. It's perhaps not surprising in a country so fond of tradition, so proud of continuity as ourselves that a feudal assembly of titled persons with so long a history and so many famous names should have survived to exert an influence upon public affairs at the present time. We see how in England the old forms are reverently preserved after the forces by which they were sustained and the dangers against which they were designed have passed away. A state of gradual decline was what the average Englishman had come to associate with the House of Lords. . . .

But now we see the House of Lords flushed with the wealth of the modern age, armed with a party caucus, fortified, revived, resuscitated, asserting its claims in the harshest and crudest manner, claiming to veto or destroy even without discussion any legislation, however important, sent to them by any majority, however large, from any House of Commons. . . .

We see the House of Lords using the power which they should not hold at all, which if they hold at all they should hold in trust for all, to play a shrewd, fierce, aggressive party game of electioneering and costing them votes according to the interest of the particular party to which, body and soul, they belong. . . .

With this speech, Churchill spent his last Radical sentiment; so was the country also drained by the continual constitutional crisis. The House of Lords, facing a possible packing of the chamber by creation of new peers, capitulated and yielded its veto power in a way not dissimilar to that in which the U.S. Supreme Court readjusted its course after F.D.R. threatened to pack its chamber. The Liberals' victory was pyrrhic, however, for the bloody fight had thinned their electoral ranks. In proving their point, the

Liberals had lost their Radical thrust. Nevertheless, the reform of the House of Lords, the high point of Radical legislation, owed not a little of its success to the grandson of a British duke.

9

WAR MINISTER

A sadder and a wiser man.
He rose the morrow morn.
—Samuel Taylor Coleridge

Although the last citadel of aristocratic oligarchy had fallen to the siege of radicalism, the victors had spent their last reserves for success. The onslaught against the Lords had antagonized the press and polarized the country. The forces of reform were losing the competition for budget requests to the armed forces, whose defense needs struck patriotic chords in all the classes. The butter of radicalism yielded to the guns of militarism.

Churchill, a soldier by training and nationalist by heritage, was not unaware of the shift in the British mood. An intellectual convert to radicalism, he had never felt completely comfortable with the Socialists and pacifists in their fight against the Lords. Although he gave it his full support, the struggle had drained his emotional sympathies for the Radical cause. Leaving the Board of Trade to be Home Secretary in 1910, Churchill further alienated himself from the left wing by his quelling of striking Welsh miners' violence with troops and his "siege of Sydney Street" caper, where, in top hat and cape, he provided an on-the-scene direction to the police's encirclement and capture of armed revolutionaries.

In July 1911, a foreign crisis broke out that gave support to those who feared for the state of national defenses. A German war vessel had docked at the Moroccan port of Agadir. Such gunboat diplomacy was seen as a German attempt to stake out a sphere of influence on the western coast of North Africa, where the British had decided to give the French a free hand in return for British control of the Suez.

During the Agadir crisis, while vacationing in Somerset, Churchill found himself himself haunted by the verse in Housman's *A Shropshire Lad*:

On the idle hill of summer
Sleepy with the sound of streams,
Far I hear the steady drummer
Drumming like a noise in dreams.

Far and near and low and louder
On the roads of earth go by
Dear to friends and fool for powder
Soldiers marching, all to die.

But the soldiers did not march in 1911. Germany, upbraided by Franco-British protest, receded from the brink. Churchill, though, had glimpsed Armageddon. With his characteristic energy, he began to brief himself on the country's state of military and naval preparedness.

Shortly thereafter, Churchill reached beyond his purview as Home Secretary and submitted to the Committee of Imperial Defence an astonishingly prescient memorandum entitled "Military Aspects of the Constitutional Problem":

It is assumed that an alliance exists between Great Britain, France, and Russia, and that if these powers are attacked by Germany and Austria, the decisive military operations will be those between France and Germany. . . . This can be found either before the full strength of the Germans has been brought to bear or after the German army has become extended. The first might be reached between the ninth and thirteenth days; the latter about the fortieth.

. . . it will be backed by sufficient preponderance of force, and developed on a sufficiently wide front to compel the French armies to retreat from their positions behind the Belgian frontier, even though they may hold the gaps between the fortresses on the Verdun-Belfort front. No doubt a series of great battles will have been fought with varying local fortunes, and there is always a possibility of a heavy German check. But, even if the Germans were brought to a standstill, the French would not be strong enough to advance in their turn; and in any case we ought not to count on this. The balance of probability is that by the twentieth day the French armies will have been driven from the line of the Meuse and will be falling back on Paris and the south.

. . . France will not be able to end the war successfully by an action on the frontiers. She will not be strong enough to invade Germany. Her only chance is to conquer Germany in France. . . .

Although the army staff called the document "ridiculous and fantastic," in three years it would all happen just as Churchill predicted. He gave the twentieth day of the German offensive as the day on which the French armies would be driven from the Meuse River and then forecast that the German army would be fully extended by the fortieth day on all fronts. That is exactly what occurred. The Battle of the Marne was lost by Germany on the forty-first day.

What gave the young Home Office Secretary the vision that the older and more experienced leaders in the War Office and the Admiralty lacked? Churchill gave the clue when he later modestly described the amazing document in *World Crisis* as "an attempt to pierce the future; to conjure up in the mind a vast imaginary situation; to balance the incalculable; to weigh the imponderable." The key to his gift of prophecy was his imagination—an uninhibited imagination that was not afraid of making mistakes. Like a Columbus, he could array the facts, sift the possibilities, and, with a full calculation of the odds, ride his conclusion far into the horizons of the future. Where the military and bureaucratic mind, confronted by an image of contingencies, would opt for the immediate and safer present, Churchill would weigh each imponderable, gauge the outcome, and proceed to the next step. Casting aside the less probable "ifs," he invaded the veiled future until the course had been resolved. Such a conclusion, unencumbered by qualifications or conditions, became, under the force of Churchill's words and the power of his description, not just a prediction, but a revelation.

The cabinet secretaries were predictably infuriated by Winston's frequent "meddling" in matters considered to be their own jurisdiction. But Asquith, who as prime minister had the overall responsibility, was increasingly impressed by his thirty-seven-year-old Home Secretary, the second youngest in history. Not long after his paper on French defenses, Churchill was invited, along with Lord Haldane, the current head of the War Office, to the Scottish summer home of the prime minister. A private man, Asquith little relished the fervent exchange of group discussion and preferred to make decisions in the cooler atmosphere of his study after reading memoranda, or, if not that, by making ministers argue their case individually and then making his decision. Asquith was casting for a First Lord of the Admiralty and dangled the role before each of them, making them, in effect, compete for the assignment. Haldane, who had reorganized the War Department with a modern army planning staff, was anxious to do the same for the navy. Winston, who had wanted the Admiralty when he had been assigned the Home Office, was brimming with ideas to make the Navy Department shipshape.

At the end of the September weekend, Churchill hauled Asquith's daughter Violet from the afternoon tea. "Will you come out for a walk with me at once?" Winston asked her breathlessly.

"You don't want tea?"

"No, I don't want tea. I don't want tea—I don't want anything—anything in the world. Your father has just offered me the Admiralty."

Churchill was overjoyed with the appointment. Destiny, he thought, had been saving him for just such a mission. That night, while undressing for bed, he picked up the Bible on the nighttable and opened it at random. His eyes lit on this passage:

Hear, O Israel, Thou art to pass over Jordan this day, to go in to possess nations greater and mightier than thyself, cities great and fenced up to heaven . . . and he shall bring them down before thy face; so shalt thou drive them out, and destroy them quickly, as the Lord has said unto thee.

To Churchill's strongly prophetic mind, it seemed an omen of reassurance.

Like a captain being given his first ship, Winston happily threw himself into the task of making the empire seaworthy against any challenge or attack. Overboard went old shibboleths on naval usage and precedent. Seniority, which Churchill almost equated with senility, was shoved aside. For his First Sea Lord he chose Prince Louis of Battenberg, whose one special laim to prominence was that he had married Queen Victoria's granddaughter.* Because of his German accent, veterans resented this career sailor in the Royal Navy, whose line would later flourish under his son, Admiral Lord Mountbatten, and his grandson Prince Philip. As Naval Secretary he appointed the young and dashing Rear Admiral David Beatty, who had startled the stiff world of the Royal Navy by taking as a bride the American heiress to the Marshall Field department store in Chicago.

Superannuated admirals were not the only ones to be scrapped. Churchill wanted to replace the thirteen-inch guns with the longer-ranged fifteen-inchers, which had greater power, and for speed, he proposed sacrificing the battle-plate armor of the old "dreadnoughts" for a lighter Cruiser squadron. Finally, to make the whole navy faster-cruising, Churchill recommended that the fleet be converted from coal to oil, thus adding maneuverability by allowing ships to be fueled at sea.

One admiral, upset by Churchill's reforms, asked him at an Admiralty meeting, "Wasn't he aware of the tradition of the Royal Navy?"

"Tradition," roared Churchill. "Tradition! I tell you what the tradition of the navy is—rum, sodomy, and the lash." When a former admiral, Lord Charles Beresford, accused Churchill on the House of Commons floor of wrecking the navy, Churchill scathingly replied, "Charles Beresford can best be described as one of those orators who, before they get up, do not know what they are saying, and when they have sat down, do not know what they have said."

---

*His affair with Lillie Langtry, which had produced a daughter, was hushed up by King Edward, who dispatched the unknowing Prince Louis to sea and Lillie to Paris to have the child.

Churchill had to convince not only admirals, but also his fellow members in the Liberal party. The reforms cost money, appropriations that would pare down the amount allotted to welfare projects dear to his once-close Radical colleagues. Lloyd George complained to him, "Winston, you've become a water creature. You think we all live in the sea, and all your thoughts are devoted to sea life, fishes, and other aquatic creatures. You forget that most of us live on land."

To the critics of his defense spending, Churchill gave this ringing answer at Glasgow, the seat of the nation's shipbuilding industry:

> The purposes of British naval power are essentially defensive. We have no thoughts, and we have never had any thoughts, of aggression; we attribute no such thoughts to other great Powers. There is, however, this difference between the British naval power and the naval power of the great and friendly empire— I trust it may long remain a great and friendly empire—of Germany. The British Navy is to us a necessity, and from some points of view the Germany Navy is to them more in the nature of a luxury. Our naval power involves British existence. It is existence to us; it is expansion to them.

If the pacifists in England were temporarily muted, the militarists in Germany flared up. The kaiser ranted at the indignity of *Luxusflotte,* the German translation of Churchill's concept. "Why should a big fleet be a luxury to us and only a necessity to them?" Churchill quickly proposed to Germany a year of no shipbuilding for both nations—"a naval holiday," he called it, "to put a blank page into the book of mutual understanding."

When the kaiser did not reply, Churchill's warning in his famous Clydeside address began taking hold in the court of public opinion. In private councils he won a compromise from the cabinet after a threat to resign; they would go along with his increased budget request for 1913 but would return to the previous level in 1914. (Of course, after the cataclysmic events of that year, no such restriction was ever imposed.)

In that fateful eleventh hour, Churchill, in both conversation and debate, was a prophet singly possessed by one vision. In *World Crisis* he described it in these romantically charged words:

Consider these ships, so vast in themselves, yet so small, so easily lost to sight on the surface of the waters. Sufficient at the moment, we trusted for their task, but yet only a score or so. They were all we had. On them, as we conceived, floated the might, majesty, dominion, and power of the British Empire. All our long history built up century after century, all our great affairs in every part of the globe, all the means of livelihood and safety for our faithful, industrious, active population depended upon them. Open the sea-cocks and let them sink beneath the surface, as another Fleet was one day to do in another British Harbour far to the North, and in a few minutes—half an hour at the most—the whole outlook of the world would be changed. The British Empire would dissolve like a dream; each isolated community struggling forward by itself; the central power of union broken; mighty provinces, whole Empires in themselves, drifting hopelessly out of control, and falling a prey to strangers; and Europe after one sudden convulsion passing into the iron grip of the Teuton and of all that the Teutonic system meant. There would only be left far off across the Atlantic unarmed, unready, and as yet uninstructed America to maintain, single-handed, law and freedom among men.

Guard them well, admirals and captains, hardy tars and tall marines; guard them well and guide them true.

When, in 1914, the World War did erupt and rage across the map of Europe, the blue that rimmed its edges was under British sway. In the hot summer days that followed the pistol shot at Saravejo, while the British cabinet debated involvement in the worsening foreign crisis, Churchill, not waiting for authorization, ordered full mobilization of the fleet. When German troops invaded neutral Belgium, Prime Minister Asquith demanded their withdrawal by August 4. To an hourly countdown at 10 Downing

Street, Asquith waited. When Big Ben struck eleven, it meant midnight in Berlin. Britain was at war. In another room at Whitehall, the First Lord was ready. As the notes of Big Ben came reverberating through the open windows, the signal for this wire was sent to all British ships: "Commence hostilities against Germany." Since Churchill had already called up and deployed the full reserves of the Royal Navy, there was never a chance for a "Pearl Harbor" strike by German U-boats and battleships. Seldom before has a defending navy been so well prepared.

Not yet forty, Churchill, as First Lord of the Admiralty, had reached the pinnacle of power as one of Britain's three most powerful leaders. He had established himself as a brilliant orator, a talented writer, and energetic administrator. Though he headed the most awesome sea force in the history of the world, Churchill was not content to confine his energies to naval problems. His creative imagination spilled over into other spheres. With the shared jurisdiction of the army, he pioneered the establishment of the first Air Force. The mind that, in World War II, would spawn devices for floating landing harbors, dispelling fog, and piping oil came up with the idea of the tank in World War I. They called it "Winston's folly" when he earmarked £10,000 for the production of "landships"; but 48 of its brothers took the field in the Battle of Thiepval. The Germans threw down their guns and fled, and land warfare underwent a lasting change comparable to that wrought on sea by the *Monitor* and *Merrimac* in the Civil War.

That is not to say Churchill was an inventor. He had hardly a schoolboy's knowledge of physics, with a disdain for "the infernal combustion engine." He was, however, inventive. The inventiveness, like his gift for prophecy, came from imagination coupled with single-minded concentration—no barrier could stop his flow of thought. Any impossibility might be wrought into a possibility. If the war was stalemated by trench warfare, why couldn't an armored car with movable track be designed? If the Normandy harbor for D-day landing was inadequate, why not make a harbor and float it across the Channel? Churchill may not have been an inventor, but he could ideate targets for those who were.

His was a mind not inhibited by the finite restrictions of bureaucrats or military technicians. From them Churchill would demand facts, not interpretations of facts. One who served under him said, "Churchill made us all write what we had to say on one side only of one piece of paper. He would call up and ask for information, but he just wanted skeletal facts. He filled out the rest from his extraordinary understanding."

Churchill had an undisguised contempt for officials who inflated the English language as a cover to hide behind for the purpose of dodging accountability. Such language he once described as "one of those rigmaroles and grimaces produced by the modern bureaucracy . . . a kind of palimpsest of jargon and officialese with no breath, no theme, and no facts."

Churchill's impatience with unwieldy words and his penchant for creating new ones led him, as First Lord of the Admiralty, to introduce new terms into the military vocabulary. By his fiat, "aeroplane" was shortened to "plane," and "hydraplane" was Anglicized to "seaplane." He dictated the term "destroyer" to describe the light unescorted "search and destroy" vessel, and "flight" to designate a squadron unit of four planes. During his stint in the Admiralty, other terms emerged which have since passed into the English language. A "naval holiday," which he proposed to Germany in 1913, became standard diplomatic usage in the Big Powers disarmament talks after World War I, and at the outbreak of the First World War, Churchill introduced to a group of civic and commercial leaders the phrase "business as usual" as a motto for their carrying on in time of crisis.

But such an innovative mind could neither brook the mediocre nor suffer the pedestrian, and Churchill would soon pay the price for his unconventionality. The England of that era was not unlike an old-line Boston bank today, where traditional conformity reigns and an aspiring young man does nothing save by stealth and guile. Young executives who tackle problems with ardor, unafraid of committing errors and prepared to accept them as the price for rapid promotion, cause suspicion and invite themselves as targets. Churchill's forte was ideas, not intrigues. He soon found that his boyish eagerness for action swiftly brought him into controversial adventures which eventually destroyed his position at the Admiralty.

The first and lesser of these was the Antwerp "Circus." Shortly after German troops rolled into Belgium, French Marshal Joffre suggested that a small British detachment land in the Belgian port to agitate the Germans on their right flank and prevent an advance to the vital seaport at Dunkirk. Churchill, whose fledgling air force, in a daringly innovative bombing raid, had just destroyed some German Zeppelin sheds and damaged a North Sea submarine base, was asked to undertake this diversionary charade. Unlike the army that seeks to do much by stealth, the not inaptly named Circus was asked to do little and parade much. To ask Churchill to draw attention to himself was like ordering a little boy to put on his first cowboy costume. The uniform he actually arrived in was that of Elder Brother of Trinity House, a ceremonial costume that made him look more like Bonaparte than Buffalo Bill. Trailing the Churchill limousine as the party drove honking into Antwerp were armored cars and a few red London buses carrying Royal Marines and yeomanry. At home the British laughed, but in Antwerp the Belgians cheered as a young Churchill strode through the lobby of his hotel headquarters to assume command.

Finding no Belgian defenses, Churchill took the army, navy, and civil defenses in his hands. For three days, he was virtually the Belgian chief of staff. From Antwerp he orchestrated darting forays behind German lines. Although the Circus actually fulfilled its mission by buying time, Antwerp finally fell; but as King Albert of Belgium later said, "Because of Churchill, the Germans never took Dunkirk." Although the French seaport was saved for British ships, Churchill's enemies in England saw it as more of a fiasco than a feat. To them it was Winston's flamboyance at its worst.

If there was a comic side to the Circus, only unrelieved tragedy could describe the Dardanelles episode. The Dardanelles are the narrow straits that are the gateway to Constantinople (now Istanbul). Ever since conflict had broken out, Churchill had argued for a combined land-and-sea invasion of the Ottoman Empire (Turkey) that would knock the "sick man of Europe" out of the war and thus shorten it by enabling Russia to attack Germany on its Eastern Front.

Then, on New Year's Day in 1915, Churchill was approached by Lord Kitchener, the virtual British commander in chief, whose face, an English version of Uncle Sam, is remembered on "We Want You" posters. It was Kitchener who had suggested the Circus at Antwerp; now he wanted Churchill to send a flotilla to bombard the Dardanelles. Churchill agreed if and only if it was to be a joint military and naval action. His tragedy was allowing this original resolution to be undermined. With the support of the prime minister and cabinet, a sea attack alone was authorized, but cannon power from the ships was not enough to subdue the Gallipoli peninsula which led to Constantinople. When, months later, British troops did arrive, the Turks had been reinforced by the Germans. Thousands of British soldiers, including the poet Rupert Brooke, died on the stark Aegean coast.

It was a classic case of "too little and too late," and the scapegoat was the First Lord of the Admiralty. As he was dismissed, Lord Kitchener said to him, "No one can take one thing from you, Winston. You had the fleet ready in 1914."

Although military historians now confirm that a successful invasion of Turkey might have ended the war in 1915, Churchill would bear the brunt of this failure the rest of his life. Cast from his office, he had himself assigned command of a battalion in the French trenches. The brutality of the ouster from office stunned Churchill. "Like a sea beast fished up from the depths, or a diver too suddenly hoisted, my veins threatened to burst from the fall in pressure. . . . At a moment when every fibre of my being was inflamed to action, I was forced to remain a spectator of the tragedy, placed cruelly in a front seat."

Not until 1917, when the American entry presaged the end of the war, was Churchill allowed back on the stage. The final release, in May, of the Dardanelles' report erased the stigma that had been laid upon him. Shortly thereafter Churchill delivered to a secret session of the House of Commons an attack on the government's war policy. He bluntly told them to wage no more costly offensives, but to conserve their strength for that moment when, with the arrival of America's vast numbers, one last massive thrust could be mounted.

Prime Minister Lloyd George, fearful of Churchill's sharp tongue in the attack, persuaded a reluctant cabinet to take back the controversial Churchill for the Ministry of Munitions, where his considerable talents could be harnessed for coordinating the logistical demands of the landing Americans. (His efforts resulted in his being awarded the Distinguished Service Cross by General Pershing, the only Englishman so honored.)

To a war-weary nation that was seeing the attrition of trench combat snuff out its young manhood, the voice of Churchill helped rally the last reserves. In that final era before radio, no head of government—not even such a dynamic personality as the now white-maned Lloyd George—could by himself inspire his countrymen. The prime minister's orations were confined to the House of Commons, except for the occasional address to a London banquet. The burden thus fell on Churchill, who proved to be as ubiquitous as he was eloquent.

Churchill launched his return to office by a speech to constituents in Dundee. Referring to Woodrow Wilson's recent call for a League of Nations, Churchill reminded his Scottish listeners:

We are the heart, the centre of the League of Nations. If we fail, all fail. If we break, all break.

The next July 4, at an Anglo-American dinner, Churchill sounded the note that would be the closing theme of the war:

Germany must be beaten; Germany must know she is beaten; Germany must feel she is beaten. Her defeat must be expressed in terms and facts which will for all time deter others from emulating her crimes and will safeguard us against their repetition.

Then he closed with this final appeal:

No compromise with the main purpose, no peace till victory, no pact with unrepentant wrong.

"No peace till victory" became the war cry. Lord Beaverbrook, who told Churchill it was his greatest speech, had it printed in pamphlet form and distributed in America. The ring of such resolute words served to dispel the lingering doubts of "defeatism," a word that Churchill took from the French language to describe the noxious pessimism of war critics.

Churchill's morale-lifting speeches around the country at bond rallies, ship launchings, factory sites, and civic dinners were in a sense a dress rehearsal for his sublime contributions a little more than twenty years later. The ending of the war brought forth words worthy of his World War II finest. In a peroration that borrowed from Bourke Cockran, Abraham Lincoln, and the Bible, he closed:

Five years of concerted effort by all classes, like what we have given in the war, but without its tragedies, would create an abundance and prosperity in this land, aye, throughout the world, such as has never yet been known or dreamt of. Five years of faction, of bickering, of class jealousies and party froth, will not merely not give us prosperity, it will land us in utter and universal privation.

The choice is in our own hands. Like the Israelites of old, blessing and cursing is set before us. Today we can have the greatest failure or the greatest triumph—as we choose. There is enough for all. The earth is a generous mother. Never, never did science offer such fairy gifts to man. Never did their knowledge and organism stand so high. Repair the waste. Rebuild the ruins. Heal the wounds. Crown the victors. Comfort the broken and broken-hearted. There is the battle we have now to fight. There is the victory we have now to win. Let us go forward together.

In the aftermath of victory the breach that needed most to be healed was the festering question of Ireland. A settlement that had been hammered out in the face of threatening German hostilities in 1914 had been shelved for the war's duration. The agreement, which did not satisfy the more extreme shades of Orange and Green, would have given home rule to all of Ireland except the

Protestant bastions of Northern Ireland. To build a lasting treaty on such elapsed understandings was the commission Prime Minister Lloyd George gave to Churchill as Colonial Secretary in the reconstituted Liberal coalition government following the war. Lloyd George picked Churchill because he, more than anyone else, had shouldered the burden of combating Ulster defiance in those uneasy moments before World War I.

This time the threat of sedition came from the Catholic south, where the Irish Republican Army, who were then less like terrorists and more like troops, as the name suggests, were conducting a full-scale civil war. The Churchill strategy for peace was far from pacific. It combined the threat of force and the flash of rhetoric with fair and even generous terms. That had been his policy for the Boer War, and even at the close of the just-finished war with Germany, Churchill was one of the few English who stood against the revanche demands of "Hang the Kaiser" jingoists.

In 1914, the concession to Ulster was that it could stay with Westminster, apart from the Dublin government, but when Orange resistance increased, Churchill, as First Lord of the Admiralty, dispatched a cruiser squadron to the coast of Northern Ireland. As the son of the man who proclaimed "Ulster will fight and Ulster will be right," he risked the name of traitor by confronting the challenge.

> But if there is no wish for peace, if every concession that is made is spurned and exploited . . . if all the loose, wanton, and reckless chatter we have been forced to listen to all these many months is in the end to disclose a sinister and revolutionary purpose—then, gentlemen, I can only say to you, let us go forward together and put these grave matters to the proof.

At the time, Lord Lansdowne, Leader of the Opposition in the Lords, approvingly described the Churchill approach of "making speeches full of party claptrap and 'no surrender' with a few sentences for wise and discerning people to see and ponder."

In the face of a probable war with Germany, wiser heads in Ulster accepted the terms, and the threat of British civil turmoil was averted, but at the end of the war it was Dublin that was rebelling against "home rule" status. As Colonial Secretary, Churchill met with Michael Collins, the Irish representative who had led an uprising in 1916.

The defiant Collins told Churchill, "You hunted me day and night. You put a price on my head." Then Churchill said, "Wait a minute, you're not the only one," and showed a framed copy of the reward offered by the Boers for his recapture. "At least you got a good price, £5000. Look at me, £25 dead or alive. How would you like that?" The relationship between the old soldiers ripened into one of mutual respect. Collins and the other leaders were handed by Churchill and Lloyd George the stark choice of dominion (like Canada and Australia) or war. They reluctantly agreed to dominion. Knowing the wrath he would incur by signing the pact, Collins said, "I expect soon to be killed." He was right. Before his assassination, he wrote one last message, "Tell Winston we could never have done without him."

Churchill, as Colonial Secretary, now had the task of presenting the Irish treaty to the House of Commons, just as he had done a little more than a decade before with South Africa.

For generations we have been wandering and floundering in the Irish bog; but at least we think that in this Treaty we have set our feet upon a pathway, which has already become a causeway— narrow, but firm and far-reaching. Let us march along this causeway with determination and circumspection, without losing heart and without losing faith. If Britain continues to march forward along that path, the day may come—it may be distant, but it may not be so distant as we expect—when, turning round, Britain will find at her side Ireland united, a nation, and a friend.

Moved by Churchill's eloquence, enough Conservatives joined to ratify the treaty. Churchill the peacemaker is not a role biographers emphasize, but it is noteworthy that Churchill, at the Colonial Office, was instrumental in securing settlement not only in Ireland but also in the Middle East—two areas where so many statesman have failed. To resolve postwar Arab demands in the wake of the defeat of Turkish rule, Churchill called a Cairo Conference, with his friend Lawrence of Arabia as chief adviser. Fearful for the Jews' tenuous hold on Palestine, Churchill maneuvered to place on the Middle Eastern thrones of Iraq and Jordan two of the Feisal family, whose moderation would check the more fanatic factions of Arab anti-Zionism.

By this Churchill wanted to insure the continuing promise of the Balfour Declaration, particularly for fleeing Russian refugees. At one point he proclaimed in the House of Commons, "It is hard enough in all conscience to make a new Zion, but if, over the portals of the new Jerusalem, you are going to inscribe the legend 'No Israelite need apply,' then I hope the House will permit me to confine my attention exclusively to Irish matters." The peace gains in Palestine and in Ireland were not without their price. The Irish treaty particularly shattered much of the Conservative party's support for Lloyd George's Liberal coalition. With the government fall, a new election was held.

But Churchill, felled by an attack of appendicitis, had to campaign from a hospital bed for his seat in Dundee. The day after his defeat in 1922, he was out of Parliament for the first time since 1900. "In the twinkling of an eye," he wrote, "I found myself without a seat, without an office, without a Party, and even without an appendix." Notwithstanding any ministerial successes, the past twelve months had constituted a milestone in his life more mournful than any other since 1895, when both his father and his beloved nanny had died. His fourth child, Marigold, had died at the age of three from a strep throat (the others were Diana, Randolph, Sarah, and Mary, who was born after Marigold's death). And two months before, in June 1921, his mother, Lady Randolph, died at age sixty-seven from complications resulting from amputation of an infested ankle. Churchill wrote, "She had the gift of eternal youth and never before have I felt this more, in these weeks of cruel pain."

Churchill was now middle-aged. Not only private sorrows, but the public memory of Gallipoli, darkened his soul. His frame bore the grief of an anguished father, mourning son, and discredited minister, whose former reputation, despite subsequent cabinet accomplishments, had not been redeemed. Though in his prime, he found himself a political has-been at the end of his odyssey in the Liberal party, which he had so brightly begun as a ministerial boy wonder.

10

CONSERVATIVE CHANCELLOR

In a Baldwin cabinet Churchill is a
Mount Everest among the sandhills.

—*Henry Asquith*

At forty-eight, Churchill was no longer a young man of promise but a relic of the past. The hair, still sandy, had thinned and made no pretense of covering the scalp except on the sides, and his slouch, which once gave his youth a purposeful cast, now seemed less a mannerism than a mirror of age. The days of adventure and greatness were behind him. At that time of life when most men find the security of career replacing the dreams of youth, Churchill had neither. The moorings were missing, not only those of politics and party, but the personal ones of property and household.

For most of his life Churchill had been rootless. He had fought in many countries, occupied many ministerial posts, and lived in many houses and apartments. As head of his family, he yearned to settle down, to seek the solace of the countryside in a home that was his own, where his children could run and romp.

On a November Sunday in 1922, he took his family on a drive from London to see an estate in Kent. Not until their return did he grinningly reveal that the house, Chartwell, was already theirs; he had bought it with the proceeds of a recent legacy from his great-grandmother, the Marchioness of Londonderry. If the Victorian manor was not an architectural splendor, the view was. A hilly crown wooded by expansive spreading chestnuts and resolute oaks overlooking the green of an English weald, it suggested much of Churchill himself. It was a scene he loved to paint—a stretch of streaming blue atop some clumps of trees that overlap into a grassy foreground where a pond gently ripples for attention. Churchill had begun painting in the summer at Gallipoli just after he had been dismissed from the Admiralty. One day, in despair, he had

147

picked up a box of his children's watercolors and experimented with them. The next day he bought an expensive set of oils and was contemplating the canvas when a voice behind him said, "Painting? Well, what are you hesitating about?" It was Lady Lavery, the wife of Sir John Lavery, who had recently completed Winston's portrait. "Let me have a brush—" she said, "a big one." And with that she slashed the canvas with bold and furious strokes. As Churchill wrote in *Painting as a Pastime*:

> Anyone could see that it could not hit back. No evil fate avenged the jaunty violence. The canvas grinned in helplessness before me. The spell was broken. The sickly inhibitions rolled away. I seized the largest brush and fell upon my victim with berserk fury. I have never felt any awe of a canvas since.

In no time, Churchill was splashing oils with gay but determined abandon. As in his oratory, he was attracted to broad sweep and rich color. An impressionist by instinct, he was almost intoxicated by cerulean blues and vibrant greens:

> I rejoice with the brilliant ones and feel genuinely sorry for the poor browns. When I get to heaven I mean to spend a considerable portion of my first million years in painting and so get to the bottom of my subject. But then I shall require a still gayer palette than I get here below. I expect orange and vermilion will be the darkest and dullest colors upon it and beyond them there will be a whole range of wonderful new colors which will delight the celestial eye.

Although, under the *nom de brush* of Charles Morin, he staged well-received exhibitions in Paris and London, the real contribution of his painting lay in its impact not on the art world but on himself. He called it his pastime, but it was more his lifeline. The outside easel and chair under a sunny sky were his decompression chamber. Painting was more than just a release from the weight of office, it was a regeneration. Churchill explained it in *Painting as a Pastime*:

Change is the master key. A man can wear out a particular part of his mind by continually using it and tiring it, just in the same way as he can wear out the elbows of a coat by rubbing the frayed elbows; but the tired parts of the mind can be rested and strengthened, not by merely rest, but by using other parts.

By calling on his physically creative side, he replenished his mental reserves. If the habit of a midday nap, developed from his Cuban sojourn, served to extend his working day, the hobby of painting generated more hours of creativity in that day. The demands of writing history and composing oratory were different from the demands of oils. After a stint of painting, Churchill found he could return to his study revived. The secret to his titanic productivity was, in no small way, due to this rhythmic rotation from library to landscape.

It is hard to realize that second only to that other giant of the English tongue, William Shakespeare, Churchill was perhaps the most prolific writer of the printed word. His histories of over one-half million words alone would crowd the shelves of most homes. Much of these chronicles, including his account of World War I and the biography of the Duke of Marlborough, were dictated at Chartwell.

The workshop for those efforts was a Tudor-beamed study where, seated at his father's mahogany table, he could gaze out through the ample bow window at the wooded downs sloping to a swan-filled pond. Besides nature, his only sources for inspiration were family and history. Peopling the top of the claw-footed writing desk were porcelain busts of Napoleon and Nelson amid a profusion of silver-framed photographs of parents, wife, and children. To his right, on the sill of the side window, rested a bronze cast of Lady Randolph's hand along with a 30-pound piece of shrapnel which in Flanders fell providentially between Churchill and his cousin the ninth Duke of Marlborough, who had inscribed it with the words: "This fragment of a shell fell between us and might have separated us forever, but now is a token of union." It was the Marlborough estate that dominated this simple, almost austere room. Hanging over the fireplace just behind Churchill's chair on his left, the massive portrait of Blenheim faced the bay window, surveying the only other grounds dear to Churchill's heart.

Churchill threw himself into the task of restoring those grounds and the manor house that rested on them during those bleak days of political limbo. Just as an orator would strike the clumsy word, revise the awkward phrase, and redress the unbalanced sentence, so Churchill hacked off the Victorian gables from the roof, sliced away the ponderous oriels of the windows, and cut away the brush of ivy on the sides to reveal the simpler tones of a Tudor house that would blend into and not dominate the gentle pastoral roll of Kent meadows.

It was not only an estate that Churchill was seeking to rebuild in those officeless years in the early twenties. He had an impaired political reputation to rehabilitate as well. The memory of Gallipoli hung over him like a dark cloud. The weapon with which he fought back was his pen. He defended the Dardanelles venture as an attempt to break the deadlock of trench warfare. He also excoriated General Munro, who had advised evacuation at Gallipoli. "He came, he saw, he capitulated." Although he admitted he should not have advocated a plan without the commensurate authority to follow it through, nevertheless the Dardanelles gamble to shorten the war was better strategy than "seeking costly offensives . . . when no answer to the machine gun existed"— offensives that decimated a generation of Europe's youth.

Although Lord Balfour, in a typical sardonicism, called *World Crisis* "an autobiography disguised as a history of the universe," a more apt description was oratory in the garb of history. That is not to demean its significance as a chronicle of World War I. Eminent historians such as Maurice Ashley and Henry Steele Commager praised the work. The book, written in Churchillian rhetoric, reverberates with the thunder of terrible events. If his previous writing experiences shaped the studied nature of his early speeches, it is the majestic sweep of Churchill the rhetorician that is heard in *World Crisis*. He didn't write it as he did *Lord Randolph* or *The River War*; he dictated it. Puffing a Havana, he would pace up and down the study declaiming in bursts, while a nervous secretary struggled to record all his rich phrases in Pitman shorthand. On the rare occasions he thought better of what he had just said, he'd roar, "Scrub it." Most of the time he would stop in admiration of his own words and contemplate the next point. On he would continue until the completion of the whole chapter or, for that matter, speech. In either case, he wanted his words before him in type-written form.

Once they were down in black and white, he could begin the endless polishing and revision. Seated at his father's desk nursing a Scotch and soda, he would eye the draft, hearing the words echo in his own imagination. In a silent reading, word repetition and un-wieldy phrases were caught, while alliterative possibilities and historical illusions presented themselves. For Churchill such liter-ary exercise was not a chore but a lark he could not bear to end by sending off to the printer, and when it returned in galley form he would view it as another draft instead of as a proof to be checked for accuracy. Galleys would be returned with margins bulging with whole new paragraphs to be inserted. If Churchill holds the record in having the most number of galleys revised, it is not due to the supine acquiescence of his editors. Only a Churchill could have so stretched their patience and their pocketbook.

But the final draft was, for the most part, well worth the cost. Listen to his conclusion of a colossal military epic when he proph-esies, with a rhetorical "nay," the spectre of nuclear apocalypse:

[War] has at last been stripped of glitter and glamour. No more may Alexander, Caesar, and Napoleon lead armies to victory, ride their horses on the field of battle sharing the perils of their soldiers and deciding the fate of empires by the resolves and ges-tures of a few intense hours. For the future they will sit sur-rounded by clerks in offices, as safe, as quiet, and as dreary as government departments, while the fighting men in scores of thousands are slaughtered or stifled over the telephone by machinery. It is established that nations who believe their life is at stake will not be restrained from using any means to secure their existence. It is probable—nay, certain—that among the means which will next time be at their disposal will be agencies and processes of destruction wholesale, limited, and perhaps, once launched, uncontrollable.

Mankind has never been in this position before. Without having improved appreciably in virtue or enjoying wiser guidance, it has got into its hands for the first time the tools by which it can unfailingly accomplish its own extermination. That is the point in human destinies to which all the glories and toils of men have at last led them. They would do well to pause and ponder upon their new responsibilities. Death stands at attention, obedient, expectant, ready to serve, ready to shear away the peoples *en masse,* ready, if called on, to pulverize, without hope of repair, what is left of civilisation. He awaits only the word of command. He awaits it from a frail, bewildered being, long his victim, now—for one occasion only—his Master.

The many-volumed word *World Crisis* and its sequel, *Aftermath,* were top sellers both in serialized and condensed form. Churchill, who plowed the royalties back into his Chartwell renovation, in untypical modesty called it a potboiler as he sent copies to friends. Lawrence of Arabia wrote back, "Some pot!" (In recounting the incident to friends, Churchill, after the initial laugh, would add, "some boiler," which no doubt was the origin of his "some chicken, some neck" aside to the Canadian Parliament in 1942.) The success of this potboiler stirred up renewed interest about its author. Yet more than being read, Churchill wanted to be listened to.

For that he needed a forum. Since the Liberal party debacle of 1922, Churchill had been without a parliamentary seat and virtually without a party. Although Churchill was still a Liberal in name, the old domestic issues of reform were faded yellowed clippings in a mind now glaringly transfixed by the recurrent headlines of war and peace. Yet even more than the weakening of his ties with the Liberal party was the weakening of the Liberal party itself. Not only had the Labourites replaced the Liberals, but what remained of the dwindling Liberal ranks had bitterly split into Asquith and Lloyd George factions. Churchill was grateful to the feisty Welsh leader who had brought him back to the cabinet after Gallipoli; though a follower of Lloyd George, he was not eager to follow him in his accommodation with the Left. It was one thing to fight the Lords, but it was another to yield to the rising union movement the power the Lords once had. To the Tory Democrat instincts of a Churchill, special privilege for any class, be it by heredity or majority, was wrong. Though he championed equality at the starting gate, he would oppose it at the finish line. Yet that was what the egalitarian tenets of British Socialism seemed to demand. If, in the face of Liberal Party disintegration, the struggle for the future lay between Labour and Conservatism, Churchill had no difficulty in making a choice.

But would the Conservative party take him back? As Churchill himself said, "It is one thing to 'rat' but another to 're-rat.'" After all, the Churchill stock was not exactly bullish. Since his defeat in Dundee in 1922, he had lost again as a Liberal at West Leicester in 1923. Nevertheless, Churchill asked the Conservative party to adopt him as the candidate when a vacancy arose in the historic seat of Westminster. Since the constituency was right in the heart of London, which included Westminster Abbey and the Houses of Parliament, it was rather like asking for the party nomination in that part of the District of Columbia where the Capitol, cabinet departments, and White House lie. Not unexpectedly he was turned down. Undaunted, Churchill created his own one-man party, the Constitutionalist, and ran anyway. Aided by his campaign manager, a young redhead named Brendan Bracken, Churchill took on the political organization of the Conservatives as well as that of the Liberal and Labour parties in what may have been the most colorful campaign in parliamentary history.

In a district that included the toughs of Soho as well as the theater set of the Strand, the poor, as well as the peers, voted. Churchill mobilized for the ten-day campaign the unlikeliest collection of political volunteers a British election had ever seen. Duchesses in diamonds went door to door, show girls stayed up all night after performances stuffing envelopes, jockeys and prize-fighters took to the stump for Churchill, "the man against the machine." Churchill himself, in a posh version of the American sound truck, rode around the district in a four-in-hand carriage with a standing uniformed trumpeter proclaiming his arrival. The American wife of a Conservative MP had hung in townhouse windows posters of Churchill's baby daughter Mary, saying, "Vote for my Daddy."

If Londoners and their press, almost all of which endorsed the Churchill candidacy, warmed to the American-style campaign, Churchill positively glowed. In earlier campaigns he had been inhibited by the strictures of party conformity, but this time he could be completely himself. He had a cause. As a centrist with his own Constitutionalist party, he would show hidebound Tories and complaisant Liberals how to fight socialism.

To his London voters, he proclaimed:

Westminster has it in its power to send to our Dominions beyond the seas, to our friends and allies, an important message. It will be a message that a new current has begun to flow—that party squabbles will not obstruct the reassertion of the national consciousness of Britain and that the British people, to whom the whole world looks for example and guidance, is not going to slide and slither weakly and hopelessly into socialist confusion.

Against the charge that the new Socialist government was seemingly mild, Churchill mockingly derided the appearance of moderation, arguing that it was due only to their lack of a ruling majority in the three-party Parliament:

How well the socialist government is doing. How moderate, how gentle they are. How patriotic Mr. Thomas's speeches. How lofty Mr. MacDonald's views of his functions. How pious is Mr. Henderson. How prudent is Mr. Snowden, how careful of the State. I say there is no correspondence between this glossy surface and the turbulent currents that are flowing beneath. These leaders can never restrain their followers. Do not be deceived. These leaders are only restrained by the fact that there is an adverse parliamentary majority against them.

But Churchill reserved his greatest contempt for the government's recent recognition of the Soviet government in Moscow:

In a few weeks a Bolshevik ambassador will reach these shores and be rapturously welcomed by the socialist minister. He will be applauded by every revolutionary, and will be conducted to the presence of the sovereign. He represents a government which has reduced a mighty and noble nation to a slavery never witnessed since the Middle Ages.

This ambassador will come as the representative of a government which has repudiated its debt and stolen all the property of British people in Russia. The two great neighbouring democracies of the United States and France have both refused to give the sanction of their authority and approbation to the existing Bolshevik regime, and it lies with the present Administration to justify to Parliament the precipitate act of recognition in which it has indulged. That act was not intended to restore trade or to reduce unemployment, but to secure a triumph for the Red Flag. It was a gesture of sympathy and approval, not indeed of the foul and bloody methods of the Bolshevists, but of the aims and principles of the Bolshevists. Friendly and allied nations find it difficult to recognize old John Bull under these repeated changes of government and prime ministers and in his new socialist trappings. Do we find it difficult to recognize ourselves? We have walked humbly in our victory since the war, but let us not lose confidence in ourselves and in our destiny. I know the present is only a passing phase, induced by war exhaustion and largely aggravated by party strife and blunders in which both parties have participated. We are still a great nation. It is not yet too late to stem these subversive and degenerating tides you see working and flowing in every direction. It is because it is not yet too late that I come to you this afternoon.

Never before had Churchill so much enjoyed the rough and tumble of political stump campaigning. For the first time hecklers failed to rattle him as they did in Dundee and Manchester. When a chorus of boos broke into his speech at one point, he shot back, "If those who interrupt me interrupted a meeting addressed by Trotsky they would spend the night in gaol."

In another speech, as Churchill was disclaiming in sepulchral tones, "I say that if another war is fought, civilisation will perish," he singled out a scoffer with his finger and theatrically intoned, "A man laughs. That man dares to laugh. He dares to think the destruction of civilisation a matter of humour!"

It was the irrepressible Churchill having fun in a way the insecure and pretentious never can. When a Conservative politician loyal to the officially endorsed candidate, Captain Nicholson, charged that Churchill was a spoiler and interloper in a district that had been represented by Nicholson's uncle, General Nicholson, since 1907, Churchill countered:

If I thought that the present Conservative candidate really represented the force of character of the constituency I should not have come forward as a candidate. And important public principle is involved. The days of family preserves and pocket boroughs ought not to be revived. It is not right that the Westminster Abbey Division should be passed on from hand to hand as if it were a piece of furniture—handed on from father to son, or from uncle to nephew.

The zest of the candidate spurred on his volunteer army of celebrities and chorus girls. Almost all the press chimed in, calling for the return to the Commons of that "debating force and volcanic energy." Finally, on the eve of the election, the onetime Conservative leader Arthur Balfour broke ranks and gave his support to his onetime tormenter from the back benches. Balfour, now an earl, was a coolly erudite Timon who, though he felt a disdain for the cant and histrionics of electioneering, recognized the uncommon talents of Churchill and indicated "his desire to see you once more in the House of Commons, once more able to use your brilliant gifts in the public discussion."

But it was not to be Westminster itself that would return Churchill to Westminster. Despite all the glamour and glitter of a spectacular campaign, he lost by 43 votes out of the 22,000 cast; but wrapped in the defeat was a victory. Churchill had fought his way back to national recognition and esteem. The Conservative Leader, Stanley Baldwin, constrained to acknowledge the potential of his leadership, assigned him a safe Conservative seat in Epping, which Churchill easily won.

When Conservatives later that year swept into office with a massive victory, Baldwin, as the new prime minister, sent for Churchill to come to 10 Downing Street. "Well, Winston," asked the bluff Yorkshireman between puffs on his pipe, "will you take the chancellorship?" Churchill, although thinking Baldwin meant the ceremonial sinecure of Chancellor of the Duchy of Lancaster, accepted in his eagerness to be welcomed back in Conservative party councils. Not until later did he realize he was being offered the powerful Exchequer. The Chancellor of the Exchequer has the prestige of a U.S. Chief Justice, with the combined power of Treasury Secretary, Budget Director, and Chairman of the Federal Reserve. The prodigal son had been awarded the most coveted seat. Churchill now donned for investiture the same black robes of the chancellorship that Lord Randolph had once worn. His mother had never returned them, but had carefully saved them for her son.

At fifty, Churchill had now reached the pinnacle his father had gained at a younger age some thirty-eight years before. As in Lord Randolph's case, it was not to be a tenure distinguished by success. At end of the ministry, Churchill said, "They said I was the worst Chancellor in history," and then after a pause he added, "You know, they're right." The Exchequer did not suit his talents. As a young man he had described his befuddled approach to the arcana of mathematics: "We were arrived in an 'Alice-in-Wonderland' world, at the portals of which stood 'A Quadratic Equation' followed by the dim chambers inhabited by the Differential Calculus and then a strange corridor of Sines, Cosines, and Tangents in a highly square-rooted condition." For the first time in his ministerial career, Churchill was wholly dependent on his advisers, the career economists of the Exchequer department. Virtually every financial expert, into whose ranks a dubious fiscal heretic named

Keynes was not admitted, recommended that Britain return to the gold standard. The deflationary move was the singular if questionable achievement in Churchill's four-year supervision of a depressed British economy.

If the mood of the British was anything but buoyant, Churchill was at last back in center stage in his most favorite theater, the House of Commons. Perhaps even more than the prime minister, the Chancellor of the Exchequer is the "point man" for the ruling government. He is not only the "abominable no-man" for any legislator's pet plan to raise welfare benefits or save a local industry, but also a one-man Internal Revenue Service who decides upon all taxes and exemptions. As Churchill himself described the onerous task of balancing expenditure and revenue: "In finance everything that is agreeable is unsound, and everything that is sound is disagreeable." As the Chancellor must regularly explain and clarify his budget program, he becomes the number one standing target in the ruling government's front bench. Churchill, peering over his glasses, could see the opposition ranks of Labourites and Liberals. To one he was a reactionary and to the other a turncoat. Even behind him on the back benches he could sense the disgruntled feelings on the part of Conservatives who questioned his claim to the chief ministry. Yet the hostile mood only served to hone his competitive verve. If some Chancellors found their Commons duties an ordeal, to Churchill they were almost sport. It took him back to his Harrovian fencing days when he used to imagine, as he practiced, warding off a horde of villainous assailants. Once, with great relish, Churchill counted up for his Commons opponents the epithets and other pejorative descriptions used of him:

> The word "robbery" or "robbed" was used 67 times; "confiscation," 10; "plunder," 10; "steal," 3—and once more by the right honourable gentleman the Member for Derby in his last remarks, but that arrived after the list was closed; "raid," 11; "theft," 2; "filch," 1; "grab," 1; and there was one "cheat." The right honourable Gentleman the Member for Spen Valley [Sir J. Simon] is entitled to the credit of that. "Breach of faith," 19; "betrayal," 5; "outrage," 1, "infamy,"

1; "rascality," 1; "perfidy," 1; "mean," 15; "paltry," 1; "despicable," 1; "shabby," 1; and "dastardly," 3. I received the following compliments; "the villain of the piece," "robber," "marauder," "cat-burglar," and "artful dodger." I think that is rather complimentary, having regard to the quarter from which it emanated. The more exuberant members of the party opposite have for some years, at elections at any rate, been accustomed to salute me by the expression "murderer," and from that point of view "robber" is a sort of promotion. It shows that I am making some headway in their esteem. Words which are on proper occasions the most powerful engines lose their weight and power and value when they are not backed by fact or winged by truth.

The fact is that for the first time in his career he had begun to enjoy the exchange of verbal thrusts in debate. Although his parliamentary repartee never reached the level of his conversational wit, the advantage of his years and experience began to manifest itself.

When the former Labourite Chancellor Philip Snowden accused his successor of switching his position, Churchill replied, "There is nothing wrong with change—if it is in the right direction."

Snowden countered, "You are an authority on that." Churchill rejoined with impish glee: "To improve is to change; to be perfect is to change often."

In his back-bencher days Churchill would come to Parliament with a carefully concocted *bon mot* and then wait sometimes for weeks for the right moment to insert it into debate or reply to a question. Now he no longer had to resort to such stratagems. Still, at times, his impish prankishness asserted itself. On the occasion of his first budget as Chancellor, he paused and filled a glass beside the dispatch box next to him, not with water, but with whiskey, saying, "It is imperative that I should first fortify the revenue, and this I shall now, with the permission of the Commons, proceed to do."

Considering the times in which he presided, Chancellor Churchill might be forgiven for resorting to spirits. The country was in depression, or as he called it, "an economic blizzard," and in

1926 a general strike paralyzed the nation. Churchill's hard line against the massive labor walkout was characterized by his statement, "I declare utterly to be impartial as between the Fire Brigade and the fire." When newspaper presses shut down, Churchill even put out a government organ. The paper, entitled *British Gazette,* gained a huge circulation, even though some felt it was a demeaning of Churchill's literary reputation. After the strike was settled, when tempers were still in a savage mood, Churchill was greeted in the House of Commons by boos from the Labour ranks. Pointing his finger at them, Churchill said, "I warn you, I warn you—if there is another General Strike"—with that the chorus of catcalls grew—"we will let loose on you"—and then he paused— "another *British Gazette.*" The peals of laughter that broke up the House revealed that the Churchill humor touched even the most trying situations.

Generally, though, the stint at the Exchequer was not a happy one for Churchill. The cause of financial orthodoxy did not invite the flair of his genius. The everyday burden of mastering budgetary details began to weary him, and he was almost relieved when the Conservative government was swept out of office in 1929. The mood of the twenties, spent by the sacrifice of war, craved mediocrity as a sign of stability. In such "normalcy" Churchill was out of joint with the times. To friends he said, "I'd quit politics altogether if it weren't for the chance that someday I might be prime minister."

11

PROPHET
IN EXILE

The voice of one that crieth
in the wilderness.
                —*Prophet Isaiah*

If the thirties were for Churchill a period of exile, it was not one regretfully entered. Churchill, in packing away the robes of Chancellor, could now again don the painter's smock and bricklayer's apron at Chartwell. Country squire was a role he had been sweetly anticipating in the last dreary days of 11 Downing Street. His relations with the stolid occupant next door, Prime Minister Stanley Baldwin, though superficially correct, were strained in a clash of temperaments. Though the chancellor is usually regarded as the heir apparent to the premier, Churchill knew his unpopularity with the Conservative party's rank and file rendered that prospect remote in the event of the party's return to power. For one thing, the canny Baldwin, whom no one ever accused of not having his ears close to the ground, considered Churchill a liability, so Churchill, seeing the pendant sword, resigned from the party's councils of leadership before it could fall on him.

The issue was India policy. Churchill, whose view of the subcontinent was more an image of Gunga Din than of Gandhi, opposed the grant of self-government. Not with his support would Britain yield the brightest jewel of its imperial crown. For the former Colonial Secretary, who had urged similar autonomous treaties with both South Africa and Ireland, it was not the most enlightened moment of a long career.

It was not contemporary affairs, however, that were engaging Churchill's attention at the beginning of the century's third decade. At long last, he could now undertake the project that had fascinated him since youth, the biography of his ancestor John Churchill, first Duke of Marlborough. This idol of Churchill's

163

boyhood had been tarnished by his readings of Macaulay while stationed in India. The glib Macaulay had written of the seventeenth-century soldier-statesman: "At twenty he made money of his beauty and his vigor; at sixty, he made money of his genius and glory." But what troubled Winston more than the historian's charge of materialism was his accusation of an opportunism by Marlborough that bordered on treason. A lead to the defense of his ancestor's conduct came from the hands of his father's friend Lord Rosebery. While Chancellor, Churchill had visited the dying Liberal statesman, who had been prime minister before the turn of the century. Rosebery, in his wheelchair, had summoned his butler and told him to fetch a particular book from his compendious library. The out-of-print manuscript went a long way in refuting the belief that John Churchill had sent intelligence to the French king of a pending British invasion. From that day, Churchill burned with the desire to write the authoritative Marlborough biography that would forever efface the blot on the family honor.

Like a general organizing his staff and coordinating his logistics for a massive military operation, Churchill assembled his researchers, including the young historian with an Oxford first, Maurice Ashley. Then, with his friend Professor Frederick Lindemann (later Lord Cherwell), he began to map a schedule of explorations of the continental terrain where the hero of Blenheim had sown his reputation.

Yet, to pursue the commander analogy, Churchill first had to secure his home base. As Chancellor of the Exchequer, he had seen the savings in the family exchequer dwindle. Politics was his occupation, but writing was his livelihood. The responsibilities of family, not to mention the maintenance of Chartwell, necessitated income.

In 1930, he wrote more than 40 articles for newspapers and magazines, nearly half of them for *The Daily Telegraph*. Besides delivering the later-published Romaines Lecture at Oxford on Parliamentary Government and the Economic Problem, he wrote the wide-selling *My Early Life,* which in America was called *A Roving Commission.* The next year he actually increased his output. An abridged version of *World Crisis* went on the stands, and then an additional volume of the World War I series entitled *The Eastern Front* (in America, *The Unknown War*). Unsurprisingly, his attendance in the House of Commons as a member from Epping was kept to the obligatory minimum. Although he made some speaking tours in America—where, in 1931, he was run over and nearly killed by a car while visiting Bernard Baruch in New York—he begrudged the trips to London away from his beloved Chartwell, where he could write and paint in the company of Clementine and his children. The older ones now, like Randolph, were already adults.

The only interruption of his journalistic labors came in 1932, when Churchill was stricken by a paratyphoid illness picked up from drinking contaminated water at the site of the Marlborough battlefield in Bavaria. Then, for the only time in his life, Churchill had to resort to the services of a ghost. His longtime administrative secretary Eddie Marsh, himself a litterateur, penned under Churchill's name "Great Stories of the World Retold" for the London tabloid weekly *News of the World*. The potboiling series, beginning with *Uncle Tom's Cabin* and ending with *Don Quixote,* was at times a pulp-magazine caricature of the Churchill style. The thirties were the heyday of magazine writing, and Churchill, according to one account, was averaging about $100,000 a year, of which most came in the form of advances from newspaper and magazine editors. The rest of his income was from the semiannual royalty checks from his book publishers and the fees from his lectures, particularly those in America.

Churchill needed every penny of those checks to support his opulent tastes. As he himself wrote, "I am easily satisfied with the best." He had by habit and desire acquired the appetites of a duke—the best horses for his stable, the finest wine for his cellar, and the richest food for his table. Even when he went on a painting jaunt, he would take along for his picnic spread wicker hampers laden with cold grouse or venison, imported fruits, cheese, caviar, and a magnum of champagne.

At home at Chartwell, his regimen in those years out of ministerial office began with reading the morning newspaper and mail in bed while consuming a breakfast considered generous by English standards. For his pressing parliamentary and commercial correspondence, he would dictate quick replies and memoranda, trying to finish the business end of his work during his morning bath. There, twirling his toes in the toasty-hot water, he would begin his literary dictation. Outside the open bathroom door the secretary would jot down his bursts of declamation. Sentences continued their staccato roll, uninterrupted by lathering, toweling, and whatever other morning ablutions were required. First he would mutter and growl snatches of phrases to himself until he had assembled the makings of a paragraph. Then he would bawl out the whole chunk, grunting his satisfaction at the end.

The costume for this singular exercise proceeded from loose-wrapped turkish towel to pink silk shorts with red cummerbund and then, anticlimactically, a white undershirt. Only occasionally was a robe put on to satisfy the delicate niceties of guests. Back in bed, Churchill, no doubt stimulated by the hot bath and strongly scented soap, continued his roar of dictation until the midmorning break of "elevenses." While the exhausted secretary braced herself with coffee, Churchill sipped a Scotch and soda. Thus fortified, he would fill up more of the secretary's shorthand tablets for transcribing until well past noon.

At lunchtime he would slip into a robe and appear in the dining room, if visitors were expected at Chartwell. But even if he stayed in his bedroom to eat from a tray the menu was uncompromisingly grand—soup, fowl or beef, washed down by a bottle of claret, to be succeeded by a glass of cognac and postprandial cigar. Then, after a stroll through his grounds, perhaps to feed the goldfish and greet the swans, he would return to his study to find a tense stenographer poised with pencil for the afternoon session.

With only a tea break at four, which for him meant brandy or a whiskey and soda, Churchill, cigar in hand, would, by puffing and pacing, turn thoughts to words. Only occasionally would he stop to check the Oxford dictionary or look at a source book propped up on a desk opposite his writing table. The rest of the time he was, to his secretary, a walking volcano whose spasmodic eruptions had to be hastily scribbled down before the torrent of phrases flooded the limits of her memory.

An hour and a half nap at five was no doubt as welcome to the stenographer as the writer. Another spicy hot tub and Churchill would be ready for dinner, the only meal he regularly dressed for. He would meet dinner guests with velvet-trimmed smoking jacket, but alone his raiment might be battle fatigues, a tunic, lounge coat, or an occasional suit.

Then, after a repast even more Lucullan than lunch, he would light up a Havana cigar for the nightly backgammon or bezique match with Clementine. When she retired at eleven, Churchill would begin his next dictation shift with a new secretary. Not until two or three in the morning, when the relief secretary was pushed to the limits of exhaustion, would Churchill himself turn in for his six or so hours' sleep.

During these Chartwell years rumors in London political circles abounded that an over-the-hill Churchill was sliding into habitual drunkenness. Churchill did nothing to scotch these stories. Unlike the alcoholic who carefully conceals his number of drinks, Churchill broadcast them, constantly pressing his guests for another round. With furtive glee, he, who never drank cocktails or mixed drinks, would hand out stiff concoctions to visitors while refreshing his own brandy or whiskey from the seltzer siphon. Yet despite the weak whiskeys, Churchill's rambling discourses seemed to reinforce the bibulous impression. Away from the public forum, his rhetorical guard was let down in conversation. His monologues on history or political issues became slathered with lisps and often shaken by a vehement stammer.

But the best refutation of those tales of gargantuan drinking bouts at Chartwell is the prodigious writing output of Churchill at that time. The principal part of that production was Churchill's massive six-volume biography of Marlborough. Though research assistants presented memoranda and collated source books, marking relevant passages for examination, it was Churchill himself who dictated the first and succeeding drafts and then revised the publisher's galleys. Unlike professional historians, who interminably delay writing in their search for new leads of documentary evidence, Churchill liked to get something down on paper early, knowing he could revise factual accuracy in later drafts. That is not to suggest that Churchill was slipshod with facts, for he was a stickler on verification and reverification of the final copy; but it does account for a productivity that far outstrips that of academic scholars.

Scholars complain, not of his facts, but of his rhetorical flourish. For in *Marlborough* Churchill the writer never frees himself from Churchill the orator. The rhythm is almost remorseless and sentences spring to attention like soldiers on parade. As if in a battle, Churchill was marshaling his adjuctival artillery for a purpose: to reclaim the lost ground in his ancestor's reputation. It was a labor of love and family piety. Of Marlborough, he writes at the beginning of the book:

> It is my hope to recall the great shade from the past, and not only to invest him with his panoply, but make him living and intimate to modern eyes. I hope to show that he was not only the foremost of English soldiers, but in the first rank among the statesmen of our history; not only that he was a Titan, for that is not disputed, but that he was a virtuous and benevolent being, eminently serviceable to his age and country, capable of drawing harmony and design from heroes, and one who only needed an earlier and still wider authority to have made a more ordered and more tolerant civilisation for his own time and to help the future.

Armed with all the private papers of his cousin at Blenheim Palace, Churchill managed to breathe life into a remote figure who hitherto had had all the one-dimensional formality of a George Washington without the American's redeeming character. If the hero of the work was the resourceful captain-general who rescued the small states of Europe from the appetites of French greed and territorial ambition, the villain was the swaggering Louis XIV.

> We have no patience with the lackey pens which have sought to invest this long, hateful process with the appearances of dignity and honour. During the whole of his life Louis XIV was the curse and pest of Europe. No worse enemy of human freedom has ever appeared in the trappings of polite civilisation. Insatiable appetite,

cold, calculating ruthlessness, monumental conceit, presented
themselves armed with fire and sword. The veneer of culture
and good manners, of brilliant ceremonies and elaborate etiquette, only adds a heightening effect to the villainy of his life's
story. Better the barbarian conquerors of antiquity, primordial
figures of the abyss, than this high-heeled, beperiwigged dandy,
strutting amid the bows and scrapes of mistresses and confessors
to the torment of his age. Petty and mediocre in all except his
lusts and power, the Sun King disturbed and harried mankind
during more than fifty years of arrogant pomp.

Possibly Churchill's description of the pompous strutting of the
seventeeth-century French autocrat was occasioned by a squalid
twentieth-century perversion now on the political horizon—the
German Fuehrer. A frustrated artist, Hitler had given up house
painting more than a decade before Churchill was learning to paint
in the south of France. Churchill's defeat in 1922 had happened a
year before the Munich putsch had landed Hitler in prison. While
Churchill was writing *World Crisis,* Hitler was putting together
Mein Kampf. At the time Churchill was reentering public life in
1924, Hitler was leaving jail to resume his political activity. Before
Hitler ever actually assumed power, Churchill was warning Britain
of German resurgence in a 1932 speech which most all of his House
of Commons audience found too pessimist or alarmist:

Now the demand is that Germany should be allowed to rearm.
Do not delude yourselves. Do not let His Majesty's Government
believe, I am sure they do not believe, that all that Germany is
asking for is equal status. . . . That is not what Germany is
seeking. All these bands of sturdy Teutonic youths, marching
through the streets and roads of Germany, with the light of
desire in their eyes to suffer for their Fatherland, are not looking
for status. They are looking for weapons, and, when they have
the weapons, believe me they will then ask for the return of lost
territories and lost colonies.

Then, a month after Hitler became Chancellor in January 1933,
Churchill began to denounce the evil character of his regime.

We watch with surprise and distress the tumultuous insurgence of ferocity and war spirit, the pitiless ill-treatment of minorities, the denial of the normal protection of civilised society to large numbers of individuals solely on the grounds of race.

Churchill's only chance of ever meeting *der Fuehrer* came in 1932 while retracing Marlborough's maneuvers on a battlefield near Munich. In the course of his stay he met Ernst Hanfstaengl, an art publisher and close friend of Hitler; but when Churchill closely questioned Hanfstaengl on Hitler's attitudes toward Jews, the proposed encounter was canceled.

Perhaps Churchill's detachment from politics and absorption with history made him, in a strong way, acutely aware of the Hitler menace. In his writing about Marlborough, contemporary parallels constantly presented themselves. Just as he himself in World War I lacked commensurate military authority, he saw the captain-general's problem as need of political support. What fascinated Churchill about his ancestor, though, was his role as Europe's first leader of a grand alliance assembling the smaller European states and principalities, together with Britain, against a common aggressor who threatened their stability. Seeing through Marlborough's eyes the military and political problems involved in maintaining a coordinated strategy gave a providential training for the comparable destiny awaiting Marlborough's descendant. Indeed, Churchill's titles for the *Marlborough* volumes in the 1930s presaged the events in the next decade: *Grand Alliance, Grand Design,* and *Lost Peace.*

Churchill has often been compared to the hedgehog of animal fable whose single-minded vision could only concentrate on the massive danger at hand, unlike that of the cunning fox who could envision a range of graduating threats. In various stages of his career one problem or issue dominated his attention: military entrenchment as a young back-bencher, naval preparedness as First Lord, the Bolshevik threat right after the war, the India question at the opening of the thirties, and now German rearmament in the middle of the decade.

In a sense it was Churchill the rhetorician shaping Churchill the orator. Just as in advocacy, he would select the single strongest argument and muster his facts in its arrayed support, so, at any given period in his life, he would focus his energies and expression on what he considered the paramount problem facing the British body politic. In the 1930s his audiences, whether in the House of Commons or in a constituency meeting, knew before he even arose to speak that Churchill would be expounding on some variation of the British preparedness theme: the resurgence of German militarism, the ineffectuality of the League of Nations to contain it, the inadequacy of the Royal Air Force, the need for Anglo-French cooperation, or the dangers of British pacifism.

There was nothing cursory or casual about these Churchill speeches. All the available statistics on comparative defenses and historic parallels with the past were brought to bear on one overriding conclusion. In this strenuous process of putting his impressions on paper for a speech, speculation became certainty and inferences turned to facts. Like a scholar who labors with his doctoral thesis or a mother with the birth of a child, Churchill had the unshakable faith in the finished product of his work that only such mental and emotional investment can bring.

To his listeners, Churchill's excess of energy seemed more like an obsession. Rearmament and the threat of another world conflict was a message a war-spent and economically depressed nation did not want to accept, particularly from one whose judgment was already suspect. Their confidence in the minister who had orchestrated the Antwerp Circus and planned the Dardanelles disaster was not unbounded. Better to trust the words of Stanley Baldwin, Ramsay MacDonald, or later Neville Chamberlain, whose dependability was never tainted by imagination and whose respectability was never sullied by genius.

But the blame rested not solely with the audience. The fervid imagination of a Churchill had its fallible side. The fulminations against Gandhi and Indian self-rule were too strident, and his misplaced loyalty to Edward VIII during the nine-day abdication crisis of 1936 was impulsively romantic. Churchill, faithful to his longtime friend the Prince of Wales, had urged him to play for time and build popular support against a prime minister who insisted that marriage with the divorced American, Mrs. Wallis Simpson, meant no monarchy. Fortunately for the nation, Edward chose to give up the throne. Churchill went to Edward's retreat at Fort Belvedere and helped him compose the abdication speech. Among the phrases he contributed were "bred in the constitutional tradition by my father" and "one matchless blessing, enjoyed by so many of you and not bestowed on me—a happy home with wife and children." As Churchill bade him farewell, the king noticed there were tears in his eyes. "I can still see him," wrote Edward later," standing at the door hat in one hand, stick in the other." Tapping out the solemn measure with his walking stick, Churchill recited (the verse is from Andrew Marvell at the time of King Charles I's execution):

> He nothing common did or mean
> Upon that memorable scene.

What was left of the Churchill prestige dwindled in the aftermath of the abdication. Churchill's loyalty, however, was not unreciprocated. Even in the exile years, he had his circle of friends and followers who made their trek to Chartwell. To them Churchill was not just a sexagenarian politician past his prime, who, like Lloyd George, was a topic of interest only as a colorful link to a bygone age. Foremost of Churchill's friends were the three B's,* Baruch, Beaverbrook, and Bracken.

Bernard Baruch was the American Jewish financier whom Churchill had met during the First World War when he was munitions minister and in the process of coordinating the war effort with the Americans. Baruch was helpful to Churchill in financial investments. Lord Beaverbrook had been born Max Aitken. A Canadian entrepreneur who suffered from asthma as well as a stutter, he had built the Tory *Daily Express* to number one in British circulation.

---

*A fourth B was Lord Birkenhead, who died in 1930. Birkenhead, an urbane barrister, very much resembled Lord Randolph in his foppish attire and acid wit. Like Randolph he died before his full promise was fulfilled.

Although the opinionated Beaverbrook often clashed with the equally resolute Churchill, the Scotch-Canadian was called by Winston his "foul-weather friend" for his steadfast loyalty in time of crisis or despair.

Brendan Bracken, the youngest of the group, came out of nowhere to help Churchill in his election campaigns in the early 1920s. In the next decade he became Churchill's eyes and ears for political intelligence as well as a one-man fan club, promoting the virtue of his leader to anyone who would listen. The fanatic loyalty of the carrot-topped, big-spectacled Bracken gave rise to the ridiculous rumor that he was Churchill's bastard son. Bracken, though, was not unhappy with the tale.

Whether it was the financial acumen of a Baruch, the newspaper mind of a Beaverbrook, or the political savvy of a Bracken, Churchill sought as his friends those who had more to contribute than just congenial amenities and social breeding. He had no time for the effete of his own background who had not proved their worth or ability.

A frequent visitor to Chartwell described the nature of the guest list there. "The full truth is, I believe, that Winston's "friends" must be persons who were of use to him. The idea of having a friend who was of no practical use to him but being a friend because he liked him had no place. . . ." The speaker was Sir Desmond Morton, who, along with Professor Lindemann, headed a second tier of advisory friends from whom Winston absorbed scientific and military data. Morton, a nearby neighbor at Chartwell, was a former aide to Field Marshall Haig in the first war. An intelligence expert, he began collecting for Churchill estimates on German industry and defense.

Lindemann, a brilliant Oxford physicist, was Churchill's interpreter of nuclear mysteries and emerging technical developments. Once a visitor bet Lindemann that he could not explain the quantum theory in five minutes. The Churchill children timed the professor with a stopwatch and applauded vociferously when he succeeded. Like the Churchill cigar, the slide rule was an appendant prop of the "Prof." At Churchill's urging the teetotaling Lindemann once calculated how many pints of champagne, in cubic feet, Churchill had consumed in a lifetime. The answer, given, while traveling on a train, was the measurement of one-half of the car, to which Churchill wistfully replied, "How much left to do and how little time to do it."

Experts like Lindemann and Morton were, in a way, human fodder for Churchill's speeches. He relied on them not only for their input of technical assessment of facts and trends, but as an audience to play back his conversational monologues, which were often rehearsals of later speeches. What Churchill was doing in these years out of ministry was organizing his own staff operation. One frequent visitor to Chartwell in the thirties was young Conservative Member Harold Macmillan. To him Chartwell seemed like a government in exile. Everywhere there were maps, charts, and graphs denoting productions of German munitions. Temporary filing cabinets bulged with folders on various aircraft and memoranda on selected members of the German high command. A European politician would arrive for an appointment and meet a scientist or military adviser on his way out. Behind every Churchill philippic on Hitler and the German threat was a juggled schedule of appointments and an assortment of white papers on German military mechanization.

Many of Churchill's warnings at the time began to focus on growing Germany's superiority in the air. As early as 1935 he told the Commons: "Germany has the power at any time henceforward to send a fleet of airplanes capable of discharging in a single voyage at least 500 tons of bombs upon London."

But the government, dismissing the threats, delayed reequipping and reinforcing a depleted RAF. Churchill, in 1937, excoriated Prime Minister Baldwin for his timid vacillation:

The government cannot make up their minds, or they cannot get the Prime Minister to make up his mind. So they go in strange paradox, decided only to be undecided, resolved to be irresolute, adamant for drift, solid for fluidity, all-powerful to be impotent. So we go on preparing more months and years—precious, perhaps vital, to the greatness of Britain—for the locusts to eat.

The British political reaction to Churchill's call ranged from skittish to spineless. The Leader of the Labourites said that Britain should disarm as an example to Hitler; and the Leader of the Liberals termed the Churchill proposal to double the RAF "the language of Malay [tribesmen] running amok." These were, in Churchill's biblical phrase, "the locust years," when the British ate up years of possible war preparation.

In 1938, after the fall of Austria, Churchill rose from his habitual front corner seat in the House and, head thrust forward, thumbs in his vest pocket, scoldingly lectured the House Conservative Government on the five years they had wasted failing to rearm:

> For five years I have talked to this House on these matters — not with very great success. I have watched this famous island descending incontinently, fecklessly, the stairway which leads to a dark gulf. It is a fine broad stairway at the beginning, but after a bit the carpet wears. A little farther on there are only flagstones, and a little further on still, these break beneath your feet. . . .
>
> . . . now is the time at last to rouse the nation. Perhaps it is the last time it can be roused with a chance of preventing war, or with a chance of coming through to victory should our efforts to prevent war fail. We should lay aside every hindrance and endeavor by uniting the whole force and spirit of our people to raise again a great British nation standing up before all the world; for such a nation, rising in its ancient vigour, can even at this hour save civilisation.

An embarrassed silence greeted Churchill as he ended. Then members anxious to turn to more pleasant thoughts rattled their papers, stood, and shuffled out to the lobby, many heading for tea. One member told his Visitor's Gallery guest, Virginia Cowles, "It was the usual Churchill filibuster — he likes to rattle the saber and he does it jolly well but you have to take it with a grain of salt."

After Austria, the next country to feel the boot of Hitler tyranny was Czechoslovakia. To avert war, Prime Minister Chamberlain traveled to see Hitler at Munich and returned to welcoming crowds proclaiming he had achieved "peace with honor." It was a settlement that dismembered Czechoslovakia.

Churchill again rose to denounce this sellout to Hitler.

All is over. Silent, mournful, abandoned, broken, Czechoslovakia recedes into darkness. I think you will find that in a period of time which may be measured by years, but may be measured only by months, Czechoslovakia will be engulfed in the Nazi regime.

. . . I do not grudge our loyal, brave people, who were ready to do their duty no matter what the cost, who never flinched under the strain of last week—I do not grudge them the natural, spontaneous outburst of joy and relief when they learned that the hard ordeal would no longer be required of them at the moment; but they should know the truth. They should know that there has been gross neglect and deficiency in our defences; they should know that we have sustained a defeat without a war, the consequences of which will travel far with us along our road; they should know that we have passed an awful milestone in our history, when the whole equilibrium of Europe has been deranged, and that the terrible words have for the time being pronounced against the Western democracies; "Thou art weighed in the balanced and found wanting." And do not suppose this is the end.

This is only the beginning of the reckoning. This is only the first sip, the first foretaste of the bitter cup which will be proffered to us year by year, unless, by a supreme recovery of moral health and martial vigour, we rise again and take our stand for freedom as in the olden time.

Churchill's was a lone voice amid the rejoicing for peace. The cheers for Chamberlain the peacemaker, however, stilled to a deadly silence when Nazi troops marched into Prague the next spring. It had not been peace but appeasement. The prediction of

Churchill at the time of Munich looked ominously right: "You were given the choice between war and dishonour. You chose dishonour, and you will have war."

The British were learning, to their consternation, that the desire for peace does not insure peace. After the laissez-faire of Baldwin, the pacifism of MacDonald, and the appeasement of Chamberlain, a day of reckoning came. A price would have to be paid for those somnolent years and squandered opportunities. The price would be war.

War came on September 1, 1939, when German panzer divisions rambled past the Polish frontier in the very early hours of that Sunday morning. A shaken Chamberlain government, desperate for unity, at least in its own ranks, asked its principal assailer to join the cabinet as First Lord of the Admiralty. To the ships at sea the wire was sent out: "Winston is back."

For Churchill the years in the wilderness had been oddly luxuriant and fruitful. Far from the corridors of power that had darkened with dishonor, he had at last ripened with wisdom and respect. His provident detachment from ministries whose mediocrity would only have encumbered him had allowed the writer to become a historian, the orator a statesman, the critic a prophet. He had chosen to await Fate, and it now was awarding him his hour.

12

PRIME MINISTER

His eloquence was worth
a thousand regiments.
— *Will Durant*

As Winston Churchill assumed his old desk in the Admiralty in September 1939, it was a case of history repeating itself not so much with a vengeance as with a pardon. For here was Churchill, once more sitting in the same chair from which he had been so ignominiously dismissed after Gallipoli in 1915. Behind him was even the same map of the North Sea on which he had then plotted the deployments of the German fleet in World War I.

In the fall of 1939, the situation hardly qualified as a full-scale war. It was, as Churchill called it, "The Trance" or the "Twilight War." On land behind the Maginot Line, French troops remained poised as if in a catatonic standstill, while in the almost perpetual dusk of the Northern and Baltic Seas the ships of Churchill's fleet passed as silent convoy through the U-boat infested waters.

As in World War I, the restlessness of the First Lord impelled him to contemplate an action whose outcome was a severe naval disaster. Churchill foresaw Germany's increasing dependence on steel supplies shipped from neutral Sweden. Thus, in a move to block the trade, he argued in 1940 for a landing at Narvik, a major Norwegian port. The operation, while damaging German shipping through British mines and submarines, failed to halt the Nazi invasion of Norway and Denmark. A quickly assembled British expeditionary force was flung ashore on the Norwegian coast. It was again a case of too little too late. Without air cover, the English troops fighting under insupportable hardships could not win and withdrew in defeat.

The political reaction bore a familiar ring. Yet, ironically, this time the dissatisfaction, triggered by what some called "the second

181

Gallipoli," brought about the dismissal of the prime minister and not the First Lord of the Admiralty. There was an odd justice to the rewriting of the Dardanelles disaster at Narvik in May 1940. If Churchill was unfairly pilloried from the cabinet in 1916, he virtually escaped the wrath of Parliament and the press in 1940. The reason had to do with the growing public perception of Chamberlain and Churchill in the spring of 1940.

With the Nazi invasion of Scandinavia, the "phony" war had ended. Now the April 4 remark of Chamberlain that "Hitler had missed the bus" had soured. The bus had trampled down England's Danish and Norwegian allies. Was Chamberlain the man to turn the tide of British defeat and rouse a united nation behind him? By his words as well as his actions Chamberlain failed to personify the resolution so desperately yearned for.

When Britain declared war after the German invasion of Poland in September 1939, Chamberlain's words were an explanation of his actions before the bar of world opinion:

> You can imagine what a bitter blow it was to me that all my long struggle to win peace had failed. Yet I cannot believe that there is anything different I could have done. . . . We have a clear conscience.

Compare the defensiveness of a Chamberlain to the defiance of a Churchill on the same day:

> The Prime Minister said it was a sad day and that indeed is true. But it seems to me there is another note which may be present at this moment. There is a feeling of thankfulness that if these trials were to come upon our island, there is a generation of Britons here now ready to prove that it is not unworthy of those great men, the fathers of our land. Here is no question of fighting for Danzig or fighting for Poland. We are fighting to save the world from a pestilence of Nazi tyranny and in defence of all that is most sacred to man. This is no war for imperial aggrandizemen' or material gain. It is a war pure in its inherent quality, a war †

establish on impregnable rocks the right of the individual. It is a war to establish and revive the stature of man.

While Chamberlain was wringing his hands, Churchill was shaking his fists. Chamberlain viewed the war as a depressing duty, but Churchill saw it as the ultimate challenge, fierce, exacting, magnificent.

In his speech to the Free Trade Hall at the beginning of 1940, the First Lord closed his speech on the naval war with a sinewy peroration of short verbal phrases sublime in their simplicity.

Come then: let us to the task, to the battle, to the toil—each to our part, each to our station. Fill the armies, rule the air, pour out the munitions, strangle the U-boats, sweep the mines, plough the land, build the ships, guard the streets, succour the wounded, uplift the downcast, and honour the brave. Let us go forward together in all parts of the Empire, in all parts of the Island. There is not a week, nor a day, nor an hour to lose.

That was a leader's tone, and all that England had begun to ask in 1940 was to be led. The defeat in Norway triggered a debate on Chamberlain's suitability as prime minister. On May 7, the veteran Conservative back-bencher Lew Amery hurled at the Chamberlain ministry the scornful words of Oliver Cromwell to the Long Parliament: "You have sat too long here for any good you have been doing. Depart, I say, and let us have done with you. In the name of God, go!"

When Chamberlain's pitiable response was that his friends should not desert him, the aging Lloyd George the next day replied, in his last great oration:

I say solemnly that the Prime Minister should give an example of sacrifice because I tell him that there is nothing which would contribute more to victory in this war than that he should sacrifice the seals of office.

On May 10, while the Hitler panzer divisions rolled his wide swath of destruction into Holland and Belgium, Chamberlain called his Foreign Secretary Lord Halifax and Churchill to discuss the prime ministership. Chamberlain preferred Halifax, even though Churchill had loyally defended the prime minister in the debate of the last two days; but Attlee, speaking for the Labour party, would not consent to a premiership from the House of Lords. So it was Churchill that King George VI called to Buckingham Palace to form a coalition government.

If the leading members of his own Conservative party were not enthusiastic about Churchill, his countrymen were. They might have shared some of the doubts that many career ministers and officials of 10 Downing Street and the Foreign Office privately expressed about his administrative ability and political judgment, but they sensed in his words the will to fight. What a now-aroused nation heard in the speeches of Churchill was the voice of England. When Churchill rose to address the Commons, the usual whispering and shuffling of papers ceased. This age-old building that had heard the voices of Cromwell, Pitt, Disraeli, and Lloyd George now readied to hear Churchill.

Never had a prime minister assumed office in such a grave hour. The blitzkrieg was sweeping like a tornado across Europe. Each hourly newscast of the BBC reported the latest tidings of disaster from Holland, Belgium, and now France. Churchill's "Inaugural" to the House of Commons was brief but brilliant in its electric effect upon the nation. "I have nothing to offer but blood, toil, tears, and sweat." These words of sacrifice he had, no doubt, adapted from his World War I work *The Unknown War,* written a decade earlier ("Their tears, their sweat, their blood, bedewed the endless plain.") This, in turn, might have been inspired by Garibaldi's speech to Italian patriots calling for "hunger, thirst, forced marches, battle and death."

Then, in perhaps unconscious emulation of the French Clemenceau, the war leader with whom he most identified ("Before Paris I wage war. In Paris I wage war. Behind Paris I wage war."), Churchill closed:

You ask, What is our policy? I will say: "It is to wage war, by sea, land, and air, with all our might and with all the strength that God can give to us; to wage war against a monstrous tyranny, never surprised in the dark, lamentable catalogue of human crime. That is our policy." You ask, What is our aim? I can answer in one word: Victory—victory at all costs, victory in spite of all terror, victory however long and hard the road may be; for without victory there is no survival.

The pent-up frustration of hundreds of days of impotence and indecision broke. Grown men wept´ not with despair but relief. They took his promises of blood, sweat, and tears as if they were grants of nobility.

If words of hope were what he had to offer, he gave them in the richest measure of English expression heard in centuries. Churchill, however, never dismissed oratory as mere words. "Of all the talents bestowed upon men, none is so precious as the gift of oratory," he had written at age twenty. "He who enjoys it wields a power more durable than that of a great King." To Churchill words were weapons, and speeches deeds. If the military arsenals of Britain were bare, the armory of its language and literature was laden with treasure.

On May 19, as French forces were reeling from the German breakthrough of their defenses at Sedan, Churchill, in his first radio address as prime minister, found reinforcement in the heroism of the biblical Maccabees.

Today is Trinity Sunday. Centuries ago words were written to be a call and a spur to the faithful servants of Truth and Justice: "Arm yourselves, and be ye men of valour, and be in readiness for the conflict; for it is better for us to perish in battle than to look upon the outrage of our nation and our altar. As the Will of God is in Heaven, even so let it be."

Then he called on the peoples of Nazi-occupied Europe to rally to the allied cause.

Behind the Armies and Fleets of Britain and France gather a group of shattered States and bludgeoned races—the Czechs,

the Poles, the Norwegians, the Danes, the Dutch, the Belgians—
on all of whom the long night of barbarism will descend unbroken even by a star of hope unless we conquer, as conquer we
must, as conquer we shall.

Churchill knew his words might spell the difference between
defeat and resistance. Any hesitation or faltering might have
meant collapse. Except for the Channel, Britain was defeated and
all Europe lay at Hitler's feet. On June 2, most of the British
troops were trapped on the beach at Dunkirk. The English people,
their will no longer unfocused, their courage tapped, responded. A
tide of English vessels and smaller craft moved across the Channel
toward French beaches and British troops. Dories, dinghies, skiffs
swelled the ranks of the 860-boat flotilla in its rescue operation.
Churchill labored that Sunday evening in the book-lined Cabinet
Room at 10 Downing Street.

On Tuesday he had to give his report on Dunkirk to the House
of Commons. At the far side of the room Mary Shearborn, his
secretary, waited at her typewriter.

Reflectively, Churchill opened:

We must be very careful not to assign to this deliverance the
attributes of a victory. . . .

Then, pacing from the fireplace at the one end to the draped
windows overlooking a garden at the other, Churchill dictated,
first muttering under his breath snatches of words to himself, then
in a burst of declamation bellowing out the complete sentence in
its full majestic panoply.

Sometimes, when the echoed resonance of the dictated passage
jarred the Churchill ear, he grumbled "Gimme," ratcheting the
paper from the typewriter to scan the offending line.

By midnight the Churchill growl had faded to a croak.

We shall not flag or fail. We shall go on to the end. . . . Even
though large tracts of Europe and many old and famous States
have fallen or may fall into the grip of the Gestapo and all the

odious apparatus of Nazi rule, we shall fight with growing confidence and strength in the air, we shall defend our island whatever the cost may be. . . .

He seemed, in the later words of his secretary, utterly spent by the effort, his head bowed and face too tired to restrain the tears that flowed at the thought of his stricken England. Then, with tremors rocking the foundation of his voice, he cried out in tones hardly above a whisper,

. . . we shall fight on the beaches, we shall fight on the landing grounds, we shall fight in the fields and in the streets, we shall fight in the hills. . . .

The words stopped. The weeping Churchill grasped the back of a chair for a couple of silent minutes. Then, like the blare of a trumpet, he roared in deafening defiance:

. . . we shall never surrender. . . .

No tears stained a voice suddenly triumphant. The Churchill phrases marched again:

. . . even if, which I do not for a moment believe, this island, or a large part of it, were subjugated and starving, then our empire beyond the seas . . . would carry on the struggle, until, in God's good time, the New World, with all its power and might, steps forth to the rescue and liberation of the Old.

One of the members of Parliament who heard those words the next day was the English essayist and man of letters Harold Nicholson. To his wife, the novelist Rebecca Sackville-West, he wrote that these were "the most magnificent words" ever uttered in the English language.*

---

*In October, 1979, a British actor, Norman Shelley, revealed he had impersonated Churchill and gave this address for the BBC. It was Churchill's habit after he delivered major

Across the Atlantic another master of words, Franklin Roosevelt, as he heard Churchill's fighting words on BBC broadcast, was moved to say to Harry Hopkins, "If we give to England, it's not money down the drain. As long as that old bastard is in charge, England will never surrender."

With the orotund phrase "The New World," Churchill coded a stark plea for intervention by an isolationist United States. Though there was a disinclination for involvement in a European conflict, the mounting sympathies of America were with the mother country. Churchill believed that the hope for Britain lay in that kindred feeling, joining with a growing perception that American vital interests would be jeopardized by a Nazi-dominated Europe and Africa.

The situation in June 1940 looked desperate, but time could be an ally. If Britain could hold on, it would survive. Never doubting the courage of the English people, Churchill questioned the American realization of that courage. They must be made to understand that Britain, unlike France, would not surrender. To that end, Churchill marshaled his literary skills and oratorical powers. His voice not only rallied his country, but would persuade a hesitant Franklin Roosevelt to move his nation toward giving aid. As the image of a valiant and persevering George Washington once brought help from Europe to America, the sight of an embattled Churchill embodying all the tenacious stoutheartedness of the English John Bull was going to win support from the New World.

But like the winter at Valley Forge, London's summer of 1940 was the severest of trials. Churchill as he sat down to the cheers for his historic Dunkirk address on June 4 was heard to murmur in an aside, "We'll beat the bastards over the head with the butts of broken beer bottles, which is bloody all we've got." At that very

---

speeches in the House of Commons, to re-deliver them on the BBC. Churchill, who wanted the United States to hear his words, recorded this speech also for the BBC. It seems that the unsophisticated taping techniques at the time must have failed, and that Shelley was called in with Churchill's permission to record excerpts for use for later broadcasts and phonographic recordings for bond rallies. Churchill, who was sorely pressed in the most severe crisis of the war, could not spare the time to do another recording.

moment the Germans had launched their second offensive, one
that would end with the capitulation of France. With the fall of
France, Britain was at last alone.

Within Churchill, the bleakness of the challenge turned into
exhilaration:

> . . . the Battle of France is over. I expect that the Battle of Britain
> is about to begin. Upon this battle depends the survival of Chris-
> tian civilisation. Upon it depends our own British life, and the
> long continuity of our institutions and our Empire. The whole
> fury and might of the enemy must very soon be turned on us.
> Hitler knows that he will have to break us in this Island or lose the
> war. If we can stand up to him, all Europe may be free and the
> life of the world may move forward into broad, sunlit uplands.
> But if we fail, then the whole world, including the United States,
> including all that we have known and cared for, will sink into the
> abyss of a new Dark Age, made more sinister and perhaps more
> protracted by the lights of perverted science. Let us therefore
> brace ourselves to our duties, and so bear ourselves that, if the
> British Empire and its Commonwealth last for a thousand years,
> men will still say, "This was their finest hour."

It was also the finest hour of Winston Churchill. The destiny that
he had always believed awaited him had now at last beckoned. The
voice that, for the last decade, had gone unheeded by his countrymen had now become their voice. By their living room radios, they
sat poised to hear that familiar delivery: the slow articulation, the
weak slurred letter *s,* the judicial pauses, and even the occasional
introductory stammer. They relished its unique pronunciation of
the words "Nazi" and "Gestapo," into whose vowels he charged
the snarl of contempt. They knew when its lifting intonation
savored a new, still more scathing portrait of Hitler, "this evil man,
this monstrous abortion of hatred and defeat, whose hands are
stained with blood and soiled with corruption," or, in mocking
tones, spoke of "his tattered lackey Mussolini at his tail," "this
whipped jackal frisking at the side of the German tiger."

There was, in his truculent cheerfulness and defiant good humor, a spirit that animated his fellow Englishmen at their hour of great peril. About the impending invasion he said, "We are waiting for the long-promised invasion—so are the fishes." When a French general asked his plan for thwarting the German's landing of a hundred divisions, Churchill replied, "We would hit them on the head as they land ashore."

If his speeches had the earthy humor of a London pub, they also had the majesty of a coronation. From London on July 11, he broadcast an address entitled "The War of the Unknown Warriors":

> And now it has come to us to stand alone in the breach, and face the worst that the tyrant's might and enmity can do. Bearing ourselves humbly before God, but conscious that we serve an unfolding purpose, we are ready to defend our native land against the invasion by which it is threatened. We are fighting by ourselves alone; but we are not fighting *for* ourselves alone. Here in this strong City of Refuge which enshrines the title-deeds of human progress and is of deep consequence to Christian civilisation; here, girt about by the seas and oceans where the Navy reigns; shielded from above by the prowess and devotion of our airmen—we await undismayed the impending assault. Perhaps it will come tonight. Perhaps it will come next week. Perhaps it will never come.

In a day before television, Churchill sought by deliberate showmanship to present a visual image behind the voice. As one who delighted in the caricatured pages of *Vanity Fair* before he could read, he made the bow tie and chained waistcoat of his father his identifiable uniform. Adding to that, he gave the cartoonists his penchant for a colorful hat and long Havana. With cigar clenched in mouth and a right hand raised in a two-fingered V for victory, his hunched frame projected a familiar silhouette that was seen everywhere those summer months of 1940 visiting factories, appraising coastal defenses, or inspecting aerodromes.

Britain and the free world looked to him for leadership, and all the pent-up energy of a lifetime burst forth. Now unleashed were the soldier's training, the historian's knowledge, and the states-man's beliefs that long had filled his mind. Seldom has the burden of leadership rested less heavily upon a man. He had plucked the sword smoothly from the stone.

From Berlin came the July 2 directive. "The Fuehrer and the Supreme Commander has decided . . . that a landing in England is possible, provided that air superiority can be attained." That inva-sion, called Operation Sea Lion, was postponed until mid-September, when Hermann Goering predicted an outnumbered and overwhelmed Royal Air Force would be wiped out. From the newly captured airfields in France, the bomber squadrons of the Luftwaffe raged across southern England. As high summer deep-ened to fall, the contrails of the world's first major air war latticed the British skies.

At the climax of what he called the Battle of Britain, Churchill, on a September Sunday afternoon, drove with his wife from the prime minister's country residence at Chequers to Uxbridge, the underground nerve center of the Royal Air Force. On the wall were electronic maps revealing the disposition of the twenty-five squad-rons of the RAF. As discs began to dot the electrified chart indicat-ing each successive wave of German aircraft swooping in from France, the Fighter Command released its squadrons one by one to meet each onslaught. Soon the red lights signaled that all 25 squad-rons were in the air. By then the British fighters were winging on their last ounce of fuel and firing their last round of ammunition.

"What other reserves have we?" asked Churchill.

"There are none," the air marshal answered.

Silence descended on the room. Of that crucial moment, Chur-chill wrote, "The odds were great; our margins small; the stakes infinite."

Then, incredibly, the discs on the wall map began to shift east-ward. The German Luftwaffe was going home. In that same underground station, Churchill had created his immortal inscrip-tion to these 800 valiant RAF pilots who had beaten back the hordes of Nazi bombers. The phrase was sublime in the perfect balance of its measured simplicity. Later incorporated into a speech in the House of Commons, it originated from a comment to Lord Ismay at a previous visit to the Uxbridge air command: "Never, in the field of human conflict, was so much owed by so many to so few."

If the glory belonged to "the few" in the Battle of Britain, the credit for the endurance of the blitz of London that followed was to "the many." Beginning in September, an air armada of 1,000 strong began to bomb London's industrial East End and docks. When Churchill visited the damaged docks, the workers cried, "Good old Winnie. We knew you'd come and see us. We can take it. Give it back." Churchill broke down and wept. As Lord Ismay was struggling to get Churchill through the crowd, he heard an old woman say, "You see, he really cares. He's crying."

In those fall days a daily torrent of Nazi bombs fell on London homes and ships; even Buckingham Palace was not unscathed. A proud Queen Elizabeth said of the near escape of the royal family, "Now I can look the East End in the face."

Because of the bombing threat, the British government persuaded a reluctant Churchill to move his command post from 10 Downing Street to the Annexe. The "Hole in the Ground" was a five-minute walk from 10 Downing Street. Originally the honeycomb of underground rooms was a repository for old documents. Churchill's operation room was the 40-foot square War Room, whose thick wooden pillars and crossbeams painted white made it seem like a ship's mess hall for officers.

At the head of the table sat Churchill, in a homely wooden chair with rounded arms and a plump cushion. In front of him were four glass inkwells, two red and two black. Between the two pairs of inkstands was an ornamental dagger used as a letter opener. The dagger, Churchill told visitors, he was saving for his personal confrontation with Herr Schicklgruber. Just past the end of the ink blotter was a propped-up cardboard sign with the words of Queen Victoria: "Please understand there is no pessimism in this house and we are not interested in the possibilities of defeat; they do not exist."

From this unlikely subterranean station, Churchill dispatched war directions by propelling hollow steel balls conveying messages through pneumatic pipelines to various government departments, with scarlet tags affixed to signal balls that contained actions to be carried out that very same day. As the blitz began, the first order designated the London tube (subway) stations as bomb shelters. Then Churchill directed the House of Commons, which met during the bomb-filled night hours, to convene in the daytime at unscheduled sittings. The Local Defense Volunteers, who began the war as coastal watchers for invasion, was rechristened the Home Guard. For these men, often aged veterans of World War I, as well as for other gallant citizenry, Churchill instituted the George Cross award to be the civilian equivalent of the Victoria Cross, which was given for bravery under fire. For the bombed-out homeless he put through a national insurance plan for compensation. Hardly a detail escaped his attention. One October directive insisted on a sufficient candy and chocolate supply for children.

Yet the directives, minutes, or telegrams, which by the end of the war numbered over a million, were not as monumentally instrumental as the speeches he composed and delivered in the heroic months of London's siege. In a September radio speech entitled "Every man to his Post" Churchill struck the theme that bespoke the mood of all Englishmen: "We shall . . . draw from the heart of suffering itself the means of inspiration and survival, and of a victory won not only for ourselves but for all. . . ."

More than a crisis of survival, it was to be a crusade. Borrowing from John Bunyan, Churchill, a few weeks later, ended a summary of the war to the House of Commons with this invocation trenchant in its intense spirituality:

Long, dark months of trials and tribulations lie before us. Not only great dangers, but many more misfortunes, many shortcomings, many mistakes, many disappointments will surely be our lot. Death and sorrow will be the companions of our journey; hardship our garment; constancy and valour our only shield. We must be united, we must be undaunted, we must be inflexible. Our qualities and deeds must burn and glow through the gloom of Europe until they become the veritable beacon of its salvation.

Churchill drafted these speeches, not in the War Room of the Annexe, but in his cell of a bedroom that was just a few feet away.

This almost monastic cubicle was furnished with the barest of furniture—a table, chair, a wardrobe, and a cot-sized bed. Only pipe ducts for heating and ventilation festooned the stark walls.

Here Churchill, in his favorite green-dragoned dressing gown, would dictate his speech while propped up by two pillows on the narrow bed. Like an oracular Buddha, Churchill periodically emitted a sentence or two between puffs of a pungently aromatic Havana whose clouds filled the small cell. At the table a tense young secretary tried to punch out on her noiseless typewriter the august words of Britain's leader.

The shorthand transmission stage had been mostly scrapped as a time-waster in the urgent demands of a war schedule. Instead, the secretary would try to transpose his message into a rough first draft, triple-spaced for massive revision by the perfectionist. The prime minister already had a rough outline in his head, which he had been mulling over days earlier—perhaps in strolls in the garden at 10 Downing Street or in the walks to and from the Annexe to Downing Street. The workings of Churchill's mind can be seen in the notes he used for an emergency Commons speech in secret session, for which he did not have time to prepare a proper address:

> We have had a couple of nights of bombing,
>   evidently much worse than that.
> Folly underrate gravity of attack impending.
> But if 100 or 150 bombers employed
>   entitled to remark:
>   Not very cleverly employed.
> Hardly paid expenses.
> Learn to get used to it.
>   Eels get used to skinning.
> Steady continuous bombing,
>   probably rising to great intensity
>   occasionally,
>   must be regular condition of our life.
> The utmost importance preserve morale of
>   people,
>   especially in the night work of factories.

A test of our nerve against theirs.
. . . essence of defence of Britain
   is to attack the landed enemy at once,
leap at his throat
   and keep the grip until the life is out of him.

The triple-spaced first draft reduced the inchoate musings in Churchill's head to paper. Back to the secretary it would go as an almost unintelligible mass — crossed-out sentences with penned-in replacements over them, and then various arrows pointing to additional paragraphs in the margin or perhaps reversing certain sentences' order.

Even though such polishing extended to a third or even fourth draft, Churchill would continue revising the final copy up until the very last minute before he left for the House of Commons, or when the BBC technicians entered the Annexe to set up a broadcast from his little cubicle. The last-minute changes exasperated a finicky Foreign Office, who insisted on their bureaucratic prerogative of approval.

The final copy, which was typed on a special octavo sheet, broke up the script into lines, as in verse. Frequently the margins held stage directions like "pause" or "emphasis." Churchill believed that rhetoric, with its appeal to the ear, should be read more as poetry than prose.

   We cannot yet see how deliverance will come
      or when it will come,

   but nothing is more certain
      than that every trace of Hitler's footsteps,

   every stain of his infected
      and corroding fingers,

   will be sponged and purged
   and, if need be, blasted
      from the surface of the earth.

To Richard Dimbleby, who, as the perennial voice of the BBC, would deliver the preliminary announcement of a prime ministerial broadcast to the radio audience, Churchill's subordination of punctuation to his own rhythmic esthetic sense was just one more example of his cavalier disregard of the accepted canons of speech delivery. Not only was the initial *s* weak, but other opening consonants were far from crisp in his slurred growl. Then too, at the end of a sentence, the Churchill intonation would generally rise instead of falling to signal a completed thought.

Yet Dimbleby acknowledged that the Churchill radio voice, possibly because of his peculiar delivery, had an incredible power of commanding rapt attention. No doubt, its rich vocabulary and majestic sweep of statement were a paramount cause of his magnetism. But Edmund Burke, with a similar style, was nicknamed the "Dinner Bell" because he emptied the House of Commons chamber when he rose to speak.

Perhaps Churchill's secret lay in his turning his speech idiosyncrasies to his own advantage. He once told President Eisenhower, who wore light, thin-rimmed spectacles, to replace them with heavy-framed dark ones like his own. "If you have a defect, make it a prop." Early in his forensic career he had done just that with his stammer. But to mask his lisp, he weakened the "s." Later he began to rob the force of other consonants. The result was an arresting combination of weak consonants and strong vowels.

Like a practiced platform speaker who lowers his voice to force his audience to strain their ears to attention, Churchill's muffled growl compelled his listeners' total concentration. Then, with his measured delivery and strategic pauses, he would guide them through his reflection on the facts to a resolve for action. Rapid-fire speakers may be more adept at raising an audience to emotional fever pitch with a frequently demagogic eloquence, yet the celerity of speech that is developed by street orators may betray an unconscious fear that the audience is going to walk away. Deliberate speakers, on the other hand, like Franklin Roosevelt, Douglas MacArthur, Everett Dirksen, and Martin Luther King seem serenely confident in their ability to hold their audience. Churchill had an undiminished faith in the worth of his message.

Moreover, the stately cadence of his delivery added a certain grandeur and profound poignancy.

As a broadcaster, his supremacy remained unchallenged. No man who appeared before the microphone in Britain has ever attracted so vast an audience, not only in his own land, but abroad in Nazi-occupied Europe, where to tune in to the BBC was an invitation to Gestapo headquarters. Even Nazis like Goebbels and Nazi collaborators like William Joyce ("Lord Haw Haw") monitored his speeches. The Germans who constantly delayed their landing plans in those months of 1940 were not inattentive to the Churchill speeches, whose fierce defiance unequivocally promised a savage resistance to any invasion force. Hitler knew that Churchill, unlike Stalin of Russia or Reynaud of France, commanded the wholehearted support of the British people. No cadre of sympathizers or defeatists could dent with half-truths or rumors the robust morale Churchill had forged with his radio addresses.

Each major speech was the result of much brooding thought. At times Churchill had to search and reach for that flash of inspiration. Sometimes it came in the special two-coach train he used as his mobile home on his tours of British factories and military bases or in the weekend car ride from London to Chequers, the official summer residence of the British prime minister.

Chequers is an Elizabethan mansion some 40 miles north of London in Buckinghamshire. With Chartwell closed for the war, Churchill took to visiting the state residence on weekends. Sometimes on Saturday or Sunday afternoons, garbed in his air-force-blue zippered siren suit, Churchill would stride the lawns dictating his thoughts to a frantic secretary struggling to write while keeping pace behind him, or late at night he would declaim from his place among the pillows. If it was a major speech, larks or thrushes might be heralding the dawn before the dictation ceased. Even then, his labor had not ended until the master craftsman had put the draft through four or five revisions. Such work done by the head of government boggles the mind. Franklin Roosevelt had the help of two or three professional writers, including such Pulitzer Prize winners as Robert Sherwood and Archibald MacLeish. The five volumes of addresses Churchill produced during the war would have taxed the energies of one if not a team of ghostwriters, yet Churchill not only wrote his own speeches but ran the war.

Yet perhaps the most exacting draft he ever dictated at Chequers was not a speech, but a letter. The July 31, 1940, cablegram of 4,000 words addressed by "Former Naval Person" to President Roosevelt pleaded for destroyers. These ships, "so frightfully vulnerable to air bombing," were crucially needed "to prevent seaborne invasion." To Churchill, the fate of Western civilization hung on the acquisition of these destroyers. "Mr. President, with great respect, I must tell you," Churchill importuned, "that in the long history of the world this is a thing to do *now*."

It was to be Churchill's longest letter, and his most successful. Soon the resourceful Roosevelt found a way, in isolationist America, to release fifty destroyers in exchange for the United States use of British naval bases in the West Indies. To Churchill it was more than destroyers that were promised—it was deliverance. The first step had been taken in the road toward U.S. involvement. Only with the total commitment of the vast American resources would the balance be tilted against the Axis powers. Churchill liked to quote the remark of Lord Grey, Britain's Foreign Secretary in the First World War: "America is like a gigantic boiler. Once the fuse is lighted under it there is no limit to the power it can generate." Now the engine had been lit.

Before Churchill ever became prime minister, he perceived that only the President of the United States could wrest his nation from its strict course of neutrality. The wooing of Roosevelt began in 1939, when Churchill, as First Lord of the Admiralty, wrote his initial letter to the American chief executive. The author veiled the secret correspondence with the cryptic signature "Naval Person." The allusion touched on a common interest between Churchill and Roosevelt, who had been an Assistant Secretary of the Navy in the First World War. The correspondence, one of whose signatories became "Former Naval Person" after Churchill was made prime minister, welded a bond between the two heads of state unparalleled in the annals of nations.

Yet as significant as these 900 or more Churchill letters were in establishing a mutual intimacy and trust, it was the Churchill speeches, particularly the Dunkirk vow to "fight on the beaches . . . fight on the landing grounds," that convinced a politically vulnerable President in an election year to nudge his country across the bounds of neutrality. A Britain that would never surrender would become the first line of American defense. Though the Neutrality Act prevented the granting of military aid, the wily Roosevelt, by citing an almost forgotten statute on the books, circumvented the Act by leasing the needed ships for British use.

When these destroyers arrived in the fall of 1940, Churchill could look beyond the smoke of dust from the bomb-destroyed docks and cities to the time when Britain would be joined by the United States in its struggle.

If the shipment of destroyers proved to be mostly symbolic, it was a symbolism not without substance. Indeed, the same could be said of the subsequent dispatch in January 1941 of Roosevelt's closest confidant, Harry Hopkins, as personal envoy to the British prime minister. Hopkins's message from the American President was the words from the Book of Ruth: "Thy people shall be my people and thy God, my God. Even to the end." Upon hearing it, a deeply moved Churchill turned his head away in tears.

In the steps of Hopkins came Wendell Willkie, the recently defeated Republican presidential candidate, whose visit under Roosevelt's auspices signaled the mounting bipartisan sympathy for the British cause. Churchill, in a broadcast from his subterranean cubicle, implored that the sympathy be undergirded by support:

The other day, President Roosevelt gave his opponent in the late presidential election a letter of introduction to me, and in it he wrote out a verse, in his own handwriting, from Longfellow, which he said "applies to your people as it does to us." Here is the verse:

> . . . Sail on, O ship of State!
> Sail on, O Union, strong and great!
> Humanity with all its fears,
> With all the hopes of future years,
> Is hanging breathless on thy fate!

What is the answer that I shall give, in your name, to this great man, the thrice-chosen head of a nation of a hundred and thirty million? Here is the answer which I will give to President Roosevelt: Put your confidence in us. Give us your faith and your blessing, and, under Providence, all will be well.

We shall not fail or falter; we shall not weaken or tire. Neither the sudden shock of battle, nor the long-drawn trials of vigilance and exertion will wear us down. Give us the tools, and we will finish the job.

To a Congress that had just heard the outlines of a Roosevelt-proposed Lend-Lease Act, a bottom line has never been expressed more succinctly. Ten weeks later, when Congress had passed and the President had signed the legislation, Churchill, calling it "the most unsordid act in the whole of recorded history," again took to the airwaves to express the gratitude of his countrymen. His closing answered Roosevelt's verse with his own lines from the British poet Arthur Clough:

Last time I spoke to you I quoted the lines of Longfellow which President Roosevelt had written out for me in his own hand. I have some other lines which are less well known but which seem apt and appropriate to our fortunes tonight, and I believe they will be so judged wherever the English language is spoken or the flag of freedom flies:

> For while the tired waves, vainly breaking,
> Seem here no painful inch to gain,
> Far back, through creeks and inlets making,
> Comes silent, flooding in, the main.
>
> And not by eastern windows only,
> When daylight comes, comes in the light;
> In front the sun climbs slow, how slowly!
> But westward, look, the land is bright.

In the early months of 1941, when British troops were being driven out of the Balkans and the Greek peninsula, the guarantee of military aid from the United States was the only good news to a bomb-ravaged Britain. At home, as the long nights of winter shortened into summer, the whine of sirens and burst of shells which for so many months had punctuated the hours of the London dark became sporadic. By June nothing heavier than a gentle English shower rained upon the British rooftops. Soon the reason for the cessation was clear: Hitler's interest had been diverted.

On June 21, while Churchill was vacationing at Chequers, the military staff telephoned him that German armored divisions were hurtling past the Polish frontier into Russia. Churchill was not surprised. Not only had he expected the attack for the last couple of months, but he had instructed his envoys to communicate that intelligence to a disbelieving Stalin. From the very outset he had been convinced that the deal between the two dictators to carve up Poland was a bond that would soon unravel from its own sleaziness.

At the Admiralty in October 1939 Churchill had delivered his epigrammatic insight into the Kremlin mind:

I cannot forecast to you the action of Russia. It is a riddle wrapped in a mystery inside an enigma; but perhaps there is a key. That key is Russian national interest.

And then he went on to suggest that German dreams for East European domination would eventually intrude in the Soviet sphere of that interest.

As Hitler's order to carry out these plans were being brutally executed by his high command, Churchill strolled the lawns at Chequers to ponder the new configuration in the geopolitical equation. His parliamentary secretary, Jock Colville, wondered aloud how the prime minister, with his record of implacable hatred of Communism, could team up with the Soviet dictator.

Churchill, between puffs of his cigar, replied, "If Hitler invaded Hell, I would make at least a favourable reference to the Devil in the House of Commons."

Then Churchill, after sending word to the BBC to schedule a broadcast from Chequers the next day, retired to his bedroom to begin dictation of the speech. The all-night work continued on through the next day, giving Churchill only a few hours for rest, finishing only minutes before the time of the broadcast.

The speech reveals Churchill's use of language not just to persuade others but to convince himself. When thoughts colored by his rich imagination were converted into printed words on paper, they were like paintings he could see and touch and possess. Just as the framed oil became more real than the ephemeral scene that occasioned the conception, so a Churchill speech sorted out his thoughts and transformed them into a doctrine or article of faith.

In this address, Churchill, the archenemy of communism, had to bring himself around to a rapprochement with its government. His imagination reached out in identification with the Russian people. The result was a speech that began almost as a lyrical ode:

I see the Russian soldiers standing on the threshold of their native land, guarding the fields which their fathers have tilled from time immemorial.

I see them guarding their homes where mothers and wives pray—ah yes, for there are times when all pray—for the safety of their loved ones, the return of their breadwinner, of their champion, of their protector.

I see the ten thousand villages of Russia, where the means of existence was wrung so hardly from the soil but where there are still primordial human joys, where maidens laugh and children play.

I see advancing on all this in hideous onslaught the Nazi war machine, with its clanking, heel-clicking dandified Prussian officers, its crafty expert agents fresh from the cowing and tying down of a dozen countries.

I see also the dull, drilled, docile brutish masses of the Hun soldiery plodding on like a swarm of crawling locusts.

I see the German bombers and fighters in the sky, still smarting from many a British whipping, delighted to find what they believe is an easier and safer prey. Behind all this glare, behind all this storm.

I see that small group of villainous men, who plan, organize, and launch this cataract of horrors upon mankind. . . .

In this choral dithyramb Churchill pulled out all the poetic stops. Even a melody of faint rhyme ("pray," "play," "prey") lingers amid the chromatic imagery of Russian folk life. Suddenly the peasant homeland is violated by the alliterative and assonant description of regimentation of German troops ("dull, drilled, docile" . . . "the cowing and tying-down"), whose brutality is painted onomatopoetically ("clanking," "heel-clicking").

Through the labors of his poetic incantation, Churchill exorcised himself of old hatreds and cast himself as the deliverer of the Russian people from the Nazi oppressors. To those, like his aide Jock Colville, who still had any question about his reaction to the German invasion of Russia, Churchill hurled out this unequivocal challenge:

We have but one aim, and one single irrevocable purpose. We are resolved to destroy Hitler and every vestige of the Nazi regime. From this nothing will turn us—nothing. We will never parley, we will never negotiate with Hitler or any of his gang. We shall fight him by land, we shall fight him by sea, we shall fight him in the air, until with God's help we have rid the earth of his shadow and liberated its people from his yoke. Any man or state who fights on against Nazidom will have our aid. Any man or state who marches with Hitler is our foe.

In no time, Churchill was fulfilling his avowal by acts. If, like the British, the Russian people could hold out for the next four or five months, the eventual victory was not improbable. For one thing, thought Churchill, "the Russian bear of a winter would hug Hitler's armies to death as it did Napoleon." So by July British convoys were regularly sailing eastward to Russian ports, carrying supplies Britain could barely spare from its own needs.

Then, in August, a different type of convoy ventured westward bearing a cargo even more vital—Churchill himself. On the battleship *Prince of Wales* the prime minister sped through the North Atlantic to a secret rendezvous with Franklin Roosevelt off the Newfoundland coast. As the *Prince of Wales* swept beside the President's ship, the *Augusta,* the chords of "God Save the King" sounded from the U.S. Marine Band. Standing, with the support of his son, was Franklin Roosevelt, his hand raised in salute. Churchill, whose romantic sense of the sea had been kindled by his nightly reading, while on voyage, of the adventures of C. S. Forester's Captain Horatio Hornblower, emerged on the deck in a peaked sailing cap and naval jacket. With a beaming smile, he said, "At long last, Mr. President." "Glad to see you aboard," hailed Roosevelt, clad in a white Palm Beach suit.

For months before the crossing Churchill had had his aides ransack the library of the United States Embassy for every book, article, or clipping on the life of Franklin Roosevelt; but after the shaking of hands, the American President recounted one incident Churchill should have remembered. It was not the first time they had met. Roosevelt was rather hurt that Churchill was not aware that he had been introduced to the then United States Assistant Secretary of the Navy at a London luncheon given in his honor by David Lloyd George at the close of World War I.

Nevertheless, the two patricians with similar interests and mutual acquaintances were immediately congenial. One of their common friends was Bourke Cockran. Cockran, the father figure who was such an influence in Churchill's forensic development, was, curiously, a decisive factor in the Roosevelt speech that catapulted his comeback to the national arena. The death in 1923 of Cockran, the greatest orator in the New York Democratic party, gave Roosevelt the opportunity to deliver the "Happy Warrior" nominating speech for Al Smith in the Democratic convention in 1924.

In the ship cabin discussions, Roosevelt was already envisioning a postwar peacemaking role like that of his World War I commander in chief, Woodrow Wilson. No doubt thinking of the

Fourteen Points, FDR brought up the notion of a common statement of principles. Responding to the idea, Churchill retired to his stateroom to work out a draft. The next day Roosevelt, with his advisers having added a few changes, okayed the Churchill composition. Thus, what was really a mimeographed press release following the meeting later became known to the world as the Atlantic Charter.

The eight-point document, though it reveals the Churchill hand, is less significant for its style than its substance. It is the first call by the Allies for a United Nations:

FIRST, their countries seek no aggrandizement, territorial or other.

SECOND, they desire to see no territorial changes that do not accord with the freely expressed wishes of the people concerned. . . .

THIRD, they respect the rights of all peoples to choose the form of government under which they will live. . . .

SIXTH, after the final destruction of the Nazi tyranny, they hope to see established a peace which will afford to all nations the means of dwelling in safety within their own boundaries, and which will afford assurance that all the men in all the lands may live out their lives in freedom from fear and want. . . .

EIGHTH, they believe that all of the nations of the world, for realistic as well as spiritual reasons, must come to the abandonment of the use of force. Since no future peace can be maintained if land, sea, or air armaments continue to be employed by nations which threaten, or may threaten, aggression outside of their frontiers, they believe, pending the establishment of a wider and permanent system of general security, that the disarmament of such nations is essential.

But more than in the Charter, Churchill found, in the Sunday church service held on the quarterdeck beneath the battle guns, a tangible expression of their common purpose. As the sun broke through the mist of that Sunday morning, the hymnal chorus of "Onward Christian Soldiers" rose to the sky in the mingled voices of two navies—"fighting men," as Churchill later retold to the House of Commons, "of the same language, of the same faith, of the same fundamental laws, of the same ideals and now to a larger extent of the same interests, and certainly, in different degrees, facing the same danger."

On his homeward voyage, Churchill's ship spied in the distance a vast flotilla of merchant ships—cargo boats, tankers, whalers, and converted passenger boats—on their way to England from America, carrying the preciously needed munitions and equipment. Churchill, whose dramatic sense of theater matched his imaginative use of words, saw his chance to say "thank you" to the ships of the merchant marine. In the fading light of sunset, the *Prince of Wales* plunged, cutting a lane through the six-columned convoy at 22 knots. Not once but twice, the British battleship plowed through the motley steel ranks. Standing on its bridge was the British prime minister, with his one hand in a V-sign and the other raised in salute to the onlooking crews, whose homely but perilous tasks were ennobled by the sight of that silhouetted figure on the distant deck.

At the historic Atlantic meeting, where the Charter was almost an afterthought, the principals and their advisers mainly discussed the emergence of Russia and Japan as crucial factors in the balance of power. Churchill, ignoring the warnings of a Japanese buildup in Singapore in the Far East, told the Americans that his paramount military objective was to drive Rommel and his Afrika Korps out of Egypt.

Three months later it would be the Americans, as well as the British, who would be surprised by the Japanese. December 7, 1941, found Churchill and his two American guests, Averell Harriman and Ambassador John Winant, at Chequers. At 9:00 P.M. they tuned in the BBC news. Immediately Churchill telephoned Roosevelt.

"It's quite true," the American president said. "They have attacked us at Pearl Harbor."

Churchill replied, "Well, we're all in the same boat now." Despite that shock, Churchill went to bed in almost a joyous exhilaration. Churchill wrote later, "I went to bed and slept the sleep of the saved and thankful." Churchill knew that, with the United States at his side, the victory he had so consistently predicted was now assured.

Hardly had the British declaration of war against Japan passed both Houses of Parliament when Churchill began to make plans to visit America. Roosevelt was not enthusiastic at first, but then acquiesced at the insistence of the adamant Churchill. Setting sail on the *Prince of York,* Churchill was consumed by one fear while he paced its decks — the idea that the Americans might now decide to concentrate on the Japanese war. Indeed, for a short time after Pearl Harbor, Lend-Lease shipments from the United States had been suspended.

Churchill's task was not only to persuade Roosevelt, but to convince a Congress whose proprietary conception of the Pacific as "the American Ocean" was now shattered by the sudden jeopardy of the Philippines, the Aleutians, and Hawaii. When Churchill arrived, he was immediately welcomed by the Roosevelts into the family Christmas celebration at the White House. Churchill found time in his Monroe bedroom on the second floor to work over a draft of his forthcoming speech to the Joint Session of Congress. Concentration was not easy since Harry Hopkins, who had the suite next door, as well as the president, kept popping in for a chat, which often evolved into a deep discussion of common war strategy. On one occasion Roosevelt wheeled into the Monroe room to find Churchill pink and naked, cigar in one hand and a whiskey and soda in the other. To a startled Roosevelt, Churchill announced unabashedly, "His Majesty's First Minister has nothing to hide from the President of the United States."

Churchill wanted to convey something of the same intimacy in his rhetorical message to Congress the day after Christmas. With an allusion to both his mother and his Revolutionary War ancestry, he opened his speech.

Members of the Senate and the House of Representatives. . . the fact that my American forebears have for so many generations played their part in the life of the United States and that here I am, an Englishman, welcomed into your midst makes this experience one of the most moving and thrilling of my life, which is already long and has not been entirely uneventful.

I wish indeed that my mother, whose memory I cherish across the veil of years, could have been here to see me. By the way, I cannot help reflecting that if my father had been American and my mother British, instead of the other way around, I might have got here on my own. In that case, this would not be the first time you have heard my voice. In that case I would not have needed an invitation, but if I had it is hardly likely that it would have been unanimous. So perhaps things are better as they are. . . .

At this deft speculation of what could have been his future in American politics, laughter rolled up toward him from the congressmen and senators. He was no longer a foreigner, a visiting head of state—but one of them, a politician with kindred roots and ties. Then, with the audience firmly in his tow, Churchill guided them around the globe in a general survey of the war situation. When he came to Japan, a silence tense with anticipation gripped his listeners.

After the outrages they have committed upon us at Pearl Harbor, in the Pacific Islands, in the Philippines, in Malaya and the Dutch East Indies they must know that the stakes for which they have decided to play are mortal. When we look at the resources of the United States and the British Empire compared to those of Japan, it becomes . . . difficult to reconcile Japanese action with prudence or even sanity.

Then, gripping his lapels, he squared his shoulders and asked the rhetorical question:

What kind of a people do they think we are?

The audience roared its reply as the members rose to their feet as one man and thunderously cheered as if they would never stop.

For minutes waves of applause flooded the chamber in a demonstration unparalleled in Capitol history.

Is it possible [Churchill continued when the uproar subsided] that they do not realize that we shall never cease to persevere against them until they have been taught a lesson which they and the world will never forget?

Then, shifting into a lofty theme for his peroration, Churchill raised again the Atlantic Charter concept of a postwar organization for keeping peace.

Duty and prudence alike command . . . that the germ centers of hatred and revenge shall be constantly and vigilantly curbed and bested in good time and that an adequate organization should be set up to make sure that the pestilence can be controlled at its earliest beginning before it spreads and rages throughout the entire earth. . . .

Then he said, in closing:

It is not given to us to peer into the mysteries of the future. Still I avow my hope and faith, sure and inviolate, that in the days to come the British and American people will for their own safety and for the good of all walk together in majesty, in justice, and in peace.

At the end Churchill stood still for a moment at the rostrum and then sat down. For an instant there was silence. Then pandemonium broke loose. Senators, congressmen, cabinet secretaries, Supreme Court justices cheered and waved, some of them exchanging V-signs with the British prime minister. Beneath the bare cherubic forehead, the apple-cheeked face of Churchill beamed, basking in the tumultuous response. "John Bull" Churchill had won the heart of Congress. On returning to the White House, he told his bodyguard Thompson, "I really hit the target." The speech had evoked the greatest reception in his long career.

But the effort took its toll. That night, while trying to open a window in his White House bedroom, Churchill felt a sudden pain in his chest. It was a mild heart attack. For reasons of security, Churchill and his doctor concealed it from the world, including his White House hosts.

Churchill, disobeying his doctor's orders, did not rest for even a day. There was too much work to do. He left his bed to continue discussions with General Marshall and Admiral King, solidifying the Churchill-Roosevelt decision to concentrate first on the German conflict. Then he boarded a train to Ottawa, where he was to address the Canadian Parliament.

After extolling the contribution of Canadian soldiers and fliers to the defense of Britain, Churchill identified all English-speaking peoples with their cousins in besieged Britain.

I should like to point out to you that we have not at any time asked for any mitigation in the fury or malice of the enemy. The peoples of the British Empire may love peace. They do not seek the lands or wealth of any country, but they are a tough and hardy lot. We have not journeyed all this way across the centuries, across the oceans, across the mountains, across the prairies, because we are made of sugar candy.

Look at the Londoners, the Cockneys; look at what they have stood up to. Grim and gay with their cry "We can take it," and their wartime mood of "What is good enough for anybody is good enough for us." We have not asked that the rules of the game should be modified. We shall never descend to the German and Japanese level, but if anybody likes to play rough we can play rough too.

Then, in the language of a Biblical prophet, he thundered a fateful judgment. "Hitler and his Nazi gang have sown the wind; let them reap the whirlwind."

Shifting tones, with a never-to-be-forgotten earthy retort, Churchill coined his own slogan:

When I warned them [the French] that Britain would fight on alone, whatever they did, their generals told their prime minister and his divided cabinet, "In three weeks England will have its neck wrung like a chicken."

Churchill paused and then roaringly hurled back the words: "Some chicken. . . ." Before he could finish, the Canadians were on their feet cheering. As the din lessened, Churchill added, ". . . some neck." The uproar doubled again amid gales of laughter. Later Churchill, who was puzzled but not unhappy with the reaction, was told that "neck" in Canadian slang meant "nerve" or "brass."

Journeying back to Washington, Churchill celebrated New Year's Eve on the train. As the train neared Brattleboro, Vermont, he strode from his compartment to the dining car, armed with cigar and brandy. To the car full of reporters and staff aides, he gave a toast: "Here's to 1942. A year of toil, a year of struggle, a year of peril. But a long step toward victory."

But the year was almost over before that first "long step" was recorded, which for the British was the turning point of the war.

On November 10, Churchill reported to the Lord Mayor's Luncheon the African victory at El Alamein by Montgomery over Rommel. In brightly recasting some lines he recalled from Bartlett's *Quotations,* "where every helmet caught some gleams of glory" (Napier) and "It's the beginning of the end" (Talleyrand) he would add his own lines to its pages.

I have never promised anything but blood, tears, toil, and sweat. Now, however, we have a new experience. We have victory—a remarkable and definite victory. The bright gleam has caught the helmets of our soldiers, and warmed and cheered all our hearts. . . .

Now this is not the end. It is not even the beginning of the end. But it is, perhaps, the end of the beginning.

As the war began its fourth year, Churchill, except for the king, was the most popular Englishman. Though his oratory stirred the

British soul, it was his personality that captured its heart. Just as in his speeches he turned his idiosyncrasies to advantage, so Churchill flaunted his personal foibles. The master of language was also the maker of legend. Tales that he outdrank as well as outate the Russians at the conference table were not denied. His eccentric pronunciation of foreign words, particularly German ones, was matched by his outlandish haberdashery. The sight of the siren-suited Churchill in steel helmet, naval cap, or panama hat was as reassuring at a factory site as the familiar grumpy growl was to listeners at the pub radio. Like the language of his speeches, Churchill would vary the workaday—his zippered one-piece garb—with dark-suit formality—bow tie and watch-chained waistcoat. He picked his wardrobe as well as his words with imagination and verve.

Not only in Britain but in America did Churchill play to the crowds. More than a few times, aides or hotel staff would be sent out scurrying to fetch a "Churchill-sized" Havana before he left the White House or hotel suite. It was as if he could not emerge from a limousine or advance to a head table unless fueled by a lit cigar and propelled by a hand waving V for victory.

Twice in 1943, Churchill traversed the Atlantic to confer with Roosevelt to discuss the time and site of a Second Front.

The second occasion, in August, followed a Big Two meeting at Quebec, where the principal topic of discussion was the political implications of the fall of Mussolini. During that stay, a presentation to Churchill of an honorary degree by Harvard University was sandwiched into a busy schedule. Both his bodyguard and his wife noted more than his customary irritability as he prepared his speech. The reason was soon evident as Churchill, in his majestically flowing robes of scarlet, reached the climax of his address on Anglo-American unity:

Twice in my lifetime the long arm of destiny has reached across the ocean and involved the entire life and manhood of the United States in a deadly struggle. . . .

The price of greatness is responsibility . . . one cannot rise to be in many ways the leading community in the civilised world without being involved in its problems, without being convulsed by its agonies and inspired by its causes. . . .

The people of the United States cannot escape world responsibility. . . . We have now reached a point in the journey where . . . it must be world anarchy or world order.

Throughout all this ordeal and struggle . . . you will find in the British Commonwealth and Empire good comrades to whom you are united by other ties besides those of state policy and public need. To a large extent they are the ties of blood and history. Naturally, I, a child of both worlds, am conscious of these. Law, language, literature—these are considerable factors. . . . The great Bismarck—for there were once great men in Germany—is said to have observed toward the close of his life that the most potent factor in human society at the end of the nineteenth century was the fact that the British and American peoples spoke the same language. . . .

Then Churchill after tracing the interwoven history, culture, and ideals of both countries delivered his breathtaking proposal:

This gift of a common tongue is a priceless inheritance, and it may well some day become the foundation of a common citizenship. . . .

It was the closest Churchill ever came to proclaiming publicly his private belief in the eventual political union between the two countries. The Harvard audience acclaimed what his wife thought was his noblest speech. The following week, Franklin Roosevelt, perhaps in an implicit concurrence with the Churchill dream, insisted that the British prime minister preside over a meeting of the Combined Chiefs of Staff of both nations in the cabinet room of the White House.

The American president, who was still vacationing at Hyde Park, had told Winston and Clementine in his absence "to treat the White House as their own home and to feel free to invite

anyone to meals." To Churchill, his use of the White House and
the occasion of his chairing the military conference in the cabinet
room was "an event in Anglo-American history."

The final fruition of the White House military discussions would
take place the next spring. On June 6, 1944, a House of Commons
tense in the eerie government silence amid rampant rumors about
landings in France, awaited the arrival of the prime minister.

An unusually serene and reflective Churchill walked to his place
at the front bench. In an offhand manner that toyed with the anxieties of the House, he opened with an announcement that was
not news:

> The House should, I think, take formal cognisance of the libera-
> tion of Rome by the Allied Armies under the Command of Gen-
> eral Alexander, with General Clark. . . . This is a memorable and
> glorious event, which rewards the intense fighting of the last five
> months in Italy. The original landing . . .

On Churchill droned, for several minutes, about the Italian
situation as the chamber grew restless with more than the usual
coughs and rustle of paper.

Then, almost casually, he shifted to a new topic.

> I have also to announce to the House that during the night and
> the early hours of this morning, an immense armada of upwards
> of 4,000 ships, together with several thousand smaller craft,
> crossed the Channel. . . .

> The battle that has now begun will grow constantly in scale and
> in intensity for many weeks to come. . . .

If the decision had been Churchill's, he would not have been
addressing Parliament that day. It was his plan, despite General
Eisenhower's opposition, to be on one of the D-Day barges crossing the Channel to France: "It is not part of your responsibility,
my dear General, to determine the exact composition of any ship's
company in His Majesty's fleet."

But then Churchill found himself stymied by a higher authority: George VI told him that if the prime minister sailed, so would the king. Like a little boy who is forbidden to watch a Fourth of July fireworks, Churchill was crushed.

As the Allied tanks pushed their way from the Channel beachheads through the Norman burgs of France in that summer's grinding advance toward Paris, the Churchill voice continued to ring out its unceasing exhortations. General Omar Bradley said, "His speeches were worth an army." This was his closing peroration on August 2:

> Let us go on, then, to battle on every front. Thrust forward every man who can be found. Arm and equip the Forces in bountiful supply. Listen to no parley from the enemy. Vie with our valiant Allies to intensify the conflict. Bear with unflinching fortitude whatever evils and blows we may receive. Drive on through the storm, now that it reaches its fury, with the same singleness of purpose and inflexibility of resolve as we showed to the world when we were all alone.

On November 11, the date of World War I's end, Churchill was at the Hotel de Ville in the same city where the armistice was announced twenty-six years earlier. In response to a presentation by Charles de Gaulle, who had just marched in the Liberation Procession with him down the Champs Elysees, Churchill said, "It gave me so much pleasure to see Paris again—this Paris which is a brilliant star shining above the world."

The French audience was told that final victory was now in sight; but one Allied leader would not see the culmination of his hopes and endeavors. For some time, Churchill, whose sturdy constitution had survived not only the unreported heart attack but two bouts with pneumonia, had watched his comrade, Franklin Roosevelt, at successive conferences literally waste away—until at Yalta, in March 1945, his face "had a transparent quality" and his eyes "a faraway look."

Past midnight into the early morning of April, Friday the thirteenth, Churchill was alone in his study at 10 Downing Street;

then he heard the news. Putting down the telephone, he frantically buzzed for his bodyguard, who was the only one in the immediate vicinity. Thompson, thinking it was a matter of security, rushed in with his revolver cocked.

"Thompson," he said numbly, staring at the rug. "Have you heard the terrible news. It's the President of the United States, your friend and mine." And then he said, with his voice breaking, "He died on the wings of victory, Thompson, but he saw the wings of it and he heard them."

On the last day of April another death shortened the struggle that had so spent the American leader. Adolph Hitler, in his underground bunker, had aimed a Walther pistol into his mouth.

A week later was VE-day. A triumphant Churchill looked out from the balcony of the Ministry of Health building at the sea of faces that bobbed up and down in the joyous pandemonium.

"God bless you all," Churchill shouted in the microphone above the din. "This is your victory!"

"No, it is *yours,*" the crowd yelled back. "It's yours."

To such a suggestion Churchill demurred. On a later occasion he would say: "I have never accepted what many people have kindly said, namely that I inspired the nation. Their will was resolute and remorseless, and, as it proved, unconquerable. It fell to me to express it and if I found the right words you must remember that I earned my living through my pen and tongue. It was the nation and race dwelling around the globe that had the lion's heart. I had the luck to be called on to give—the Roar."

It was his roar of savage defiance that had rallied his countrymen, reassured friends, and deterred foes. In 1940 his words were weapons, when they were almost the only words. His personal motto, which he used as his inscription for his history of World War II, was:

In War: Resolution
In Defeat: Defiance
In Victory: Magnanimity
In Peace: Good Will

He might well have added: "In Crisis: Eloquence."

13

CHAMPION
OF FREEDOM

He has sounded forth
the trumpet that
shall never call retreat.
Julia Ward Howe,
"The Battle Hymn of the Republic"

(Churchill's favorite hymn was
to be played at his memorial service.)

A few months later the VE cheers rang hollow in Churchill's ears. While attending the Potsdam meeting with the new U.S. President Harry Truman and Premier Joseph Stalin, Churchill awaited the results of the July election, held following the dissolution of the wartime coalition government. Announcement of the final counts was delayed pending the mailed military ballot. One morning Churchill awoke from a nightmare in which he had seen himself wrapped in a sheet with his feet protruding from the bottom—a corpse. It was the omen of the unexpected Labourite victory which dismissed Churchill from office. To Churchill, the actual impact of the losing returns a couple of days later struck like "a physical blow."

How could the English people whom he had so recently led to triumphant victory reject him in such a stunning defeat? The bannered postmortems of the British press were hardly balm to the Churchill wounds. First, they said it was his very fame as a world statesman that had toppled him from office. Somehow, Churchill the war leader could not be pictured as absorbed by the homely problems of a job for the returning veteran, a better pension for Dad, or relief for Mom's mounting doctor's bills. Then, in an even more ironic twist, the newspaper pundits assigned the blame for the Conservative defeat on, of all things, Churchill's oratory!

They said that Churchill's partisan diatribes against the "monster" of socialism was a two-edged sword that sliced at his own credibility. Swing voters as well as Socialists were apparently infuriated by an eve-of-the-election charge by Churchill: "I declare to you, from the bottom of my heart, that the socialist system cannot be established without a political police. . . they would have to fall back on some kind of Gestapo, no doubt very humanely directed in the first instance."

His former Socialist allies in the coalition government expressed hurt at the ill-considered comparison, but Churchill had wounded himself more than his Labourite opponents. A national hero had abased himself through political cant. From political hack, the commentators deemed, it was but a short step to political has-been.

To Churchill, the defeat was more than a surprise; it was a shock. Not since Gallipoli had he sustained such a crippling blow. His wife, thinking of his advancing age and his health, tried to console him.

"Winston," she said, "it may well be a blessing in disguise."

"At the moment," replied Churchill, "it seems quite effectively disguised."

King George VI wanted to appoint him a peer of the realm—the Duke of London—but Churchill would not retire from the House of Commons. His Majesty then suggested the conferral upon Churchill of the palace's highest honor, the Knight of the Garter. Churchill had this reaction: "I could not accept the Order of the Garter from my Sovereign when I had received the 'Order of the Boot' from his people."

The kings and queens of Norway, Denmark, and Holland, who invited him to their courts, were also spurned. Conservative leaders tried to map a global tour of the British Empire, as well as Europe, for him. More than a few cities in Canada and Australia as well as in Britain were ready to offer him their ceremonial gold keys, with the accompanying appropriate civic celebrations to honor the war's most heroic figure. Churchill saw these tributes, though, as another not-so-subtle-hint that he resign his leadership of the Conservative party. "I refuse," said Churchill, "to be exhibited like a prize bull whose chief attraction is his past prowess."

When the time came for his furniture to be carted out of 10 Downing Street, he moved into Claridge's, the hotel whose most sumptuous suite, that of the chairman of the Savoy Hotel Group, had been vacated to make room for the former prime minister. Churchill, though, was uneasy with the balcony outside the apartment, which had an 80-foot drop. "I don't like sleeping near a precipice like that. I've no desire to quit the world, but thoughts, desperate thoughts, come into the head."

"Black Dog," Churchill's name for his recurrent depression, filled hours no longer seized with the challenge of power. To recuperate, Churchill decided to fly to Italy, where Field Marshal Alexander had asked him to stay at his villa on Lake Como. After a week in which no mail was brought and no newspapers delivered, the glazed numbness began to thaw. Three decades earlier, he had taken up painting on his spiritual escape from the Gallipoli disaster; now, armed with his oils, Churchill went in search of a painting. He discovered his scene in a ferryboat ride across the lake, where a bright yellow kiosk shaded by willows contemplated its reflection in blue Italian waters.

By the end of his stay Churchill had found, if not peace, a quickening of purpose. He philosophized to the young military aide provided by General Alexander: "Out of a life of long and varied experience, the most valuable piece of advice I could hand to you is to know how to command the moment to remain."

Upon his return to London, the purpose took shape when a letter arrived inviting him to speak at a small American college in an obscure Midwestern town. But the town was in Missouri, the home state of President Truman, who, because of an old political debt to the college president, was asking Churchill to accept.* Even if the town of Fulton had hardly more than a 7,000 population, a speech with the President of the United States in attendance had the makings of a world forum.

Though the date of the address, March 5, 1946, was a half-year away, the opportunity triggered Churchill's imagination. He might have been out of office, but he was still the world's foremost figure, whose words could still command attention in the world's leading nation. The thought buoyed his spirits as he resumed his role as Leader of the Opposition.

---

*Major-General Harry Vaughan, President Truman's military aide, was a long-time friend of Westminster College and its President, Dr. F. L. McCluer. Vaughan had brought the letter of invitation, which was sent to the White House to the attention of the President. Truman forwarded the letter to Churchill with this inscription: "It's a fine college in my state. Come and I'll introduce you."

If Churchill, as head of a defeated party, had no power, he still had a forum, as well as the greatest and most eloquent voice to fill that forum. The voice that had commanded armies around the globe could still move the forces of world opinion. Clearly Churchill, far from being a liability, was an asset to the Conservative party, perhaps its only asset. Grumblings from the rank-and-file Conservatives began to cease as a more sober analysis of the Conservative defeat shifted the blame from the wartime premier to the party that had only reluctantly chosen him under the constraint of a national crisis.

The mistakes of Munich were not his, but his party's. The British electorate had not so much defeated Churchill as they had defeated the many Conservative party members who had held office in the inglorious two decades before the war. Though Churchill was nominally a Conservative in that feckless time, he was also the Conservatives' most effective opponent. In 1945 the British people compared the two parties—one that had a plan to one that had been devoid of any plans for social reform for twenty years. In the end they chose the program of one over the personality of the other.

Churchill now went to work, to build such a program as well as the party. He appointed a task force to develop a domestic program under the leadership of R.A.B. (Rab Butler) and assigned Lord Woolton the task of revamping the party at the grass roots. For himself he charted a personal program of writing a history of World War II and playing the role of world statesman.

In early March, Churchill sailed on the *Queen Elizabeth* to New York and then took a train to Miami for some sun and sand before journeying to Washington. There he holed himself up in a British Embassy bedroom in Washington rewriting his Fulton speech, which he had entitled "Sinews of Peace." The title was a play on Cicero's phrase "sinews of war." Churchill was striking his familiar theme that only preparedness could ensure peace: the Soviet political and military encroachments could be stopped only by a united West under the resolute leadership of the United States. He wanted to jerk America out of its cozy worship of the United Nations and its intellectual make-believe. The mask of democratic pretensions had to be ripped from the Kremlin face and its naked imperialism revealed. Since the government in Washington, as well as his own in London, were reluctant to topple the illusion of peace that existed between the wartime allies, Churchill saw that it was his duty to do so. As an out-of-office world statesman, he could sound the alarm that Truman and Attlee hesitated to utter.

One American who he called into the British Embassy to discuss the text was Dean Acheson, Truman's Under Secretary of State. Lester Pearson, the Canadian Ambassador in Washington, had suggested Acheson to Churchill as one who had not only a sound diplomatic head but also a keen ear for the elegant phrase. Acheson found Churchill in the second-story bedroom, garbed in his dragon dressing gown, swathed in cigar smoke, and sipping Scotch and soda as he polished and repolished the lines he had dictated in London before he had left. Acheson had this comment on the master craftsman at work: "If genius is the infinite capacity for taking pains, Churchill is overqualified." Acheson's one suggestion was to eliminate the reference to World War II as "the unnecessary war." Quite wisely, Acheson thought that right-wing Republicans would seize on the phrase as support for their past opposition to Roosevelt and as justification for continuing isolationism. The revised sentence now read: "There never was a war in all history easier to prevent by timely action."

On March 4, Churchill joined the presidential party aboard the B&O's special train from Washington's Union Station to Jefferson City, Missouri. When Truman noticed Churchill studying the presidential seal that is always carried with a traveling Chief Executive, the American president proudly pointed out that he had changed the seal and directed that the eagle be turned to look toward the olive branch instead of the arrows.

Churchill, whose speech the next day would cast shadows on the roseate glow of the immediate postwar peace, could not quite give the new seal his full approval. He told the American president: "Why not put the eagle's neck on a swivel so that it could turn to the right or left as the occasion presented itself?"

The train had hardly embarked when it was discovered that the cache of liquor in the presidential stateroom was laden with

Truman's favorite Bourbon but no Scotch. At Silver Spring, the first suburban stop in Maryland, Harry Vaughan, Truman's military aide, stepped off to make a quick purchase of Johnnie Walker Black. Churchill told Vaughan, "When I was a subaltern in South Africa, the water was so bad we had to add whiskey to it to make it palatable. With diligence and effort I learned to like it."

As the B&O train rolled through the Cacoctin countryside of western Maryland, Churchill regaled Truman as he once had Roosevelt with the twelve-stanza rendition of "Barbara Frietchie." Then Churchill retired to his stateroom for a nap and more work on his speech. When he emerged from his room to rejoin the president for dinner he offered this criticism on American habits: "Why do you Americans stop your drinking at dinner?" Truman replied with a reference to the aid to Britain that was now being debated in Congress. "The cost of supplying you with wine would mean a bigger loan." Churchill retorted, "You Americans keep trying to twist the 'loan's' [lion's] tale."

When the presidential train arrived in Jefferson City, an open limousine awaited the president and the former prime minister. The procession of the motorcade was temporarily delayed until a long Havana could be purchased at a Jefferson City tobacco store for the propless Churchill. At the arrival at Westminster College, lunch was offered at the home of the college president, Dr. F. L. McCluer. The speech was given in the college gym, with about 2,600 in attendance. In introducing Churchill, President Truman was his characteristic blunt self.

> Mr. Churchill and I believe in freedom of speech. I understand Mr. Churchill might have something useful and constructive to say.

Typically, Churchill opened on a light but warm note that immediately won the affection of his audience. With his hands clasping the sides of his scarlet Oxford robes, honorarily earned, he peered over his black spectacles and harrumphed in his habitual stutter style.

I am glad to come to Westminster College. . . . the name Westminster is somehow familiar to me. I seem to have heard of it before. Indeed it was at Westminster that I received a very large part of my education. . . .

Then Churchill, gesturing with palms upturned as if to show that he was not stripped of power, offered a disclaimer that was meant to anticipate his cool reception in official Washington and London quarters:

Let me . . . make it clear that I have no official mission of any kind and that I speak only for myself.

He continued by stating that the paramount mission facing the world was the prevention of another global war. Raising his forefinger twice in emphasis, he pointed to two institutions that would play major roles in the maintenance of peace: a strengthened United Nations Organization and the continuing "special relationship between Britain and America."

Then, with the epic foreboding of a Milton, Churchill began his celebrated description:

A shadow has fallen upon the scenes so lately lighted by the Allied victory.

The darkness was that cast by a looming "iron curtain." The passage, which Churchill had added sometime in the night as the train hurtled through Kentucky, was not included in the advance texts. Thus, some of the leading papers such as the *Washington Post* failed to mention the phrase in their coverage of the speech. Even the movies missed capturing it because the cameramen chose to wind their cameras at that point of the speech. (Indeed, there was almost no oral recording of the historic address, as the speaker system went dead for a couple of seconds; but an alert onlooker found, as he kneeled down behind the podium to check the wiring, that when he touched the wires the speaker system resumed. For the rest of the speech he held on to the wires in his crouched position, and the Churchill speech was duly heard and recorded.)

The phrase, which made its debut in this Fulton address, had been used before. In a telegram to President Truman on May 6, 1945, Churchill had written of his profound misgivings over the withdrawal of the American army to the occupation line: "this bringing Soviet power into the heart of Western Europe and the descent of an iron curtain between us and everything to the eastward." Indeed, at Potsdam Churchill had confronted Stalin with the phrase "iron fence." Stalin's reply was: "All fairy tales!" Some commentators think that Churchill may have first seen the phrase in a news account of a German reporter translated in a London *Times* dispatch dated May 3, 1945.

But it was Churchill who made "iron curtain" part of the English language. In a majestic sentence perfect for its balance and sweep, Churchill introduced the phrase after marking the curtain's bounds with the names of two rhyming seas:

From Stettin in the Baltic, to Trieste in the Adriatic, an iron curtain has descended across the continent.

At the mention of "iron curtain" Churchill's clenched fists shook in angered dismay. Then, one by one, with finger pointing in mute chorus, he recited the litany of occupied cities behind the curtain:

Behind that line lie all the capitals of the ancient states of Central and Eastern Europe: Warsaw, Berlin, Prague, Vienna, Budapest, Belgrade, Bucharest, and Sofia, all of these famous cities and the populations around them lie in what I must call the Soviet sphere, and are all subject in one form or another, not only to Soviet influence but to a very high and, in many cases, increasing measure of control from Moscow.

He then followed with an insight into the Kremlin mind which has never been surpassed in succeeding years:

I do not believe that Soviet Russia desires war. What they desire is the fruits of war and the indefinite expansion of powers and doctrines.

For such Soviet imperialism he offered this prescription:

From what I have seen of our Russian friends and allies during the war, I am convinced there is nothing they admire so much as strength, and there is nothing for which they have less respect than weakness, especially military weakness.

Then he reinforced his postwar summons to action with a reminder of his prewar warning:

Last time I saw it all coming and cried aloud to my own fellow-countrymen and to the world, but no one paid any attention. Up to the year 1933 or even 1935, Germany might have been saved from the awful fate which has overtaken her and we might have all been spared the miseries Hitler let loose upon mankind. There never was a war in all history easier to prevent by timely action than the one which has just desolated such great areas of the globe. It could have been prevented in my belief without the firing of a single shot, and Germany might be powerful, prosperous, and honoured today; but no one would listen, and one by one we were all sucked into the awful whirlpool.

Though President Truman had no comment on the speech, protests were delivered to Moscow the next day on Soviet actions in Iran and Eastern Europe. Thus ended the era of Roosevelt's policy of blind trust in Russia. Churchill had persuaded Americans that their very security was again threatened by tyranny abroad. The shuddering clang of the iron curtain coming down rang dissonantly in Western ears.

At first, however, the speech brought mainly criticism. The widow of the late President Roosevelt was disapproving. Three Democratic senators called a press conference to denounce the speech as "shocking." In Britain, when Prime Minister Attlee was asked if he endorsed the speech, he said he was not called upon to express any opinion on a speech delivered in another country by a private individual.

But if the speech gave the jitters to the British Foreign Office and U.S. State Department, Churchill, in his role as traveling world statesman, was as happy as a boy let out of school. Free from the constrictions that the responsibility of high office imposed, Churchill could hurl out challenges without worry of offending Whitehall's overly delicate sense of diplomatic niceties.

Two months after Fulton he was at the Hague addressing the States-General of the Netherlands. There he told the Dutch what he had told the Belgians months previously:

> I see no reason why . . . there should not ultimately arise the United States of Europe.

Then, in September 1946, he astounded a Swiss audience at Zurich University by voicing the unthinkable hardly a year after World War II had formally ended:

> I am now going to say something that will astonish you. The first step in the re-creation of the European family must be a partnership between France and Germany. In this way only can France recover the moral leadership of Europe. There can be no revival of Europe without a spiritually great France and a spiritually great Germany.

The inclusion of Germany in the future of Europe hardly a year after the nation's defeat startled Churchill's audience at a time when the havoc of Nazi destruction still greeted the eye and the horrors of Buchenwald were only first being heard at the Nuremberg trials. Such prescience by Churchill was rare and courageous statesmanship.

In some ways the immediate postwar years were the happiest in Churchill's long and eventful life. Chartwell, which he had closed down at the outbreak of war with the intention of selling, had been purchased by friends and given to Britain, with a life estate reserved for Winston and Clementine. If the old Kent manor had been an ideal place for his children to run and romp in the twenties and thirties, it was to be the favorite haunt for his grandchildren in the forties and fifties. By the end of the war Mary, his youngest and last to marry, had wed Captain Christopher Soames of the Coldstream Guards. Her children joined Randolph's Winston* and Arabella, and those of Diana, who had married Duncan Sandys, a rising and respected Tory politician.

At Chartwell Churchill recharged the enervated batteries of the wartime years. The first task was the chronicling of World War II. Like Caesar before him, he assembled a team of amanuenses for compilation and research. Young historians fresh from university training together with former staff assistants, were pressed into duty under the baton of Churchill's orchestration. Sheet by sheet, galley proof by galley proof, Churchill would subject the copy to at least six editions of revision, much to the dismay of the publishers. The first volume, *The Gathering Storm,* came out in 1948. The other volumes followed in successive years.

For Churchill, the penning of history, which was but memoirs written on a world scale, was not a chore but a pleasure. Listen to him as he sums up 1940 in the second volume of the chronicle, entitled *Their Finest Hour*:

> We may, I am sure, rate this tremendous year as the most splendid, as it was the most deadly, in our long English and British history. It was a great, quaintly organised England that had destroyed the Spanish Armada. A strong flame of conviction and resolve carried us through the twenty-five years' conflict which William III and Marlborough waged against Louis XIV. There was a famous period with Chatham. There was the long struggle against Napoleon, in which our survival was secured through the domination of the seas by the British Navy under the classic leadership of Nelson and his associates. A million

---

*Winston is the son of Randolph and Pamela Digby, who is now Mrs. Averell Harriman. Mrs. Harriman married the American producer Leland Hayward after her divorce from Randolph. The issue of Randolph's second marriage with June Osborne was Arabella.

Britons died in the First World War. But nothing surpasses 1940. By the end of that year this small island, with its devoted Commonwealth, Dominions, and attachments under every sky, had proved itself capable of bearing the whole impact and weight of world destiny. The citadel of the Commonwealth and Empire could not be stormed. Alone, but upborne by every generous heartbeat of mankind, we had defied the tyrant in the hour of his triumph.

Writing was not the only pleasure that the sojourns at Chartwell yielded to Churchill. There was his painting, and he was over-joyed when two of his offerings, anonymously submitted, were accepted by the Royal Academy. Horses were a hobby too for the once-ranking polo player. Just before his seventy-fourth birthday, he donned jodhpurs after fortifying himself with some rum punch. Then, hoisted to a horse, he galloped off to the hounds, waving his square-crowned Russell hat with the inevitable cigar clenched in his teeth. But it was his last hunt. The love of horses bred in his years as a cavalry subaltern now found vent in his purchase of a race horse, Colonist II, which, under the chocolate and pink colors of Lord Randolph, would win 13 races and considerable earnings. On one occasion late in Colonist II's career, the highly favored horse didn't finish in the running. When Churchill was asked to explain, he said, "I told him—this is a very big race and if you win it, you will never have to run again. You will spend the rest of your life in agreeable female company." Then Churchill added, "Colonist II could not keep his mind on the race."

It often seemed that Churchill preferred the four-legged mammals to the two-legged ones as his companions. Rufus, a small brown poodle, was the recipient of many confidences and muttered asides until he was run over by a bus in Brighton while his master was addressing a Conservative conference there in 1947. For days Churchill was desolate at the loss, but Rufus I was replaced by another poodle, Rufus II, a gift from Walter Graebner of *Life* magazine, which was about to serialize Churchill's World War II history. His poodle friend, if clearly the favorite at court, was not the only quadruped who treated Chartwell as his domain.

There was the tawny cat with the appropriate name of Marmalade, and for a short while a foul-smelling black lamb had the run of the house, much to the dismay of Churchill's wife. Then, in addition to the mammalian pets, there were the black swan and golden carp that policed the Chartwell ponds.

Chartwell was the only real home Churchill ever had. The house, with its books and mementoes, and the grounds, with their scape for painting and range for the run of animals, allowed physical expression of all his loves and interests. When Churchill was there all of his manifold sides had outlets. Like a giant chestnut tree with room to spread, Churchill had sunk his roots deep in Chartwell.

The speeches and his writings were the bloom and fruit of the tree. But in those works can be seen the many facets of Churchill's personality that found reflection at Chartwell. Who but a painter would have given such a perspective in the Dunkirk speech. "We shall fight on the beaches, we shall fight on the landing grounds, we shall fight . . . in the streets, we shall fight in the hills." Like an artist he moves from the beaches in the foreground to the hills in the distance.

Or after the victory at El Alamein, perhaps only one with an artist's eye would have said, "The bright gleam has caught the helmets of our soldiers. . . ."

The imagery of animals, which he sometimes doted on, splashed across his speech canvas. Mussolini was a "whipped jackal frisking at the side of the German tiger." The British Commonwealth was "the old lion with the cub at its side." In a radio address in 1943, he warned, "If the Nazi villains drop down upon us from the skies . . . you will make it clear to them that they have not alighted in the poultry run or on the rabbit farm or even in the sheepfold, but in the lion's den at the zoo!"

But even more than the lion, Churchill, like the bulldog, stood as the symbol of English tenacity. "The nose of the bulldog has been slanted backwards so it can still breathe without letting go." Indeed, Churchill's description of his friend Lord Birkenhead could well apply to himself: "He had all the canine virtues—courage, fidelity, vigilance, and love of the chase—and all the defects—pugnacity, obstinacy, a loud bark, and thrusting muzzle."

For the wicked and evildoers, Churchill, like the ancient scripture, would switch from mammal to reptile. Witness his denunciation of appeasement in 1938: "Each one hopes that if he feeds the crocodile enough, the crocodile will eat him last." Or his description of the Third Reich as "a boa constrictor that befouled its victims with saliva before engorging them."

Chartwell, if a playground for his animals, was also a gallery for his ancestors. Portraits of Lord Randolph and the first Duke of Marlborough, along with the painting of the Blenheim battle, are testament to the Churchillian reverence for history. Beside the pictures were the hundreds of tomes in his library, chronicling the histories of countries such as France, Germany, and Russia. Churchill wrote:

Knowledge of the past is the only foundation from which to peer into and try to measure the future. Expert knowledge, however indispensable, is no substitute for a generous and comprehending outlook upon the human story with all its sadness — with all its unquenchable hope.

Only a Churchill, in reporting to the House of Commons on a naval base in the Portuguese Azores in 1943, would have taken his audience six centuries back in time.

I have an announcement to make to the House arising out of the treaty signed between this country and Portugal in the year 1373 [pause] between His Majesty King Edward III and King Ferdinand and Queen Eleanor.

It is also typical Churchill style to say of the RAF in 1940:

The knights of the Round Table, the Crusaders, all fall back into the distant past: these young men going forth every morn to guard their native land and all that we stand for, holding in their hands these instruments of colossal and shattering power.

Who but Churchill could have asked the British and American generals and admirals before the D-day landing, "When did William go?" It took a moment before the top military strategists realized that he was talking of the Conqueror. Churchill knew the details of that epic landing. He told them that the Allies would be landing at the Bay of Seine, just where William had started out with his invasion boats.

If history was a series of tableaux for Churchill, words were jewels—antique ones, classic ones, old ones refurbished or placed in a new setting, or sometimes even new ones. The unabridged Oxford English Dictionary in his Chartwell study was well thumbed by his search for the right word. He called those critics of the intelligentsia who attacked his call to arms in early 1940 "thoughtless dilettanti" and "purblind worldlings"—the word "purblind" hardly having been used since Chaucer.

At times Churchill loved to roll off certain Latinate phrases from his tongue. He could declaim alliteratively of "the plenitude of power" or declare "I have not become the king's first minister in order to preside over the liquidation of the British Empire."

The avowal was as much to history as to posterity. In a sense it was an answer to Edward Gibbon in his own language. For if Shakespeare was the favorite author on Churchill's Chartwell bookshelves, Gibbon was the historian he most revered. In an essay he wrote at Chartwell on the pleasures of painting he almost echoes the stately rhythm of the English historian:

> Painting is a friend, who makes no undue demands, excites to no exhausting pursuits, keeps faithful pace even with feeble steps, and holds her canvas as a screen between us and the envious eyes of Time or the surly advance of Decrepitude.

"Decrepitude" is more regal than "decay," more noble than "decline." Thus an old man's cantankerous resistance to the creeping infirmities of age is sublimely expressed.

Quite early in his career, Churchill revealed an interest in prolixity as a tool for humor. In 1906, he coined with the orotundity of a future Dirksen "terminological inexactitude" as an eleven-syllable synonym for "lie." It was verbosity at its deftest. Similarly, he termed his return to the Conservative party, from which he had once deserted, a "tergiversation," a euphemistic rendering of the political jibe "re-ratting."

If some words were intellectual games, others were the ritual gems whose Elizabethan beauty beat a repeated tattoo on the memory of a schoolboy enjoined to attend the obligatory Church of England service. Churchill may not have been the most devout of Anglicans, but God's words as written in the King James Bible and the Common Book of Prayer never lost their majestic awe. That the two books stood on his shelves more for their literary than spiritual guidance does not diminish their significance in his life.

Churchill knew his Bible. In 1944 when Churchill sailed to Alexandria to see Roosevelt at a secret conference, the American President radioed his reservations about the appropriate meeting place in Egypt. Churchill returned this verse citation: "See St. John 14: 1–4.

> Let not your heart be troubled; he believe in God,
>   believe also in me.
> In my Father's house are many mansions: if it were
>   not so, I would have told you. I go to prepare
>   a place for you.
> And if I go and prepare a place for you, I will come
>   again, and receive you unto myself; that where
>   I am, there ye may be also.
> And whither I go ye know, and the way ye know."

To the Chamberlain government he said after Munich, "Thou are weighed in the balance and found wanting." And to the people of Birmingham who returned him after a closely contested election, he thanked them by telling the scriptural tale of the hospitable Shunamite woman who was asked by a prophet if he could speak to the king in her behalf. "No," she said. "I dwell among my own people."

Only Churchill among the World War II leaders denounced Hitler with the righteous fervor of a prophet: "This wicked man. . ." On another occasion he called Naziism "wickedness, enormous, panoplied, embattled, . . . justice cast from her seat." Churchill's sense of Old Testament retribution was never more evident than in his judgment after the London blitz: "They have sown the wind; let them reap the whirlwind."

To Churchill, words, like jewels, were not one-dimensional. Beyond their intrinsic definition or worth there was the extrinsic glow or sound. In his twenties he said to his friend Lady Violet Bonham-Carter, "Don't you think words have a magic independent of their meaning?

Lady Violet responded with a poetic passage:

> "Charmed magic casements, opening on the foam
> Of perilous seas, in faery lands forlorn."

"Oh, that's marvelous," Churchill replied. "What's it from?"

"Don't you know?" she asked. "It's Keats' 'Ode to a Nightingale.'"

When she next ran into Churchill a month later, he insisted on sitting her down and reciting to her all of Keats' Odes, which he had committed to memory in the interval.

From the early days of his youth when he was thrust from the security of his home and nanny into a boarding school, Churchill made poetry his playmate. With no Mrs. Everest to read him verse or tell him rhymes, he learned to recite by himself. To hear the sounds that spilled from his mouth fall into a measured beat and then come to attention with a rhyming halt was like watching soldiers forming ordered ranks in dress parade.

The memorizing of poems or plays for dramatic rendering was Churchill's first stretching of his mind. But if it was good mental exercise for Churchill, it was also pure escape.

It was his ticket to ancient battles and faraway places and was his companion when all alone.

Poetry permeated his speeches—not only the echoes of familiar lines, but excerpts cited in the midst of an address. The libraries of Chartwell are full of scores of English poets—famous ones like Milton, Pope, Dryden, Keats, Shelley, Wordsworth, Coleridge, and lesser knowns such as Rupert Brooke, Arthur Clough, W. E. Healy, A. E. Housman, and Siegfried Sassoon.

In his role as Opposition Leader, Churchill could recite a couplet of an obscure poet, William Camden, in telling the Labourites it was not too late to mend their ways:

> "Betwixt the stirrup and the ground
> Mercy asked, mercy found."

Then in a Pilgrims' dinner honoring Mrs. Roosevelt, he drew on the words of an unfamiliar Scottish poet, Lindsay Gordon, in memory of her late husband:

> "We tarry on; we are failing still
> He is gone and he fares the best
> He fought against the odds; he struggles uphill
> He has fairly earned his season of rest."

But most of the time he stuck to his favorites, like Blake, Byron, Fitzgerald (Omar Khayyam), Kipling, Tennyson, and Bobbie Burns. In the midst of an exchange at the House of Commons, Churchill defined the role of his political mission by quoting the Scottish bard:

> "To make a happy fireside clime
> For weans and wife
> There's the true pathos and sublime
> Of human life."

Or this quote from Tennyson, attacking the socialists for their wholesale revamping of settled laws in the name of social planning:

"Some reverence for the laws ourselves have made
Some patient force to change them when we will."

But in the thousands of speeches, remarks, toasts, and presentations that he had delivered since before the turn of the century, there was one whose words he quoted almost more than all the rest put together: Shakespeare.

Typical was the line from *The Merchant of Venice* that he cited in 1947 to praise the work of the newly developing United Nations:

"So shines a good deed in a naughty world."

Or on October 22 of that year he signaled observance of the engagement announcement of Princess Elizabeth to Lieutenant Philip Mountbatten with the sweet words from *Troilus and Cressida:*

"One touch of nature makes the whole world kin."

For Churchill, a line of verse could be not only a dart of love but a shaft of wit. As Leader of the Opposition, he used poetry as part of his armory as he rallied his Conservative troops in their rise from defeat in 1945. The Labourite disarray, under the divided counsel of such leaders in the cabinet as Aneurin Bevan, Hugh Dalton, and Sir Stafford Cripps, prompted Churchill to paraphrase Tennyson's "Charge of the Light Brigade" and tease Herbert Morrison that their numbers after the next election might be reduced to less than 400.

Crippses to the right of him: Daltons to the left of him;
Bevans behind him volleyed and thundered
What tho' the soldiers knew
Someone had blundered . . .
Then, they came back, but not the four hundred.

At the same time in 1947 he paraphrased Sir Walter Scott. After calling socialism "Government of the duds, by the duds, and for the duds," he said they would vanish "unwept, unhonored, unsung, and unhung."

The gales of laughter that swept over the House of Commons were not confined to the Conservative benches. Churchill was not just Leader of the Opposition, he was a legend. He was more than just the foremost British politician, he was a world personality whose idiosyncrasies they now indulged almost as much as he himself did.

On the walls leading up the staircase from the Chartwell library were political cartoons of him by Low, Shepherd, and others, as well as a few framed portrait caricatures from *Vanity Fair*. Churchill not only laughed at the often unkind treatment of his foibles, he gloried in them. As a British aristocrat he had the security to nurse and pursue his own unconformities, and as a half-American he had the lack of inhibition to flaunt them.

In earlier days of his career members had laughed at him, but now they laughed with him. Churchill was now a character who so dominated his stage, the Commons, that he didn't have to be speaking to hold center stage. Protracted yawns or even a short snooze could be as effective an answer to Labourite attack as an eloquent speech. Once, while Hugh Gaitskell was addressing the House, Churchill drained all attention away from him by scurrying on all fours underneath the front benches. When Gaitskell asked about the commotion, he replied, "I'm looking for my jujube" (since the trade name of one of these lozenge tablets was Pastille, the press called the incident "Fall of the Pastille").

It was not that he couldn't come up with the clever retort when the occasion required. Far from it; his wit was never more ready or rapier-sharp. A Labourite, Denis Palings, whose name describes the pointed picket fence around the House of Commons or the White House on which one can be "impaled," once called Churchill a "dirty dog capitalist." Churchill replied that his reaction was that of any "dirty dog" toward a "palings."

Long shrouded in the past were those days when Churchill, frozen by the cut and thrust of parliamentary exchange, would have to work out his bon mots beforehand, waiting for the opportune time to slip them in. With David Lloyd George's death in 1945, there were no members who could recall the self-conscious Churchill in his early, formative years. He was not so much an institution as the Commons itself.

When the Leader of the Opposition rose, he could, with his puckish grin and twinkling eyes peering above the eyeglasses set far down on his nose, set up a laugh as much as any Jack Benny or Groucho Marx. Then, after seizing the stage, he would haltingly open discourse in that jocular style, a combination of chuckle and stutter, that would launch the first titters, which then ripened into guffaws. It was not only what he said, but how he said it.

When Gaitskell, as Minister of Fuel, in 1947 said as an inducement for saving coal, "I have never had a great many baths myself," Churchill rose to interrupt with this comment:

When Ministers of the Crown speak like this on behalf of His Majesty's Government, the Prime Minister and his friends have no need to wonder why they are getting increasingly into bad odour.

I have even asked myself, when meditating on these points, whether you, Mr. Speaker, would admit the word "lousy" as a Parliamentary expression in referring to the administration, provided, of course, it was not intended in a contemptuous sense but purely as one of factual narration.

A. P. Herbert, no mean wit himself, who was in the House of Commons at the time, said Churchill was the greatest British humorist of his day, outranking Noel Coward, P. G. Wodehouse, and Hillaire Belloc. Herbert himself was a recipient of the Churchill wit. When he gave his first speech, a provocative one, in the House of Commons, Churchill said: "Call that a maiden speech? It was a brazen hussy of a speech. Never did such a painted lady of a speech parade itself before a modest Parliament." Herbert, speaking of those years when he saw Churchill perform on the front bench, said that few could calculate Churchill's power of wit by just reading the anecdotes in cold print "without some knowledge of the scene, the circumstances, the unique and vibrant voice, the pause, the chuckle, the mischievous and boyish twinkle on the face and all the tiny signs that something grander than wit is on parade."

Wit is a weapon too few leaders on the right ever possess. Humor can puncture the pretensions of the social planners when the dour economics of Conservatives only reinforce the public stereotype of the soulless businessman.

By the end of 1949, the British people were registering their weariness with socialism by voting Conservative in a series of by-elections. Churchill was feisty at the thought of returning to power. On November 30, the morning of his seventy-fifth birthday, the press waited for him outside his London home at 28 Hyde Park Gate. A photographer said, "I hope, sir, that I will shoot your picture on your hundredth birthday." Churchill replied, "I don't see why not, young man. You look reasonably fit and healthy."

The coming year of the mid-century mark looked promising for Churchill's prospects. *Time* magazine, which featured him in its January 3 cover story as "Man of the Century," predicted that he would soon return as prime minister. Hardly a week later, King George announced the dissolution of Parliament for the election to be held in late February.

Churchill, in a speech in Cardiff, Wales, hit out against the Orwellian dreariness of the British Socialist state as his campaign theme. As a lover of the English, he reserved his strongest contempt for the bureaucratic "newspeak" of Labourite social planners.

> I hope you have all mastered the official socialist jargon which our masters, as they call themselves, wish us to learn. You must not use the word "poor." They are described as "the lower income group."

> When it comes to a question of freezing a workman's wages, the Chancellor of the Exchequer speaks of "arresting increase in personal income". . . . There is a lovely one about houses and homes. They are in the future to be called "accommodation units." I don't see how we are to sing our old song "Home Sweet Home"—"Accommodation Unit, Sweet Accommodation Unit." I hope to live to see the British democracy spit all this rubbish from their lips.

On election day, the British people did unseat scores of Labourite members who came to office in the landslide of 1945. But though the sizable gains by Conservatives shattered the overwhelming Labourite majority, it was not quite enough to return them to power.

Churchill could not consider it a personal defeat. Polls taken to compare his popularity with that of Clement Attlee, the Labourite prime minister, showed that he was still a most respected and beloved figure in Britain.

Still, Churchill yearned for the test of another election, which by the nature of Labour's slim hold could not be far in the future. His eagerness to return to 10 Downing Street was no longer fired by a zeal to redeem his loss of 1945. It was lit by a new dream to find an accommodation between East and West that would lift the threat of nuclear conflict and conflagration. The leader who had climaxed his long career by waging war wanted to close it by making peace.

Churchill first unveiled his hope of arranging a conference with the Soviets at a speech in Edinburgh in early 1950.

> Still I cannot help coming back to this idea of another talk with Soviet Russia upon the highest level. The idea appeals to me of a supreme effort to bridge a gulf between the two worlds, so that each can live their life, if not in friendship, at least without the hatreds of the cold war. . . . It is not easy to see how things could be worsened by a parley at the summit.

"Parley at the summit," "summit meeting," "summit conference"—it was not the first time Churchill would capture the popular imagination by use of a graphic phrase that challenged prevailing beliefs. If "iron curtain" dominated the lexicon of the cold war,* "summit meeting" would become the phrase most associated with détente.

Perhaps Churchill is most remembered by his wartime phrases— slogans like "blood, sweat, and tears" in World War II or "Business as usual" in World War I, or newly coined words like "Quisling" for traitor or "destroyer" for a light-armed vessel; or even newly minted old words like the "underbelly of Europe" for the Balkans. But when Churchill proposed a Naval Holiday for the arms race in 1912, he proved that his mind was no less fertile for

---

*There are those who believe Churchill coined the phrase "cold war," but with this Churchill himself credited his friend Bernard Baruch.

the causes of peace. Late in his career he would popularize "peaceful co-existence" in a speech to the National Press Club in Washington in 1954.

In America, critics from the Right thought a proposal for a summit meeting and particularly the "co-existence" that such a meeting suggested were tantamount to appeasement, just as attackers from the Left had found his "iron curtain" description belligerent.

Churchill had this to reply to those who suggested he had gone soft with his call for a "summit conference at the highest level." "You remember Fulton," he said. "I got into great trouble being a bit in front of the weather that time. But it's all come out since — I won't say all right, but it's all come out." As a statesman he knew it doesn't always pay to be right too soon. As an artist he knew that perspective is deceptive — a figure in a portrait or photograph may seem closer to the right or left when, actually, he is only in the forefront.

When Churchill first issued his call for a parley at the summit in February 1950, the Left in Britain was also scornful. The Socialists denounced it as an election-eve stunt, and the matter seemed closed, as Clement Attlee narrowly kept his premiership.

But Churchill knew the bid had potent appeal to an electorate made edgy by a cold war intensified by the invasion of South Korea in June 1950. Only a Churchill could deal face to face with his former wartime ally Joseph Stalin.

It was an appeal that he would raise again in the next general election. That came in September 1951. The ailing King George persuaded Prime Minister Attlee to have an election in the fall before the king was scheduled to go into the hospital for removal of a cancerous lung.

In October 1951, Churchill again called for a meeting at the highest level, referring back to his speech early in the previous year. What convinced Churchill to consider the possibility of high-level negotiation was not so much the increasing intransigence of Russia, but the developing resurgence of Western Europe. In March 1950, Churchill had startled Britain by his suggestion that Germany become part of the European Army. Though the idea was attacked, it gradually caught on. The foundations now being laid for NATO were the evidence of strength that might eventually move the Kremlin toward considering some accommodation with the West. The key was the rearming of Britain and Western Europe. As Churchill said, "I do not hold that we should rearm to fight. I hold that we should rearm to parley."

But when Churchill issued his second offer to go to the mountaintops in the name of peace, Labour had its countercharge ready. "Whose finger do you want on the trigger, Churchill's or Attlee's?" So asked the Labour-oriented *Daily Mirror*. The cry was picked up by Labourites, notably Aneurin Bevan:

> I do not think Churchill wants war. The trouble with him is that he does not know how to avoid it. He does not talk the language of the twentieth century, but of the seventeenth. He is still fighting Blenheim all over again.

Churchill was stung by the charge, but the veteran political warrior carefully orchestrated his response. First, he answered the personal attack by some invective of his own. At a rally in his own constituency of Woodford, Churchill rose to give his home folks and friends a bit of political fun at the expense of the Socialists. He opened with a slogan alluding to certain Labourite mistakes in foreign policy as well as by its most flamboyant minister:

> Abadan, Sudan, and Bevan—they are a trio of misfortune.

The crowd roared its approval.

Then he turned his sights on Clement Attlee, the prime minister whom he had once called "a modest man with much to be modest about." In his mock-heroic style, he fixed on a recent statement of the Labourite prime minister.

> Mr. Attlee, speaking of the achievements of his government, has said . . . "How can we clear up . . . the mess of centuries?" "The mess of centuries!" The remark is instructive because it reveals with painful clarity the socialist point of view and sense of proportion. Nothing happened that was any good until they

came into office. We may leave out the great struggles and achievements of the past—Magna Carta, the Bill of Rights, parliamentary institutions, constitutional monarchy, the building of our Empire—all these were part of "the mess of centuries." Coming to more modern times, Gladstone and Disraeli must have been pygmies. Adam Smith, John Stuart Mill, Bright, and Shaftesbury, and in our lifetime, Balfour, Asquith, and Morley, all these no doubt were "small fry." But at last a giant and Titan appeared to clear up "the mess of centuries."

Pausing to let the howls of laughter subside, he continued:

Alas, he cries, he has only had six years to do it in. Naturally, he was not able to accomplish his full mission. We have endured these six years. They have marked the greatest fall in the rank and stature of Britain in the world which has occurred since the loss of American colonies nearly two hundred years ago. Our Oriental Empire has been liquidated, our resources have been squandered, the pound sterling is only worth three-quarters of what it was when Mr. Attlee took over from me, our influence among the nations is now less than it has ever been in any period since I remember. Now the Titan wants another term of office!

For a direct answer to the Bevan warmonger charge, he took the high road. On election eve he journeyed to Plymouth to campaign for his son, Randolph, who was standing for election there. He said that he remained in public life because he thought he could still make a lasting contribution to peace. "I pray indeed," he allowed, "that I may have this opportunity. It is the last prize I seek to win."

14

WORLD SYMBOL

The man is noble
and his fame folds
in the orb of the earth.
— *William Shakespeare*

The election the next day was almost an exact replay of the 1951 results, a standoff except for one thing. This time it was Churchill who squeezed in. When the king sent for him, the word in Westminster went out: Winston was back. Holding a bare majority, Churchill made good his election promise to try to form a national government. Although the Liberal party decided not to join his administration, he did appoint a few Liberals, like Lloyd George's son Gwylym, appointed Minister of Food and Fuel. Other nonparty people, like his old scientific friend Lord Cherwell (Frederick Lindemann) came into the government. There was the full share of deserving Conservatives. The still dapper Anthony Eden became Foreign Secretary again, and R.A.B. Butler was appointed Chancellor of the Exchequer. Some younger men, too, were included; Harold Macmillan was Minister of Housing, and Lord Home Secretary of State for Scotland.

Although it is now academically as fashionable to downplay the second Churchill ministry as it is to rate the Eisenhower presidency, of roughly the same period, as less than distinguished, both tenures, if anticlimactic in the careers of both men, were times of sunny stability and fruitful consolidation for their nations. Historians such as A. S. Rowse and Sir Alan Moorehead credit Churchill for presiding over one of the most felicitous administrations in British history.

The iron and steel industries were denationalized. Controls went out and most of rationing was lifted. The only somber note was the declining health of King George. Churchill went with the king to the airport to see his daughter, Princess Elizabeth, and her husband, Prince Philip, off on her African tour on a raw January morning in early 1952. As the plane carrying his daughter soared up, George broke precedent by suggesting that a bit of whiskey might be in order to ward off the chill.

Churchill readily agreed, saying, "When I was younger I made it a rule never to take a strong drink before lunch. It is now my rule never to do so before breakfast."

It was the last time Elizabeth would ever see her father. The king died in his sleep on February 6. Churchill paid tribute to the gallant king a day later on the BBC:

> The last few months of King George's life, with all the pain and physical stresses that he endured—his life hanging by a thread from day to day—and he all the time cheerful and undaunted— stricken in body but quite undisturbed and even unaffected in spirit—these have made a profound and an enduring impression and should be a help to all. He was sustained not only by his natural buoyancy but by the sincerity of his Christian faith. During these last months the king walked with death, as if death were a companion, an acquaintance, whom he recognized and did not fear. In the end death came as a friend; and after a happy day of sunshine and sport, and after "good night" to those who loved him best, he fell asleep as every man or woman who strives to fear God and nothing else in the world may hope to do.

Nineteen fifty-three emerged radiant and refulgent amid the splendid hopes of a coronation year. It was, in Churchill's life, the crest of an Indian summer of content made glorious by the Duke of York's daughter, Elizabeth. January witnessed another accession, that of his old friend Dwight Eisenhower, whom he journeyed to see for talks just before the Washington inauguration. In April, the young queen made her venerable prime minister Knight Companion. She announced the Knight of the Garter honor on April 23, the day of England's patron saint, George. The date was felicitously appropriate for the redoubtable champion who had slain dragons of his own in defense of his country. It was apt in another way. He was now the second Sir Winston Churchill, the first having been his ancestor of the seventeenth century, who served in Parliament, attended King Charles II, and fathered John, Duke of Marlborough.

The circle was closing for the seventy-eight-year-old parliamentarian who had begun his career in the reign of the last queen. On the date of coronation, June 2, a day filled with interspersed sun and rain, the new Sir Winston was the only one to ride from Buckingham Palace in an open carriage that circled round past the joyously waving crowds that lined and packed Hyde Park and other thoroughfares along the procession route to Westminster.

From his privileged place within the Abbey, Churchill, robed in the resplendent bemedaled purple befitting the Queen's First Lord of the Treasury, witnessed the solemn grandeur of the ancient crowning rite. For a moment the clock turned back to the colors and glories of the age of chivalry. The dour grayness of the immediate postwar years was suddenly effaced, just as the bright heritage of the American bicentennial would later burst, closing the dark decade of Vietnam behind it.

The coronation festivities closed with an address from the palace by the new queen, introduced by Her Majesty's first minister:

> The splendours of this second of June glow in our minds. Now as night falls, you will hear the voice of our sovereign, herself crowned in the Abbey and enthroned forever in our hearts. Here at the summit of our worldwide community is the lady whom we respect because she is our queen and whom we love because she is herself. Gracious and noble are words familiar to us all in courtly phrasing. Tonight they have a new ring, because we know they are true about the gleaming figure whom Providence has brought to us, and brought to us in times when the present is hard and the future veiled.

The words echo what he wrote of the first Queen Elizabeth. "She had a capacity for inspiring devotion that is perhaps unparalleled in British sovereigns. . . . It is not for nothing that she has come down to history as Good Queen Bess."

Perhaps it is not idle to suppose that when Sir Winston listened to the new monarch, he allowed himself a sigh of regret that he was not a young man embarking on a career to add to the luster of the reign of Queen Bess the Second.

The celebration following the coronation had hardly passed before Sir Winston was felled by a severe stroke. The prime minister, doubling as Foreign Secretary in the absence of Eden, who was recovering from abdominal surgery he had undergone in Boston, was in the midst of preparing for a Bermuda Conference with President Eisenhower and the French premier.

At a June 26 dinner at 10 Downing Street for Premier de Gasperi of Italy, where Sir Kenneth Clark, the art critic, was a guest, his wife Jane noted that the prime minister had slumped over in his seat. Churchill took her hand and said, "I want the hand of a friend. They put too much on me. Foreign affairs . . ." and then his voice faded. The Clarks immediately sought Sir Winston's daughter, Mary, and the ailing prime minister was put to bed. The next day an announcement was issued from 10 Downing Street that Sir Winston, on the advice of the doctors, was to rest for a month. What the country did not know was that doctors at first feared that the paralyzed Churchill would never talk, much less walk, again.

But the old warrior rallied. Nursed by his devoted Clementine, Churchill was, by July, seeing his key ministers at Chartwell and signing the necessary papers. At the end of the summer he went to the races as the guest of the queen, who then invited him to vacation with her at her Scottish castle in Balmoral.

In October he was notified of his winning the Nobel Prize for Literature, which would be awarded in Stockholm in December. The citation had described him as a Caesar who wielded Cicero's stylus.

I notice [he commented on the award] that the first Englishman to receive the Nobel Prize was Rudyard Kipling and that another equally rewarded was Mr. Bernard Shaw. I certainly cannot attempt to compete with either of those. I knew both quite well and my thought was much more in accord with Mr. Rudyard

Kipling than with Mr. Bernard Shaw. On the other hand, Mr. Rudyard Kipling never thought much of me, whereas Mr. Bernard Shaw often expressed himself in flattering terms.

Announcement of the prize seemed to swell the hints that he would resign as party leader. On the occasion of the annual Conservative Party Conference at Margate later that month, Churchill kept appearances to the minimum and husbanded his strength for his keynoting speech at this convention of party officials.

At the convention hall the old warrior, when introduced for the principal address, rose amid cheers from his place at the rostrum and walked with measured step to the podium. In a pace slow but unbroken in rhythm, he carefully set out the accomplishments of his government in mid-administration. For the government, he said he had no intention of calling an early election. For himself, he declared that he had no thought of resignation:

> If I stay, for the time being, bearing the burden at my age, it is not because of love for power or office. I have had an ample share of both. If I stay it is because I have the feeling that I may, through things that have happened, have an influence on what I care about above all else—the heralding of a sure and lasting peace.

At the end of his hour-long address the convention of Conservative dignitaries and party officials rose to their feet and roared their salute to this tour de force of stamina by their indomitable leader. For Churchill it was a sovereign display of will power over physical disability. His spirit was invincible, his resolution a triumph over age.

As Churchill entered his seventy-ninth year, he was an old man in a hurry. He could not afford to rest or tarry, as so little time availed for him to scale his last remaining peak, a "summit" conference. The one they had called a warmonger yearned to be the harbinger of peace. The death of Stalin the previous March offered a possible foothold. It was worth a try. He would strain every last ounce and bend every effort to make it. The Nobel Prize he coveted was the one for Peace.

But he would fail to convince his friend, President Eisenhower, of the wisdom of such a conference with Premier Malenkov, Stalin's successor. Eisenhower's doubts were fortified by his Secretary of State, John Foster Dulles. Churchill, who respected Dulles, described the obdurate American diplomat in a moment of exasperation as "the only bull who carries a china closet with him."

For Eisenhower, who in 1959 would meet Krushchev at Camp David, the clincher against such a conference with Premier Malenkov was the latter's insistence that the Red Chinese be included.

When Churchill returned from his Bermuda conference in January 1954, he was resigned to his fate that the future of a possible détente lay in other hands than his. His call for an "era of peaceful co-existence" had triggered the charge of appeasement from many former American admirers, but Churchill had not softened his hatred of tyranny, nor changed his convictions on how to deal with it. He still believed that strength was the key to peace and the requisite for negotiation.

To achieve that strength, he had urged the arming of Germany and had had Britain test its own atomic bomb. To Churchill, "the mutual terror of the bomb" on both sides of the curtain could lead to some modus vivendi. Although he supported the Korean action, he didn't think the West should drain itself by involvement in the developing Indochina crisis in the spring of 1954. Again Churchill was attacked for not favoring the extension of military aid to the French in Dienbienphu. Yet Eisenhower eventually sided with the Churchill posture, a posture that in hindsight grows increasingly prescient in the light of the bloody cost that was to be paid in the next decade.

For the prophet-statesman's eightieth birthday on November 30, there was an unprecedented celebration in the House of Commons, equaled only by that for Victoria's Jubilee. In Westminster's hall, around which the whirl of ten centuries of history had revolved, people of all parties assembled to pay tribute to the man who was the living embodiment of Parliament. The V-sign was tapped out in Morse code on a drum as Sir Winston and Lady Churchill entered from St. Stephen's entrance and descended the staircase to be seated between the Lord Chancellor and the Speaker of the House of Commons. Among the many gifts received by Churchill was the portrait of him by Graham Sutherland, which he admitted privately he did not like, and the royally monogrammed wine coasters from the queen, which he cherished.

Contrary to much speculation, the old man would not announce his retirement on the birthday occasion. His influence and prestige were still needed. In February 1955, he committed Britain to the development of an H-bomb, which he believed would lessen the possibility of war with the Soviets.

Despite his age, Churchill, perhaps more by memory than mental reflexes, could parry any of the sharp jabs at question time. With the droll geniality of a Dickensian Mr. Pickwick, he easily dispatched the thrusts of parliamentary picadors. One voluble member who became enmeshed in the complexity of his own interrogatory was advised: "Try one question at a time." When another persistent member proffered a series of questions with "Isn't it a fact . . ." Churchill brushed him aside, saying, "The honourable gentleman seems more desirous of imparting information than securing it."

But the old man's powers were ebbing. He had run his course, and he knew it. His final words to a questioner were on March 31: "I think the closer contacts between the United States and Europe the better." His last speech as prime minister had been three days earlier to present, as a former "lieutenant," a monument in honor of his old mentor and chief, David Lloyd George.

It now remained for him to pass the leadership to his lieutenant Anthony Eden, who in 1952 had taken in second marriage Churchill's niece Clarissa, daughter of his brother, John. As he said facetiously, "I must retire. Anthony won't live forever." On the night of April 4, the queen, in an unprecedented action, came to dinner at 10 Downing Street to toast her prime minister.

The crowds that gathered outside 10 Downing Street that night saw the venerable prime minister assist the young queen to her limousine. Then, with Churchill's deep bow of homage and Lady Churchill's graceful curtsy, the waving queen was driven off. For a moment, while Sir Winston, in white tie and with the blue Knight of the Garter sash, stood framed against the 10 Downing Street doorway, the onlookers were silent, as if reverently participating in a historic ceremony. Then they cheered. The next day he went to Buckingham Palace to resign.

Churchill repaired to Chartwell to do some painting and resume authorship of his *History of the English-Speaking Peoples,* which the Second World War had interrupted. The first two volumes of the four-volume series came out in 1956. (Clement Attlee thought the title should have been *Things in History Which Have Interested Me.*) Sir Winston still continued to represent his Woodford constituency in the House of Commons. An election in May 1955, following Eden's accession to the premiership, was a Conservative victory that bore witness to the successful policies of the postwar Churchill ministry; but the visits of Sir Winston to the House were becoming more infrequent, touched with more symbolism than substance.

There were other symbolic pilgrimages to make. In 1958, Churchill journeyed to France for a reunion, or perhaps even a reconciliation, with President Charles de Gaulle, who made him a Companion of the Liberation, the highest honor given to one of the Resistance movement. The next spring he would take his final trek to the U.S. capital. In Washington, President Eisenhower joined his White House guest in a visit to Walter Reed Hospital, where the two men made a poignant call on General George Marshall and John Foster Dulles, both of whom were shortly to die of cancer. From Walter Reed, the limousine sped to Andrews Air Force Base for the return to London. In halting tones, the old warrior, his eighty-five years now supported by a cane, delivered to his American well-wishers a "good-by to the land of my mother."

It was a time for farewells and the finishing of old business. In October at Woodford, Churchill would stand for the last time. Prime Minister Harold Macmillan, who succeeded Sir Anthony Eden after the Suez misadventure, had called for a general election. The crowd that gathered at the outside rally for his one campaign speech got a glimpse of a hunched-over, blanketed Churchill who was staring vacant-eyed from a platform chair. Many thought he could scarcely make it to the platform, much less speak from it.

Yet once the old campaigner was helped to his feet, his sense of theater took over and the old impishness lit up the sagging features.

"Among our socialist friends there is great confusion about private enterprise," he said, assembling each word carefully into place. Then, raising his arms as if aiming a rifle, he continued, "Some see it a predatory tiger to be shot. Others," he said, changing his hands to the pumping of a milker, "see it a cow to be milked." As the crowd cheered his antics, he went on, "Only a handful see it for what it really is—the strong and willing horse that pulls the whole cart along." It proved to be the final campaign speech of the old Tory, and it ended not with a whimper but with laughter.

Macmillan and the Conservatives won, but only rarely would Churchill now come to the Commons. When he did, it was an occasion. On one such visit in 1961, a Conservative member briefed Churchill on the speech in progress, but he got no response. A colleague said in a whisper to the young man, "He can't hear you; he's very deaf." Then, from ahead of him, the whisperer heard the familiar lisping drawl, "Yes, and they say the old man is gaga too!"

It was Churchill's attempt to counter rumors that he had become senile; but he could not deny the ravages of close to nine decades. The lapses of memory grew more frequent, and more painful to a man of eloquence was the stroke-inflicted difficulty of summoning up even the most common words of expression. He knew his only remaining public role was like a monarch's; he was a symbol embodying certain values: freedom and the courage to fight for it.

Sir Winston, on April 12, the sixteenth anniversary of Roosevelt's death, had come to America for a final look. The Onassis yacht, *Christina,* sailed past the Statue of Liberty into New York harbor. Joining Churchill on the yacht were U.S. Ambassador Adlai Stevenson and his old friend Bernard Baruch. While the evening dinner was in progress, a call from the White House came. Churchill, whose first conversation with a U.S. President was with William McKinley, would now speak with John Kennedy, who would later die much as McKinley had. Kennedy wanted Churchill to visit the White House, and proposed sending a special plane to bring him.

Because there was news that his beloved Clementine had become sick, the old man declined. He wanted to return immediately by plane to London. At the Pan American terminal of Kennedy Airport a crowd of three hundred cheered the arrival of Churchill. He looked around, slightly startled, his eyes in an unfocused daze and the few tufts of his white hair whipping in the wind. Then he lifted his hat. The simple gesture was completely Churchill, and the people behind the gate waved back their response.

On April 9, 1963, President John Kennedy would salute Churchill in a more tangible way when he proclaimed him the first honorary American citizen of the United States by Act of Congress. "By adding his name to the rolls," said the President, "we mean to honor him—but his acceptance honors us far more, for no statement nor proclamation can enrich his name now—the name of Sir Winston Churchill is already legend."

Churchill, in a letter generously accepting the honor, delivered his valedictory:

I reject the view that Britain and the Commonwealth should now be relegated to a tame and minor role in the world.

It was the parting roar of the old Empire lion.

Just before the adjournment of the House of Commons in 1964, Churchill made his last visit there, on July 27. He had lost weight and the pale sallowness of death was on him. Two fellow Members of Parliament helped him into the chamber and supported him when he made the customary bow of recognition to the Speaker. He smiled and nodded and took his place on the front bench. He had not come to speak but to say good-by. Harold Macmillan said what was in everyone's heart: "The life of the man we are today honouring is unique. The oldest can recall nothing to compare with it and the younger ones among you, however long you live, will never see the like again."

The next month, when he was hospitalized, Sir Winston was visited by General Eisenhower. The former president had been

touring in Europe, participating in various ceremonies commemo-
rating the twentieth anniversary of the D-day landing.

To some, the affection between the two men seemed
incongruous—the one a Kansas farmboy from a Mennonite-like
religious sect and the other a scion of the ducal house of Marlborough. Yet beneath their superficial contrasts there were many
similarities. Each had been schooled at a military academy. Then
both, as fathers, had suffered the heartbreaking loss of a child.
Dwight Doud, an infant, had died in 1921, about the same time as
Churchill's three-year-old Marigold.

For both, the thirties had been years in the wilderness—Churchill
out of office in Chartwell, and Eisenhower a restive lieutenant colonel serving under the autocratic MacArthur in the Philippines.
With the war, both surged into worldwide fame. Afterward each
was called back to lead his nation in the 1950s.

Eisenhower entered the Churchill suite at Saint George's Hospital. There, propped up in the bed, was an enfeebled, dying Churchill. The flaccid features of his face showed little response except
for the glimmer when their eyes met. The recognition prompted his
only movement. The right hand, in almost a cherubic gesture,
reached to the bedside table next to him. His old comrade advanced
to the table and clapsed the frail pink hand in his own. For three,
five, then eight minutes, there were no words spoken, just two
friends, holding hands in mute eloquence.

No words could have better expressed the bond of the English-
speaking peoples than the clasp between these two men who were
among the most gallant heroes their respective nations had ever
summoned for service. Churchill unclapsed his tiny hand and waved
good-by in a V-sign. Fewer spoken farewells have ever been more
ineffably sublime.

By his ninetieth birthday on November 30, he was back at Hyde
Park Gate. To accommodate the crowd of well-wishers he appeared
briefly at the window. Greetings had come to him from kings,
queens, presidents, prime ministers, and simple people from all
over the globe. One that reached him was addressed only to "The
Greatest Man Alive in the World."

The close was gentle. As he himself had written some thirty years earlier about the last days of John Churchill, first Duke of Marlborough:

> The span of a mortal is short, the end universal; and the twinge of melancholy which accompanies decline and retirement is in itself an anodyne. It is foolish to waste lamentations upon the closing phase of human life. Noble spirits yield themselves willingly to the successively falling shades which carry them to a better world or to oblivion.

On Saturday evening, January 9, 1965, an ailing Sir Winston declined his nightly ritual of cigars and brandy. He said to his family, "The grand journey has been well worth making—once." The sleep that evening turned into a coma from which he never awoke. Nine days later, a London *Times* editorial commented on the effect of his latest stroke, "Life is clearly ebbing away, but how long it will be until the crossing of the bar it is impossible to say."

The *Times* was wrong. One knew, and that was Churchill. Long ago he had predicted to Jock Colville, his wartime secretary, that he would die on January 24, the same day his father Lord Randolph had died. Randolph had died around eight in the morning, and shortly after eight o'clock on Sunday morning, January 24, 1965—exactly seventy years after his father's death—Sir Winston Churchill ceased to breathe.

The old soldier who, in the previous century, had narrowly escaped being killed on three different continents, had died in his own bed. The one who had barely survived the last cavalry charge had lived to supervise Britain's coming into the atomic age. The span of he whose parliamentary career overlapped the years of Queen Victoria and Lyndon Johnson was over. The greatest of British statesmen, who played a paramount role in not one, but two world wars, now belonged to the ages.

The final tribute to him was not so much a funeral as it was a festival celebrating the greatness of one man's humanity. Like the noble-domed St. Paul's where the service was held, the attendance of leaders of nations from across the globe was recognition of the soaring heights the human spirit can reach in its fullest flowering. The presidents and princes were not bowed in grief, but stood straight in proud salute to the memory of a man.

For to the rites of Churchill no burden of sorrow was carried. If men wept, it was for the passing of an age where one man by himself could fire the free world.

The most eloquent expression of pride came from the London dockside by the Thames on which Churchill was borne to his final resting place in the country churchyard at Bladen, beside his mother and father. More poignant than the words of tribute or the refrains of anthems like his favorite, the American "Battle Hymn of the Republic," more moving than the muffled beat of black-draped drums in procession on the street or the winged flight of old RAF pilots in the sky, was the dipping of the boat cranes as the barge bearing Churchill's body slipped past.

In their own simple and spontaneous way, the London workers were expressing what the other titan of their language had written in the first Elizabethan age, "Whence shall come another."

Appendix I

WIT AND WISDOM

In the profession of politics the voluminous record of Winston Churchill's speeches from 1897 to 1963 is unsurpassed by that of any statesman in history. Indeed few, if any, writers could match his mountainous productivity as a historian, not to mention his contributions as a journalist.

The titanic output of his work is staggering to those editors and anthologists who try to select for readers the choicest of his wit and wisdom. Among writers in the English language, perhaps only Shakespeare offers more quotable lines. The axioms of political conduct Churchill framed, the historical judgments he rendered, and his insights into human fame and folly deserve more than cursory reading. There are more gems to be gleaned in the writings and speeches of Churchill than in the sayings of Mao or the observations of Machiavelli.

Saints and Sinners

Anne, Queen of England
She moved on broad, homely lines. . . . She was not very wise nor clever but she was very like England.

Clement Atlee, Labourite Prime Minister
He is a modest man with much to be modest about.

Stanley Baldwin, Conservative Prime Minister
Occasionally he stumbled over the truth but hastily picked himself up as if nothing had happened.

263

Lord Beaverbrook,
Press Magnate and War-Time Cabinet Minister
  He is a foul-weather friend.

Aneurin Bevan, Labourite politician
(The flamboyant Welsh left-winger was Churchill's most vicious foe.)
  He is a merchant of discourtesy.

Joseph Chamberlain, British Statesman
(Chamberlain was, at the turn of the century, a high tariff imperialist. He was the uncle of Neville Chamberlain.)
  Joe Chamberlain loves the working man. He loves to see him work.

Neville Chamberlain, Conservative British Prime Minister
(Chamberlain negotiated the infamous Munich Settlement)
  He has a lust for peace.

· · ·

  An old town clerk looking at European affairs through the wrong end of a municipal drainpipe.

Sir Stafford Cripps, Labourite Chancellor of the Exchequer
(The Socialist Cripps was a Calvinist with strict vegetarian and teetotaling habits.)
  He has all the virtues I dislike and none of the vices I admire.

· · ·

  There but for the Grace of God goes God.

· · ·

  His chest is a cage in which two squirrels are at war, his conscience and his career.

Charles de Gaulle, President of France
  We have all our crosses to bear. Mine is the Cross of Lorraine.

· · ·

  He looks like a female llama who has just been surprised in her bath.

John Foster Dulles, U.S. Secretary of State
He is the only bull I know who carries his china closet with him.

Farouk, King of Egypt
King Farouk was wallowing like a sow in a trough of luxury.

Sir Cedric Hardwicke, British actor
You are my fifth favourite actor. The first four are the Marx brothers.

Adolf Hitler
Into that void strode a maniac of ferocious genius, of the most virulent hatred that has ever corroded the human breast . . . Corporal Hitler.

. . .

This wicked man, the repository and embodiment of many forms of soul-destroying hatred, this monstrous product of former wrongs and shames . . .

Harry Hopkins, F.D.R.'s aide and trouble-shooter
I dub you "Lord Root of the Matter."

Thomas "Stonewall" Jackson, Confederate General
Jackson came of Ulster stock, and settled in Virginia. His character was stern, his manner reserved and usually forbidding, his temper Calvinistic, his mode of life strict, frugal, austere. He might have stepped into American history from the command of one of Cromwell's regiments.

John, King of England
When the long tally is added, it will be seen that the British nation and the English-speaking world owe far more to the vices of John than to the labours of virtuous sovereigns; for it was through the union of many forces against him that the most famous milestone [Magna Charta] of our rights and freedom was in fact set up.

Lawrence of Arabia
. . . a man, solitary, austere, to whom existence is not more than a duty, yet a duty to be faithfully discharged. He was indeed a dweller upon the mountaintops where the air is crisp and rarefied and where the view commands all the Kingdoms of the world and the glory of them . . . He was not in complete harmony with the normal.

Lenin
Lenin was sent into Russia by the Germans in the same way you might send a phial containing a culture of typhoid or cholera to be poured into the water supply of a great city, and it worked with amazing accuracy.

Louis XIV, King of France
Better the barbarian conquerors of antiquity, primordial figures of the abyss, than this high-heeled, beperiwigged dandy, strutting amid the bows and scrapes of mistresses and confessors to the torment of his age. Petty and mediocre in all except his lusts and power, the Sun King disturbed and harried mankind during more than fifty years of arrogant pomp.

Ramsay MacDonald, Labourite British Prime Minister
He is a sheep in sheep's clothing.

. . .

He has the gift of compressing the largest amount of words into the smallest amount of thought.

Vyacheslav Molotov, Soviet Diplomat
I have never seen a human being who more perfectly represented the modern conception of a robot.

Viscount Bernard Montgomery ("Monty"), British General
Indomitable in retreat, invincible in advance, insufferable in victory.

Richard the Lion-hearted, King of England

His life was one magnificent parade, which, when ended, left only an empty plain.

Franklin D. Roosevelt

Meeting him was like opening your first bottle of champagne.

George Bernard Shaw, Irish playwright

Few people practice what they preach and no one less than Mr. Bernard Shaw. . . . His dissolvent theories of life and society have been sturdily banished from his personal conduct and his home. No one has ever led a more respectable life or been a stronger seceder from his own subversive imagination. He derides the marriage vows and even at times the sentiment of love itself; yet no one is more happily or wisely married. He indulges in all the liberties of an irresponsible chatterbox, babbling gloriously from dawn to dusk and at the same time advocates the abolition of parliamentary institutions and the setting up of an Iron Dictatorship, of which he would probably be the first victim.

George Washington

Lord Cornwallis once observed after Yorktown that the military fame of George Washington would rest not on the Chesapeake but on the Delaware. It was that marvelous bitter nerve-racking campaign that revealed the fortitude and constancy of the American leader. . . .

. . .

Is not the courage and civic fidelity which Washington showed in every situation heeded as much today in the anxieties of modern times as it was ever in the fires of bygone wars?

Maxims and Mottoes

Anxiety

Worry is a spasm of the imagination. The mind seizes hold of something and simply cannot let it go.

Boredom
Broadly speaking, human beings may be divided into three classes: those who are billed to death; those who are worried to death; and those who are bored to death.

Conservatism
We must beware of needless innovations, especially when guided by logic.

Courage
Courage is the first of human qualities because it is the quality which guarantees all others.

Democracy
Where there is a great deal of free speech, there is always a certain amount of foolish speech.

. . .

Democracy is no harlot to be picked up in the street by a man with a tommy-gun.

. . .

Democracy is the worst form of government except for all those other forms that have been tried from time to time.

Expediency
There are two kinds of success: initial and ultimate.

Facts
You must look at the facts because they look at you.

Fanatic
A fanatic is one who can't change his mind and won't change the subject.

Future
It is a mistake to look too far ahead. Only one link in the chain of destiny can be handled at a time.

History

The farther backward you can look, the farther forward you can see.

. . .

We cannot say "the past is past" without surrendering the future.

Institutions

We shape our buildings; thereafter they shape us.

Justice

One ought to be just before one is generous.

Legends

There are a terrible lot of lies going about the world, and the worst of it is half of them are true.

Order

I decline utterly to be impartial as between the Fire Brigade and the Fire.

Perfection

The maxim—Nothing avails but perfection—spells paralysis.

Prophet

A hopeful disposition is not the sole qualification to be a prophet.

Responsibility

The price of greatness is responsibility.

Survival

It is no use saying, "We are doing our best." You have got to succeed in doing what is necessary.

Wisdom

All great things are simple, and many can be expressed in a single word: freedom; justice; honour; duty; mercy; hope.

. . .

All wisdom is not new wisdom.

War and Peace

Allies

There is only one thing worse than fighting with allies and that is fighting without them.

Ambassadors

The reason for having diplomatic relations is not to confer a compliment, but to secure a convenience.

Appeasement

It is no use leading the other nations up the garden path and then running away when the dog growls.

. . .

The belief that security can be obtained by throwing a small state to the wolves is a fatal delusion.

. . .

An appeaser is one who feeds a crocodile hoping it will eat him last.

China

The tail of China is large and will not be wagged.

Communism

It is better to have a world united than a world divided; but it is also better to have a world divided than a world destroyed.

Defense

I do not hold that we should rearm to fight. I hold that we should rearm to parley.

Dictatorships

Dictators ride to and fro upon tigers from which they dare not dismount.

. . .

The world is divided into peoples that own the government and governments that own the peoples.

Disarmament
False ideas have been spread about the country that disarmament means peace.

Foreign Policy
A nation without a conscience is a nation without a soul. A nation without a soul is a nation that cannot live.

. . .

Moral force is unhappily no substitute for armed force, but it is a very great reinforcement.

Pacifists
I have always been against the pacifists during the quarrel, and against the Jingoists at its close.

Realpolitik
The only real sure guide to the actions of mighty nations and powerful governments is a correct estimate of what they are and what they consider to be their own interests.

Soviet Union
I do not believe that Soviet Russia desires war. What they want are the fruits of war and the indefinite expansion of their power and doctrine.

. . .

From what I have seen of our Soviet friends and allies during the war, I am convinced that there is nothing they admire more than strength and nothing for which they have less respect than weakness, particularly military weakness.

. . .

Trying to maintain good relations with a Communist is like wooing a crocodile. You do not know whether to tickle it under the chin or beat it over the head. When it opens its mouth, you cannot tell whether it is trying to smile or preparing to eat you up.

. . .

I cannot forecast to you the action of Russia. It is a riddle wrapped in a mystery inside an enigma; but perhaps there is a key. That key is Russia's national interest.

United Nations
The U.N. was set up not to get us to Heaven but only to save us from Hell.

Capitalism and Socialism

Budget
In finance everything that is agreeable is unsound, and everything that is sound is disagreeable.

. . .

Expenditure always is popular; the only unpopular part about it is the raising of the money to raise the expenditure.

Bureaucracy
There is no surer method of economizing and saving money than in the reduction of the number of officials.

. . .

Bureaucratic management cannot compare in efficiency with that of well-organized private firms. The bureaucrats suffer no penalties for wrong judgment; so long as they attend their offices punctually and do their work honestly they are completely disinterested in the correctness of their judgment.

Deficit Spending
All social reform which is not founded upon a stable medium of internal exchange becomes a swindle and a fraud.

Free Enterprise
If you destroy a free market, you create a black market.

. . .

The production of new wealth must precede common wealth; otherwise there will only be common poverty.

Planners
Those whose minds are attracted or compelled to rigid and symmetrical systems of government should remember that logic, like

science, must be servant and not the master of man. Human beings and human societies are not structures that are built or machines that are forged. They are plants that grow and must be treated as such.

Profit Motive

It is a socialist idea that making a profit is a vice; I consider the real vice is making a loss.

Socialism

We must beware of trying to build a society in which nobody counts for anything except a politician or an official, a society where enterprise gains no reward and thrift no privileges.

. . .

The inherent vice of Capitalism is the unequal sharing of blessings; the inherent virtue of Socialism is the equal sharing of miseries.

. . .

You may try to destroy wealth and find that all you have done is to increase poverty.

. . .

Socialism is the philosophy of failure, the creed of ignorance, and the gospel of envy.

. . .

"All men are created equal," says the American Declaration of Independence. "All men shall be kept equal," says the British Socialist Party.

Taxation

The idea that a nation can tax itself into prosperity is one of the crudest delusions which has ever befuddled the human mind.

Politics and Public Service

Campaigning

A candidate is asked to stand, he wants to sit, and he is expected to lie.

. . .

Politics are almost as exciting as war, and quite as dangerous. In war, you can only be killed once, but in politics, many times.

Criticism
Eating words has never given me indigestion.

. . .

I am always ready to learn, although I do not always like being taught.

. . .

It would be a great reform in politics if wisdom could be made to spread as easily and as rapidly as folly.

Defeat
Although always prepared for martyrdom, I prefer that it shall be postponed.

Expediency
Nothing is more dangerous in wartime than to live in the temperamental atmosphere of a Gallup Poll, always feeling one's pulse and taking one's temperature.

. . .

It always looks so easy to solve problems by taking the line of least resistance. What looks like the easy road turns out to be the hardest and most cruel.

Legislature
The congestion of Parliament is a disease, but the futility of Parliament is a mortal disease.

Opponent
I like a man who grins when he fights.

Pragmatism
The high belief in the perfection of man is appropriate in a man of the cloth, but not in a prime minister.

Problems

In critical and baffling situations, it is always best to recur to first principles and simple action.

. . .

In my experience of large enterprises I have found it is often a mistake to try to settle everything at once.

Qualifications

The main qualification for political office is the ability to fore-tell what is going to happen tomorrow, next week, next month, and next year—And to have the ability afterwards to explain why it didn't happen.

Statesmanship

People who are not prepared to do unpopular things and defy clamour áre not fit to be ministers in times of stress.

. . .

We shall not escape our dangers by recoiling from them.

Books and Learning

History

A good knowledge of history is a quiver full of arrows in debate.

Reading

There is a great deal of difference between the tired man who wants a book to read and the alert man who wants to read a book.

University

He who has received a university training possesses a rich choice. He need never be inactive or bored, there is no reason for him to seek refuge in the clack and clatter of our modern life. He need not be dependent on the headlines which give him something new every day. He has the wisdom of all time to drink from, to enjoy as long as he lives.

. . .

Take full advantage of the years when wisdom of the world is placed at your disposal, but do not spend too much time in buckling on your armour in the tent. The battle is going on in every walk and sphere of life.

. . .

Young people study at universities to achieve knowledge and not to learn a trade. We must all learn how to support ourselves, but we must also learn how to live. We need a lot of engineers in the world, but we do not want a world of engineers.

Writing

Writing a book is an adventure: to begin with it is a toy and an amusement, and then it becomes a mistress, and then it becomes a master, and then it becomes a tyrant, and the last phase is that just as you are about to be reconciled to your servitude, you kill the monster and fling him about to the public.

Pleasures and Pastimes

Alcohol

All I can say is that I have taken more out of alcohol than alcohol has taken out of me.

Brandy

Good cognac is like a woman. Do not assault it. Coddle and warm it in your hands before you gently sip it.

Champagne

A single glass of champagne imparts a feeling of exhilaration. The nerves are braced; the imagination is agreeably stirred; the wits become more nimble. A bottle produces a contrary effect.

Cheese

Stilton and port are like a man and wife. They should never be separated. Whom God has joined together, let no man put asunder. No, nor woman either.

Dinner

My idea of a good dinner is, first have good food, then discuss good food, and after this good food has been elaborately discussed, to discuss a good topic with myself as chief conversationalist.

Enjoyment

If this is a world of vice and woe, I'll take the vice and you can have the woe.

Exercise

I get my exercise being a pall-bearer for those of my friends who believed in regular running and calisthenics.

Flying

The air is an extremely dangerous mistress. Once under the spell most lovers are faithful to the end, which is not always old age.

Golf

Golf is like chasing a quinine pill around a cow pasture.

Luxuries

We shall forego our luxuries—but not our pleasures.

Nap

A man should sleep sometime between lunch and dinner in order to be at his best in the evening when he joins his wife and friends at dinner. My wife and I tried two or three times in the last few years to have breakfast together, but it was so disagreeable we had to stop.

Painting

When I get to heaven, I mean to spend a considerable portion of my five million years in painting, and so get to the bottom of my subject. But then I shall require a still gayer palette than I get here below. . . . There will be a whole range of wonderful new colours which will delight the celestial eye.

. . .

I prefer landscapes. A tree doesn't complain that I haven't done it justice.

Tastes
My tastes are simple; I am easily satisfied with the best.

Tobacco
Tobacco is bad for love; but old age is worse.

But consider! How can I tell my temper would have been as sweet or my companionship as agreeable if I had abjured from my youth the goddess Nicotine.

Whiskey
When I was a young officer in the African campaign, the water was not fit to drink. To make it palatable, we had to add whiskey. By diligent effort, I learned to like it.

Life and Death

Children
You must have four children. One for Mother, one for Father, one for Accident, one for Increase.

Family
Where does the family start? It starts with a young man falling in love with a girl. No superior alternative has yet to be found.

Life
(When Sarah Churchill told her father she was resolved to marry the comedian Vic Oliver, Churchill imparted this advice.)

Do what you like, but—remember—like what you do.

Middle Age

We are happier in many ways when we are old than when we are young. The young sow wild oats. The old grow sage.

Old Age

It is foolish to waste lamentations upon the closing phase of human life. Noble spirits lead themselves willingly to the successive falling shades which carry them to a better world or to oblivion.

Valedictory

What is the use of living, if it be not to strive for nobler causes and to make this muddled world a better place for those who will live in it after we are gone?

Last recorded words of Sir Winston Churchill

The grand journey has been well worth making—once.

Appendix II

ESCAPADES
AND ENCOUNTERS

In a sense, it is misleading to recount many of the delicious anecdotes about Winston Churchill. They could serve to distract from the greatness of his accomplishments. Churchill is more than a lovable character. For character can slip into caricature. The result may be a distorted emphasis on the bibulous Churchill, which is as wrong as seeing Benjamin Franklin only as an amiable lecher. Perhaps if Abraham Lincoln had not been martyred, the impression of him as a teller of earthy stories would be dominant.

But as Lincoln proved, the knack of taking one's cause but not oneself seriously is surely a trait of leadership sorely missed in the Presidents of today. The humorless politician may smack of the pompous prig or ideological fanatic. Such personalities are, in the long run, ill-suited to the compromise and tolerant give and take of democratic life. The lusty and even ribald wit of a Churchill is an antidote to the cant and inflated promises of political rhetoric.

The stories, even if not all of them can be documented, reveal the colossal richness of the Churchill personality. Perhaps a few of the stories that follow are apocryphal or altered slightly to heighten a point, but they would be difficult to pinpoint. Many of them, which cannot be authoritatively supported, were told me by members or friends of the Churchill family. But the humorous accounts of his encounters with the great and not-so-great are more than just insights into the Churchill character. Many of them touch on the human condition in general, such as the vices of hypocrisy and arrogance or the vicissitudes of old age and in-law problems.

Another Man's Poison

At a weekend party given by the Duke of Marlborough at Blenheim Palace, Churchill found himself seated next to Lady Astor. The beautiful American-born Nancy had been angered at some of Churchill's savage attacks on the Baldwin government and had fought him in House of Commons debates.

When coffee was served, the acid-tongued Nancy said,

"Winston, If I were your wife, I'd put poison in your coffee."

"Nancy," Churchill replied to the acid-tongued lady member of Parliament, "If I were your husband, I'd drink it."

Bare Facts

During Churchill's first visit to the White House, the British prime minister was surprised one morning by an unexpected visit by President Roosevelt to his bedroom. F.D.R., propelling himself in his wheelchair, found his guest stark naked and gleaming pink from his bath. Faced with this vision the American president put his chair into reverse. But Churchill stopped him, saying,

"Pray enter. His Majesty's First Minister has nothing to hide from the President of the United States."

Birds of a Feather

When Churchill returned to 10 Downing Street in 1951, he soon scheduled a trip to inspect the N.A.T.O. defenses. On his way by plane to meet the head of Cypress, Archbishop Makarios, he asked his Defense Minister, Harold Macmillan, what kind of man the Archbishop was.

"Is he one of those priestly ascetics concerned only with spiritual grace or one of those crafty prelates concerned rather with temporal gain?"

"Regrettably," replied Macmillan, "the Archbishop seems to be one of the latter."

"Good," replied Churchill, rubbing his hands. "He is one of our kind, and we can work together."

Brush-Off

After his escape from capture in the Boer War, Churchill made plans to stand for Parliament. To make himself look older he grew a moustache. A friend of his mother's was not, however, enthusiastic.

"Winston," she scolded when she encountered him at a dinner party, "I approve of neither your politics nor your moustache."

"Madam," replied Winston, "You are not likely to come in contact with either."

Cheap and Nasty

When the first destroyers arrived in the fall of 1940 under America's Lend-Lease Program to Great Britain, Prime Minister Churchill went to inspect them. He was joined by F.D.R.'s right-hand man, Harry Hopkins. Churchill, looking at the decidedly over-aged ships, grumbled in a whisper, "Cheap and nasty." Hopkins, who was startled by the remark, queried, "What was that?" Churchill amended aloud, "Cheap for us and nasty for the Germans."

Dead Birds

While sitting on a platform waiting to speak, the seventy-eight-year-old Churchill was handed a note by an aide. Churchill glanced at the message, which advised: "Prime Minister—your fly is unbuttoned."

Churchill then scrawled beneath it, "Never fear. Dead birds do not drop out of nests."

Equal Time

In May 1955, a debate was conducted over the BBC entitled "Christianity vs. Atheism." Churchill objected to the programming. The BBC spokesman responded.

"It is our duty to truth to allow both sides to debate."

Churchill shot back. "I suppose then that if there had been the same devices at the time of Christ, the BBC would have given equal time to Judas and Jesus."

To Err Is Human

During the wartime coalition, the President of the Board of Trade was the austere Calvinist, Sir Stafford Cripps. Cripps both tithed and teetotaled. He was even a vegetarian. His only concession to pleasure was smoking cigars.

This habit too he swore off during the war, when he announced at a rally that he was now giving up cigars as a "salutary example of sacrifice."

Prime Minister Churchill, who was seated on the same platform, leaned over to a colleague and whispered—"Too bad—it was his last contact with humanity."

Flying High

In the 1930s, a Liberal party statesman spoke at a London dinner on the League of Nations. The speaker soared to rhetorical heights as he depicted the day when there would be no war amid an era of international brotherhood. Afterward, a listener asked Churchill who attended the dinner what he thought of it.

"Well," he commented. "It was good. It had to be good, for it contained all the platitudes known to man with the possible exception of 'Prepare to meet thy God' and 'Please adjust your trousers before leaving.'"

High Spirits

In 1941, Prime Minister Winston Churchill visited General Montgomery at the front. After a morning session of inspecting the troops, the Prime Minister offered a nip of whiskey.

Monty refused, pounding his chest with the boast, "I neither drink nor smoke and I'm 100 percent fit."

Churchill put down his cigar and lifted his glass, replying, "I both drink and smoke and I'm 200 percent fit."

"Johnny Bull" Reb

Churchill was once visiting in Virginia when he was asked what it felt like to be in a city that played such a great role in the Revolutionary War against the English.

"Revolution against the English! Nay, it was a reaffirmation of English rights. Englishmen battling a Hun king and his Hessian hirelings to protect their English birthright. Such a struggle against a German despot is a scene not unfamiliar to English-speaking peoples who twice this century have triumphed over Teutonic tyranny."

Morning After

One night in the House of Commons, Churchill, after imbibing a few drinks, stumbled into Bessie Braddock, a corpulent Labourite Member from Liverpool. An angry Bessie, straightened her clothes and addressed the British statesman.

"Sir Winston," she roared. "You are drunk, and what's more, you are disgustingly drunk."

Churchill, surveying the obese Bessie, replied, "And might I say, Mrs. Braddock, you are ugly and what's more disgustingly ugly. "But tomorrow," Churchill added, "I shall be sober."

The Mouse That Roared

One weekend, while Churchill was resting at Chequers, the official country home of the British prime minister, the minister found Churchill retouching with his brush and oils Rubens's masterpiece of the ensnared lion being rescued by a mouse.

Like a naughty boy caught in the act, Churchill looked sheepish. Then he muttered in defense,

"Poor little mouse! If he were to gnaw the ropes and rescue the lion, he had to be made bigger."

No Ifs, Ands, or "Butts"

After the deliverance at Dunkirk, Churchill rallied Britain with his most memorable speech.

"We shall fight on the beaches, we shall fight on the landing grounds, we shall fight in the fields and in the streets, we shall fight in the hills. We shall never surrender."

Then, as the House of Commons thundered with cheers at this stirring rhetoric, Churchill muttered in a whispered aside to a colleague.

"And we'll fight them with the butt ends of broken beer bottles because that's bloody well all we've got!"

No Rush Job

In early 1945, President Roosevelt wrote to Churchill about the agenda for the six-day conference of the Big Powers at Yalta. F.D.R. saw there was no reason why the plans for establishing the U.N. could not be completed in the conference session.

Churchill was doubtful.

"I don't see any way of realizing our hopes for a World Organization in six days," he wrote F.D.R. "Even the Almighty took seven."

Nothing at Stake

At the Casablanca Conference in 1942, Churchill and Roosevelt met with Charles de Gaulle, the prickly leader of the French Resistance.

Brendan Bracken, who was in charge of Churchill's arrangements at the hectic three-day meeting, at one point vented his frustrations at his boss.

Churchill replied, "Well, Brendan, you have only one cross to bear. I have a double cross—the double cross of Lorraine."

"The General's problem," sympathized Bracken, "is that he thinks he is the reincarnation of Joan of Arc."

"No, the problem is," concluded Churchill, "*my* bishops won't burn him."

Not Hung-up Over It

Once Churchill was sitting in an outside platform waiting to speak to crowds who had packed the streets to hear him. Beside him the chairlady of the proceedings leaned over and said:

"Doesn't it thrill you, Mr. Churchill, to see all those people out there who came just to see you?"

Churchill replied, "It is quite flattering, but whenever I feel this way I always remember that if instead of making a political speech I was being hanged, the crowd would be twice as big."

One at a Time

During the wartime coalition, Churchill assigned to some Labourites a few of the more ceremonial but less meaningful ministries. One of these plums was given to Lord Privy Seal, whose responsibilities included the supervision of state papers. A particular document needed the signature of the prime minister, and the Lord Privy Seal dispatched his young aide to track down Churchill.

Churchill was finally traced to the House of Commons lavatory, where clouds of billowing cigar smoke behind a stall door signalled his presence.

"Mr. Prime Minister," the aide said, rapping on the door, "the Lord Privy Seal requests your signature at once on a document important to the Crown."

Churchill, annoyed at being pestered by a man he thought he had carefully shelved, bellowed,

"Tell the Lord Privy Seal that I am sealed in my 'privy'." Then he added, "And I can only deal with one shit at a time."

Overshadowed

Churchill did not get along with Lord Reith, the dour head of the BBC. Reith's gloomy presence was enhanced by his towering six-foot-four frame. Once, when the huge dark-visaged Scot was seated next to the prime minister, Churchill grumbled,

"Who will rescue me from this 'Wuthering Height'?"

Paper Thin

After a cross-country tour of the United States in the 1930s, Churchill was questioned in a Canadian press interview.

"Mr. Churchill," a Canadian reporter asked, "Do you have any criticism of America?"

Churchill thought and then replied, "There are only two things I dislike about America. Its toilet paper is too thin and its news-papers too fat."

Prepositional Nitpicking

A priggish civil servant had corrected and returned a Churchill memorandum pointing out that the prime minister had mistakenly ended a sentence with a preposition.

Back it went to the officious bureaucrat, with this Churchill note appended in the margin.

"This is the sort of pedantic nonsense up with which I will not put."

Prime Time

When Winston Churchill returned to 10 Downing Street for the second time in 1951, there was some criticism about his advanced age. A year later a reporter cornered the seventy-eight-year-old prime minister and asked him if he was going to make his announcement to retire soon.

Churchill growled, "Not until I'm a great deal worse and the Empire a great deal better."

Prince Consort

At a formal banquet in London, the attending dignitaries were asked the question "If you could not be who you are, who would you like to be?" Naturally everyone was curious as to what Churchill, who was seated next to his beloved Clemmie, would say. After all, Churchill couldn't be expected to say Julius Caesar or Napoleon. When it finally came Churchill's turn, the old man, who was the dinner's last respondent to the question, rose and gave his answer.

"If I could not be who I am, I would most like to be"—and here he paused to take his wife's hand—"Lady Churchill's second husband."

Private Enterprise

Once a British parliamentarian was droning on about the accomplishments of socialism. As an example, he cited the increase in general population under the previous three years of the Labourites' administration. Churchill's ears pricked up as he heard the figure and rose to ask the speaker a question.

"Wouldn't the honourable gentleman concede that the last statistic about population is due to private enterprise?"

Rain Check

George Bernard Shaw wired Churchill in 1931. "Am reserving two tickets for you on opening night of my new play. Come bring a friend—if you have one."

Churchill composed the return telegram.

"Impossible for me to attend first performance. Would like to attend second night—if there is one."

Reciprocal Trade

During a visit by Churchill to Richmond, a memorial sculpture to the wartime prime minister was dedicated. A southern lady of Rubenesque proportions gushed to Churchill when she met him in a receiving line.

"Mr. Churchill, I want you to know I got up at dawn and drove a hundred miles for the unveiling of your bust."

"Madam," replied Churchill, gazing at her amply endowed figure, "I want you to know that I would happily reciprocate the honor."

Red "Paleface"

Mrs. Ogden Reid of *The New York Herald Tribune* once attacked Churchill for his colonialist views on India.

"The Indians," she charged, "have suffered years under British oppression."

Churchill replied:

"Before we proceed further, let us get one thing clear. Are we talking about the brown Indians in India who have multiplied alarmingly under benevolent British rule, or are we speaking about the Red Indians in America who, I understand, are now extinct."

Rendezvous with Destiny

On his seventy-fifth birthday, a reporter encountered Churchill as he left his London Hyde Park residence.

"Mr. Churchill, do you have any fear of death?"

"I am ready to meet my Maker," Churchill replied, and then he added with a twinkle, "But whether my Maker is prepared for the great ordeal of meeting me is another matter."

Super Service

Late in his life, Sir Winston took a cruise on an Italian ship. A journalist from a Rome newspaper encountered the former prime minister to ask him why he chose to travel on an Italian line when the stately Queen's line under the British flag was available.

Churchill gave the question his consideration and then gravely replied.

"There are three things I like about Italian ships. First, their cuisine, which is unsurpassed. Second, their service which is quite superb." And then Sir Winston added, "And then there is none of this nonsense about women and children first."

Taking the In-Law into Your Own Hands

Sarah Churchill, Churchill's oldest daughter, married Vic Oliver, a music-hall comedian. At a family dinner at Chartwell, Oliver, who brought along a guest, tried to draw out his famous father-in-law from one of his periodic silent moods.

"Winston, who, in your opinion, was the greatest statesman you have ever known?"

"Benito Mussolini" was the unexpected reply.

"What? Why is that?" said a surprised Oliver.

"Mussolini is the only statesman," grumbled Churchill, "who had the requisite courage to have his own son-in-law executed."

(Count Ciano, the former Italian Foreign Secretary who married Mussolini's daughter, was shot in 1942.)

Teetotaling Ships

As First Lord of the Admiralty in the First World War, Churchill reportedly was asked by a temperance group to reconsider the Royal Navy's practice of christening ships by breaking a bottle of champagne across its bow.

"But Madam," replied Churchill, "the hallowed custom of the Royal Navy is indeed a splendid example of temperance. The ship takes its first sip of wine and then proceeds on water ever after."

White Meat

At a New York reception in Churchill's honor, cold fried chicken was served along with champagne. Churchill asked for a breast, whereupon his hostess, a lady of Victorian sensibilities, gently chided him.

"We say instead the term 'white meat'."

The next day, a corsage arrived at the lady's home. Attached to it was a card—"Winston Churchill, p.m." On the other side he had scrawled a note.

"I would be most obliged if you would pin this on your 'white meat'."

Appendix III

BARBS AND BLASTS

To catch the full flavor of Churchill's repartee, one must picture the scene of the House of Commons. The distance between the Government and the Opposition Party benches is the combined reach of two outstretched swords, to literally keep them from being at sword's points. Churchill himself said that "the object of Parliament is to substitute argument for fisticuffs." The formal language of Parliament, restricting remarks to the third person, is also a procedure to keep attacks from becoming too personal. Yet the frequent and heated exchange between members is characteristic of the Commons, and offers a healthy a lusty contrast to the "canned" speeches of our Congress.

It is important to remember, however, that Churchill was not always skilled at parliamentary repartee. Though he habitually bubbled with wit at the dinner table, he would freeze up on the parliamentary benches, at least early in his career. In those beginning years he would often devise a bon mot in the leisure of his bedroom and then wait patiently for the right moment to spring it in debates. At least one prime minister thought this ploy "unsporting" and told him so.

The exchanges reported here come mostly from the latter part of his career, when material for a reply could be summoned from his lengthy experience or prodigious memory. Such a comeback or deflecting reply, coupled with the sheer force of the Churchillian personality, was enought to deflate a personal jibe or attack.

Bombs Away

On Question Day in the House of Commons, the British Prime Minister and Cabinet Members traditionally answer inquiries about government policy. Some of the more technical and involved questions are, as a matter of courtesy, submitted beforehand and dropped into a special box to allow adequate preparation.

After the accession of Queen Elizabeth, certain Scottish nationalists were upset at her designation as Elizabeth II, since the Stuarts ruled Scotland at the time of Elizabeth I's reign. Some radicals were even putting bombs into the concrete pillar or mail boxes which were imprinted with the queen's insignia.

Churchill was ready when a Scottish member asked, "Is the Prime Minister aware that there is strong feeling in Scotland being taken to the title Queen Elizabeth II?"

"I shall be very glad to hear from the honorable member," he answered matter-of-factly. Then, allowing a grin to wreathe his features, he added "if he will put his question into the pillar box."

Containment Policy

A Labourite, in the midst of his attack on the policies of the Conservative government, suddenly lost his train of thought. Churchill interceded with this sympathetic suggestion:

"My right honorable friend should not develop more indignation than he can contain."

Creeping Senility

When a veteran parliamentarian rambled disjointedly against Churchill's wartime policies, the prime minister delivered this medical assessment:

"I must warn him that he will run a very grave risk of falling into senility before he is overtaken by age."

Drip-Out

His perennial Labourite foe, Emanuel Shinwell, once interrupted a Churchill speech with a rebutting fact; Churchill shrugged it off, saying,

"I do not challenge the honorable gentleman when the truth leaks out of him by accident from time to time."

Dry Run

Sir Oswald Mosley, the British Fascist, bored more than scared his British audiences. After a speech to the Commons that was haltingly tedious, Churchill offered this mock sympathy:

"I can well understand the honorable member's wishing to speak for practice. He needs it badly."

General Nuisance

When Churchill was President of the Board of Trade in 1909, he was target for criticism by Conservative members, whose party he had left. Churchill had this retort ready when one of the senior members of the opposition attacked his handling of certain ministry matters.

"I admire the martial and commanding air with which the right honourable gentleman treats the fact. He stands no nonsense from them."

Involuntary Action

During a long session in the House of Commons, one of Churchill's opponents was droning on in a long speech. Churchill slumped in his seat and closed his eyes. The speaker said, "Must the right honorable gentleman fall asleep when I am speaking?" Churchill blithely replied, "No, it is purely voluntary."

Unhappy Coincidence

Richard Crossman was a left-wing political gadfly who often crossed swords with Churchill, both in his regular newspaper column and on the floor of the House.

Churchill once punctured an attack by Crossman by remarking, "The Honorable Gentleman is never fortuitous in the coincidence of his facts with truth."

Appendix IV

MOCKERY AND PARODY

In the United States the art of political invective is a lost skill. We remember Franklin Roosevelt and his "Fala" speech, or others of his vintage such as John L. Lewis or Bob Kerr of Oklahoma. The biting wit of Churchillian invective makes us realize how vapid our congressional debate is compared to that of the House of Commons.

Churchill was, of course, a virtuoso, but his skills were honed by crossing wits with others. Beginning with their debating experience at Oxford or Cambridge, aspiring British politicians look upon speaking as a form of literary expression as well as persuasion.

Churchill had, in his father, a superb model. But although he could occasionally be as cruelly devastating as Randolph, he preferred irony to the savage thrust. The fable, be it Chinese or classical, was often his favorite vehicle for satire.

Churchill, like other British public figures, also worked at becoming a skilled practitioner of the after-dinner speech. In America this genre has been extinct since the days of Mark Twain and Chauncy Depew. Traditionally, such a speech is comprised of four-fifths wit, with the last fifth being serious or sentimental. One might hear an example of it today listening to the British Ambassador waxing on the qualities of the Scots to a St. Andrew's Society dinner. In one of the excerpts citing Churchill's opening lines in a St. George's Society speech, we can almost hear the crowd's laughter punctuating each finely chiseled sentence as he depicts the modern diplomat negotiating with the dragon. Be it an after-dinner address or political invective, Churchill reveals the technique of capitalizing on the absurdities of an opponent's incompetence or mistakes.

The Bear Hug

The disarmament talks between nations in the 1920s prompted this Aesopian parable by Churchill.

Once upon a time all the animals in the zoo arranged that they would disarm and they arranged to have a conference to arrange the matter. So the Rhinoceros said, when he opened the proceedings, that the use of teeth was barbarous and horrible and ought to be strictly prohibited by general consent. Horns, which were mainly defensive weapons, would, of course, have to be allowed.

The Buffalo, the Stag, the Porcupine, and even the little Hedgehog all said they would vote with the Rhino. But the Lion and Tiger took a different view. They defended teeth and claws which they described as honorable weapons of immortal antiquity. The Panther, the Leopard, the Puma, and the whole tribe of small cats all supported the Lion and the Tiger.

Then the Bear spoke. He proposed that both teeth and horns should be banned and never used again. It would be quite enough if animals were allowed to give each other a good hug when they quarreled. No one could object to that. It was so fraternal and that would be a great step toward peace.

Chinese Parable

In 1942, Churchill's leadership of the war was coming under attack. To deflect the criticism, Churchill tried to strike a humorous tone with a recital of this tale of ancient China.

There was a custom in Ancient China that anyone who wished to criticize the government had the right to memorialize the Emperor and provided he followed that up by committing suicide, very great respect was paid to his words and no ulterior motive was assigned. That seems to me to have been from many points of view a very wise custom, but I certainly would be the last to suggest that it should be made retroactive.

Dox Quixote and Sancho Panza

Churchill saw, in Cervantes' tale, an apt description of the odd couple Prime Minister Ramsay MacDonald and his Foreign Secretary Sir John Simon made. MacDonald was an idealistic pacifist, and Simon was a political opportunist.

When MacDonald accepted an invitation to visit Mussolini in Rome in a quixotic hope to dissuade the Italian dictator from his course of conquest, Churchill saw elements of burlesque in the spectacle.

Lastly there is the visit to Rome. I do not wish to treat it too seriously. No doubt it was a pleasant expedition. No doubt it gave Signor Mussolini a great deal of pleasure; the same sort of pleasure that a thousand years ago was given to a pope when an emperor paid a visit to Canossa. It was certainly a striking spectacle to see these two heads of governments, the master of sentimental words and the master of grim and rugged action, meeting together in such friendly intercourse. I welcome the Prime Minister back. We have got our modern Dox Quixote home again, with Sancho Panza at his tail, bearing with him these somewhat dubious trophies which they have collected amid the nervous twitterings of Europe.

Hush of Fear

In the ominously quiet months between Munich and the invasion of Poland, Churchill delivered a warning to Europe in a radio address. With poetic imagery, he depicted a silence broken only by the tramp of Fascist bootsteps. Again, tone is mock-heroic as he sardonically derides the Fascist version of liberation.

But to come back to the hush I said was hanging over Europe.
What kind of hush is it? Alas! It is the hush of suspense, and in
many lands it is the hush of fear. Listen! No, listen carefully; I
think I hear something—yes, there it was quite clear. Don't you
hear it? It is the tramp of armies crunching the gravel of the
parade-grounds, splashing through rain-soaked fields, the tramp
of two million German soldiers and more than a million
Italians—"going on maneuvers"—yes, only on maneuvers! Of
course it's only maneuvers—just like last year. After all, the Dictators must train their soldiers. They could scarcely do less in
common prudence, when the Danes, the Dutch, the Swiss, the
Albanians—and of course the Jews—may leap out upon them at
any moment and rob them of their living-space, and make them
sign another paper to say who began it. Besides, these German
and Italian armies may have another work of Liberation to perform. It was only last year they liberated Austria from the horrors
of self-government. It was only in March they freed the Czecho-
slovak Republic from the misery of independent existence. It is
only ten years ago that Signor Mussolini gave the ancient
kingdom of Abyssinia its Magna Carta. It is only two months ago
that little Albania got its writ of Habeas Corpus, and Mussolini
sent in his Bill of Rights for King Zog to pay. Why, even at this
moment, the mountaineers of the Tyrol, a German-speaking
population who have dwelt in their beautiful valleys for a thousand years, are being liberated, that is to say, uprooted, from the
land they love. No wonder the armies are tramping on when there
is so much liberation to be done, and no wonder there is a hush
among all the neighbors of Germany and Italy while they are
wondering which one is going to be "liberated" next.

Land of Topsy-Turvydom

Churchill felt the best antidote to the Hitler "Big Lie" technique
was sarcasm. A factual rebuttal of Nazi propaganda made it seem
like an answer in a debate and thus lent a semblance of dignity to

such lunatic absurdity. Churchill, in this 1939 radio address, mocked Goebbel's version of history.

Goebbels and his Propaganda Machine have their own version of what happened twenty-five years ago. To hear them talk, you would suppose that it was Belgium that invaded Germany! There they were, these peaceful Prussians, gathering in their harvests, when this wicked Belgium—set on by England and the Jews—fell upon them; and would no doubt have taken Berlin, if Corporal Adolf Hitler had not come to the rescue and turned the tables. Indeed, the tale goes further. After four years of war by land and sea, when Germany was about to win an overwhelming victory, the Jews got at them again, this time from the rear. Armed with President Wilson's Fourteen Points they stabbed, we are told, the German armies in the back, and induced them to ask for an armistice, and even persuaded them, in an unguarded moment, to sign a paper saying that it was they and not the Belgians who had been the ones to begin the war. Such is history as it is taught in topsy-turvydom.

Minister of Disease

In 1947, Aneurin Bevan, as Minister of Health in the Labourite Government, charged that Conservatives were "lower than vermin." Churchill, as leader of the Conservative opposition, rose to counter-attack.

At the very moment he has chosen to bring the National Health Service into existence, he calls half of his countrymen "lower than vermin" and gives vent to the burning hatred with which his mind is seared. We speak of the Minister of Health, but ought we not rather say Minister of Disease, for is not morbid hatred a form of disease, a mortal disease in a highly infectious form? Indeed, I can think of no better move for the inauguration of the National Health Service than that the man who so obviously needs psychiatric attention should be among the first of its patients.

St. George and the Dragon

At a St. George's Society dinner in 1928, Churchill mocks the ineffectuality of the League of Nations and the naivete of pacifist politicians by telling the tale of St. George and the dragon in contemporary diplomatic context.

St. George would arrive in Cappodocia accompanied not by a horse but by a secretariat. He would be armed not with a lance, but with several flexible formulas. He would of course be welcomed by the local branch of the League of Nations Union. He would propose a conference with the dragon—a Round Table conference, no doubt—that would be more convenient for the dragon's tail. He would make a trade agreement with the dragon. He would lend the dragon a lot of money of the Cappodocian taxpayers. The maiden's release would be referred to Geneva, the dragon receiving all his rights meanwhile. Finally St. George would be photographed with the dragon.

Appendix V

PREDICTIONS AND PROPHECIES

Edward R. Murrow once introduced a volume of Churchill recordings by saying, "The voice you are about to hear is that of the only man who ever prophesied history, made history, and recorded history."

The world is well aware of the Churchill warnings against the rise of Nazi Germany in the 1930s and the erection of the Soviet iron curtain a decade later. What is not so deeply etched in the public mind are the many other uncanny predictions he made in his sixty-five years in Parliament. At the turn of the century, during the Boer War, he was outlining the dimensions of World War I. During World War I he was forecasting the effect of air power in the next World War. In the 1920s, he foresaw not only the nuclear missile era but also the energy crisis of today's world.

Insight was not the only ingredient in his prophetic ability. Courage and diligence were equally important. Conceptions only vaguely conceived hardened into prophecies when tempered in the many drafts and revisions of his speeches. Unlike many leaders of today, Churchill did not have any nervous bureaucrat or overly cautious aide ghost a "safe" talk for him. He had the courage to state unpalatable facts or unpopular warnings. He did not hedge. He did not let the qualifying conditions so often imposed by the military or political technocrats deter him from riding his perception to its ultimate conclusion. The speaker who wishes to provoke new thinking rather than echo the old can learn from Churchill.

World War I (1901)

A European war can end only in the ruin of the vanquished and the scarcely less fatal commercial dislocation and exhaustion of the

311

conquerers. Democracy is more vindictive than Cabinets. The wars of peoples will be more terrible than those of kings.

Israel (1905)

I recognize the supreme attraction to a scattered people of a safe and settled home under the flag of tolerance and freedom. Such a plan contains a soul. . . I do not feel that the noble vision ought to be allowed to fade, and I will do what I can to preserve and fill it.

Welfare Legislation (1906)

The State should increasingly assume the position of the reserve employer of labour. The State must increasingly and earnestly concern itself with the care of the sick and the aged, and above all, of the children. I look forward to the universal establishment of minimum standards of life and labour. I do not want to see impaired the vigour of competition, but we can do much to mitigate the consequences of failure.

Eight-Hour Day (1908)

The general march of industrial democracy is not towards inadequate hours of work, but towards sufficient hours of leisure. People are not content that their lives should remain alternations between bed and the factory; they demand time to look about them, time to see their houses by daylight, to see their children, time to think and read and cultivate their gardens; time, in short, to live.

German Invasion (1911)

The decisive military operations will be those between France and Germany. . . . . The balance of probability is that by the twentieth day the French armies will have been driven from the line of the Meuse and will be falling back on Paris and the south.*

---

*The same memorandum also correctly foretold that by the fortieth day, the German army would reach its farthest penetration and that at such a point the two armies would entrench themselves.

World War I Stalemate (1914)

I think it quite possible that neither side will have the strength to penetrate the other's lines in the Western Theatre. . . . My impression is that the position of both armies is not likely to undergo any decisive change, although no doubt several hundred thousand men will be spent to satisfy the military mind on that point. Are there not any other alternatives than sending our armies to chew barbed wire in Flanders?

Air Power (1914)

One cannot doubt that flying, to judge from the position which it has reached today, must in the future exercise a potent influence, not only upon the habits of men, but upon the military destinies of states.

Stalin-Hitler Pact (1919)

Our policy must be directed to prevent a union between German militarism and Russian Bolshevism, for if that occurred these tyrants would swiftly crush the little weak states which lie between.

Nuclear Missiles (1921)

Might not a bomb no bigger than an orange be found to possess a secret power . . . to blast a township at a stroke . . . guided automatically by wireless and other rays without a human pilot.

Nuclear Destruction (1923)

It is probable—nay, certain—that among the means which will next time be at their disposal will be agencies and processes of destruction wholesale, unlimited, and perhaps, once launched, uncontrollable.

[Mankind] has got into its hands for the first time the tools by which it can unfailingly accomplish its own extermination.

Energy Crisis (1929)

We used to be source of fuel; we are increasingly becoming a sink. These suppliers of foreign liquid fuel are no doubt vital to our industry, but our ever-increasing dependence on them ought to arouse serious and timely reflections. The scientific utilization by liquefication, pulverization and other processes, of our vast and magnificent deposits of coal, constitutes a national objective of prime importance.

Nazi Conquest (1932)

Do not let His Majesty's government believe . . . that all that Germany is asking for is equal status. That is not what Germany is seeking. All these bands of Teutonic youths, marching through the streets and roads of Germany with the light of desire in their eyes to suffer for their Fatherland—when they have the weapons, believe me, they will then ask for the return of lost territories and lost colonies, and when that demand is made, it cannot fail to shake and possibly shatter to their foundations every one of those [Western European] countries.

Munich Settlement (1938)

Do not suppose that this is the end. This is only the beginning of the reckoning. This is only the first sip, the first foretaste of a bitter cup.

Germany—Part of that European Community (1946)

I am now going to say something that will astonish you. The first step in the re-creation of the European family must be a partnership between France and Germany.

No World War III (1952)

The third World War is unlikely because, it would be entirely different from any other war that has ever taken place. Both sides know that it would begin with horrors of a kind and on a scale never dreamed of before by human beings.

Détente (1953)

These fearful scientific discoveries cast their shadow on every thoughtful mind, but, nevertheless, I believe that we are justified in feeling that there has been a diminution of tension.

I say this in spite of the continual growth of weapons of destruction such as have never fallen before into the hands of human beings. Indeed, I have sometimes the odd thought that the annihilating character of these agencies may bring an utterly unforeseeable security of mankind.

Deterioration of the United Nations (1957)

I do not throw in my lot with those who say that Britain should leave the United Nations. But it is certain that if the Assembly continues to predicate its discussions on grounds of enmity, opportunism, petty jealousy and petulance, the whole structure may be brought to nothing.

Appendix VI

MILESTONES
IN CHURCHILL'S LIFE

1874, November 30	Birth of Winston Churchill at Blenheim Palace.
1884, April 17	Enters Harrow.
1893, June 28	Enters Royal Military College, Sandhurst, as cavalry cadet.
1894, December	Graduates from Sandhurst.
1895, January 24	Death of Lord Randolph Churchill.
1895, July 3	Death of Mrs. Everest (Churchill's nanny).
1895, April 1	Commissioned as lieutenant in the Fourth Queen's Own Hussars.
1895, November 30	Observes fighting during visit to Cuba.
1896, October 3	Arrives in India and settles down in military cantonment at Bangalore. Reads avidly.
1897, September 4	Takes part in fighting on the Indian Northwest frontier.
1898, September 2	Takes part in charge of Twenty-first Lancers at Omdurman, the last cavalry charge.
1899, July	Presents himself as Conservative candidate at by-election in Oldham and is defeated.
1899, October 14	Sails to South Africa as war correspondent of *The Morning Post*.
1899, December 13	Escapes from prison in Pretoria, South Africa.

1900, October 1	Elected Conservative Member of Parliament from Oldham.
1901, February 14	Takes his seat in the House of Commons.
1901, February 18	Makes his maiden speech in Parliament.
1901, May 13	Attacks the army estimates of the Conservative government.
1904, May 31	Joins Liberal Party.
1905, December 9	Becomes Under Secretary of State for the Colonies.
1908, April 24	Joins Asquith's cabinet as President of the Board of Trade.
1908, September 12	Marries Clementine Hozier.
1910, November 8	Welsh mine strike quelled.
1911, January 3	Battle of Sidney Street.
1914, June 28	Assassination of Archduke Franz Ferdinand at Sarajevo.
1914, August 1	Orders mobilization of the Royal Navy.
1914, August 4	Great Britain declares war on Germany.
1914, October 3–6	Churchill in Antwerp, organizing Belgian defense called the Antwerp Circus.
1915, January 3	With Lord Kitchener, proposes naval and military attack on the Dardanelles.
1915, March 18	Naval attack on the Dardanelles.
1915, May 28	Resigns as First Lord of the Admiralty following Dardanelles defeat.
1915, November 19	Commands Second Battalion of the Grenadier Guards in France; later commands a battalion of the Sixth Royal Scots Fusiliers.
1917, July 16	Becomes Minister of Munitions in Lloyd George's government.
1918, November 11	Armistice signed.
1919, January 15	Becomes Secretary of State for War and Minister of Air.
1921, February 15	Becomes Colonial Secretary and begins negotiating settlements in Ireland and Middle East.

1921, June 29	Death of his mother Lady Randolph Churchill.
1921, August 23	Death of his daughter Marigold.
1922, October	Defeated; out of Parliament first time since 1910.
1922, November	Buys Chartwell Manor near Westerham, Kent.
1924, November 7	Becomes Chancellor of the Exchequer in Stanley Baldwin's government.
1933, August	Warns against German rearmament.
1938, October	Attacks Munich Agreement.
1939, September 1	Hitler invades Poland.
1939, September 3	Britain and France declare war on Germany. Churchill joins Chamberlain's government as First Lord of the Admiralty.
1940, April 9	Germany invades Denmark and Norway.
1940, May 10	Churchill becomes prime minister. Germany invades Holland and Belgium.
1940, May 13	In his first speech as prime minister Churchill offers the House of Commons nothing but "blood, toil, tears, and sweat."
1940, August 10– September 15	Battle of Britain. The RAF hurls back the German Luftwaffe.
1941, August 10	Atlantic meeting with President Roosevelt on board *Prince of Wales*. Atlantic Charter signed two days later.
1941, December 7	Japan attacks Pearl Harbor and Singapore.
1943, November 28– December 1	Meets Stalin for the first time at the Teheran Conference.
1944, June 6	D-day. Allied invasion of Normandy.
1945, February 4–12	Yalta Conference.
1945, April 12	Death of President Roosevelt.
1945, May 8	VE-day. Unconditional surrender of all German armed forces.

1945, July 26	Defeated in general election, he resigns premiership.
1945, August 14	VJ-day. Japan surrenders.
1946, March 5	Delivers "iron curtain" speech at Westminster College, Fulton, Missouri.
1951, October 26	Becomes premier for second time.
1953, December 10	Awarded Nobel Prize for Literature.
1955, April 5	Resigns from premiership.
1963, April 9	President Kennedy declares him an honorary citizen of the United States.
1964, July 28	Presented with Vote of Thanks by House of Commons.
1965, January 24	Dies in his home at Hyde Park Gate in his ninety-first year on the 70th anniversary of the death of his father, Lord Randolph.

BIBLIOGRAPHY

Acheson, Dean. *Present at the Creation.* New York: W. W. Norton, 1969.

Adler, Bill. *Churchill Wit.* New York: Coward McCann, 1965.

Ashley, Maurice. *Churchill as Historian.* New York: Charles Scribner's Sons, 1952.

Bardens, Dennis. *Churchill's Parliament.* Cranbury, N.J.: Barnes, 1967.

Berlin, Isaiah. *Mr. Churchill in 1940.* Boston: Houghton Mifflin, 1964.

Bibescu, Princess Marthe. *Sir Winston Churchill: Master of Courage.* New York: John Day, 1963.

Bloodworth, Dennis. *An Eye for the Dragon.* New York: Farrar, Straus & Giroux, 1970.

Bocca, Geoffrey. *The Adventurous Life of Winston Churchill.* New York: Julian Messner, 1958.

Blunt, Wilfred Scawen. *My Diaries.* London: Martin Secker, n.d.

Broad, Lewis. *Winston Churchill: The Years of Preparation.* New York: Hawthorn Books, 1958.

———. *Winston Churchill: The Years of Achievement.* New York: Hawthorn Books, 1963.

Bryant, Arthur. *The Turn of the Tide.* New York: Doubleday, 1957.

———. *Triumph in the West.* London: Collins, 1959.

Burrow, E. J. *The Early Life of Winston Churchill.* London: E. J. Burrow, 1942.

Carter, Violet Bonham. *Winston Churchill: An Intimate Portrait*. New York: Harcourt Brace and World, 1965.

Cawthorne, Graham. *The Churchill Legend*. London: Cleaver-Hume Press Ltd., 1965.

Churchill, Randolph. *Winston S. Churchill: Youth, 1874–1900*. Boston: Houghton Mifflin, 1966.

———. *Winston S. Churchill: Youth*. Companion Volumes Part I (1874–1896) and Part II (1896–1900). Boston: Houghton Mifflin, 1967.

———. *Winston S. Churchill: The Young Statesman, 1901–1914*. Boston: Houghton Mifflin, 1967.

Churchill, Sarah. *A Thread in the Tapestry*. New York: Dodd, Mead, 1967.

Coote, Colin R. (ed.). *A Churchill Reader*. Boston: Houghton Mifflin, 1954.

Cowles, Virginia. *Winston Churchill: The Era and the Man*. New York: Harper and Brothers, 1953.

Czarnomsk, F. B. (ed.). *Wisdom of Winston Churchill*. London: George Allen & Unwin, 1956.

David, Richard Harding. *The Young Winston Churchill*. Austin, Texas: Pemberton Press, 1904.

Dilks, David. *Sir Winston Churchill*. London: Fernhill, 1965.

Eade, Charles (ed.). *Churchill, by His Contemporaries*. New York: Simon and Schuster, 1954.

Emmert, Kirk R. *The Political Thought of Winston Churchill*. (thesis) University of Chicago, 1962–63.

"Ephesian," (Bechofer Roberts). *Winston Churchill*. London: Mills and Boon, 1927.

Fedden, Robin. *Churchill and Chartwell*. Oxford, Pergamon Press, 1968.

Fishman, Jack. *My Darling Clementine*. New York: David McKay, 1963.

Gardner, Brian. *Churchill in His Time*. London: Methuen, 1968.

Germains, H. V. *The Tragedy of Winston Churchill*. London: Hurst & Blackett, 1931.

Gilbert, Martin. *Winston S. Churchill*. Boston: Houghton Mifflin, 1971, 1975, 1977. Vol. 3, *The Challenge of War, 1914–1916*.

Vol. 4, *The Stricken World, 1916–1922*. Vol. 5, *The Prophet of Truth, 1929–1939*. (Continuation of Randolph Churchill's official biography. See above.)

Guedalla, Phillip. *Mr. Churchill: A Portrait*. London: Hodder and Stoughton, 1945.

Halle, Kay (ed.). *Irrepressible Churchill*. Cleveland: World Publishing Company, 1966.

————. *The Grand Original: Portraits of Randolph Churchill by His Friends*. Boston: Houghton Mifflin, 1971.

Halle, Kay. *An English-Speaking Union*. New York: Walker & Co., 1963.

Harrity, Richard, and Martin, R. G. *Man of the Century: Churchill*. New York: Duell Sloan & Pearce, 1962.

Howells, Roy. *Churchill's Last Years*. New York: David McKay, 1965.

James, Robert Rhodes. *Churchill: A Study in Failure*. New York: World, 1970.

James, Robert Rhodes (ed.). *Speeches of Winston Churchill, 1897–1963*. 8 vols. London: 1977.

Jones, R. V. *Winston Leonard Spencer Churchill*. London: The Royal Society, 1966.

Kraus, Rene. *Young Lady Randolph*. New York: G. P. Putnam's Sons, 1943.

————. *Winston Churchill: A Biography*. Philadelphia: J. B. Lippincott, 1940.

Leech, H. J. *Mr. Winston Churchill M.P.* Manchester: Abel Haywood, 1907.

Leslie, Anita. *The Remarkable Mr. Jerome*. New York: Henry Holt, 1954.

Leslie, Sir Shane. *Long Shadows*. London: John Murray, 1966.

Liddell, Kenneth C. *Winston Churchill and the Battle of Britain*. London: Michael Slains, 1965.

Liddell-Hart, B. H. *History of the Second World War*. New York, G. P. Putnam's Sons, 1970.

Longford, Elizabeth. *Winston Churchill*. New York: Rand McNally, 1974.

MacMillan, Harold. *The Blast of War*. New York: Harper & Row, 1968.

Marsh, John. *The Young Churchill*. London: Evans, 1955.

Martin, Ralph G. *Jennie: The Dramatic Years*. Englewood Cliffs, N.J.: Prentice-Hall, 1971.

————. *Jennie: The Romantic Years*. New York: New American Library, 1969.

McGowan, Norman. *My Years with Churchill*. London: Souvenir Press, 1958.

McGurrin, James. *Bourke Cockran*. New York: Charles Scribner's Sons, 1948.

McKibben, Margaret. *Mr. Churchill's Secretary*. New York: Coward McCann, 1958.

Mendelssohn, Peter de. *The Age of Churchill: Heritage and Adventure 1874–1911*. New York: Alfred A. Knopf, 1961.

Moir, Phyllis. *I Was Winston Churchill's Secretary*. New York: Wilfred Funk, 1941.

Moorehead, Alan. *Winston Churchill in Trial and Triumph*. Boston: Houghton Mifflin, 1955.

Moran, Lord. *Churchill*. Boston: Houghton Mifflin, 1966.

Morton, H. V. *Atlantic Meeting*. London: Methuen, 1943.

Nel, Elizabeth. *Mr. Churchill's Secretary*. New York: Coward-McCann, 1958.

Owen, Frank. *Tempestous Journey: Lloyd George, His Life and Times*. London: Hutchinson, 1954.

Oxford and Asquith, Earl of. *Memories and Reflections*. 2 Vols. Boston: Little Brown, 1925.

Patterson, Carolyn Bennett. "The World Pays Final Tribute," *National Geographic*. Aug. 1965.

Pilpel, Robert H. *Churchill in America, 1895–1961*. New York: Harcourt, Brace, Jovanovich, 1976.

Plumb, J. H. *Churchill Revised: The Historian*. New York: Dial Press, 1969.

Rowse, A. L. *The Early Churchills*. New York: Harper & Brothers, 1956.

————. *The Later Churchills*. London: MacMillan, 1958.

Scott, A. McCallum. *Winston Churchill in War & Peace*. London: Newnes, 1916.

Sherwood, Robert E. *Roosevelt and Hopkins.* New York: Harper & Brothers, 1948.

Stewart, H. L. *Sir Winston Churchill as Writer and Speaker.* London: Sidgwick & Jackson, 1954.

Sykes, Adam, and Sproat, Iain. *The Wit of Sir Winston.* London: Leslie Frewin, 1965.

Taylor, A. J. P., and others. *Churchill Revised: A Critical Assessment.* New York: Dial Press, 1969.

Taylor, Robert Lewis. *Winston Churchill: An Informal Study of Greatness.* Garden City, N.Y.: Doubleday, 1952.

Thompson, R. W. *The Yankee Malborough.* London: George Allen & Unwin, 1963.

Thompson, Walter H. *Assignment Churchill.* New York: Farrar Straus and Young, 1965.

Wheeler-Bennett, J. M. (ed.). *Action this Day: Working with Churchill.* New York: St. Martin's, 1969.

Wilmot, Chester. *The Struggle for Europe.* London: Collins, 1966.

Young, Kenneth. *Churchill and Beaverbrook.* London: Eyre & Spottiswoode, 1966.

Further bibliography is found in the Works of Churchill.

INDEX